Sunday Night Concert at the Casino (Author's Collection)

Rough Point, Great Hall (Newport Restoration Foundation, Newport, Rhode Island)

Rough Point, Drawing Room (Newport Restoration Foundation, Newport, Rhode Island)

Rough Point, see page 68

Rough Point, Music Room (Newport Restoration Foundation, Newport, Rhode Island)

Marble House, Chinese Teahouse Rendering (Author's Collection)

Marble House, see page 82

Marble House, Entrance Hall and Staircase (Photo Richard Cheek for the Preservation Society of Newport County)

Marble House, Gold Room (Photo Richard Cheek for the Preservation Society of Newport County)

Marble House, Mrs. Vanderbilt's Bedroom (Courtesy of the Preservation Society of Newport County, Richard Cheek Photographer)

Marble House, Dining Room (Courtesy of the Preservation Society of Newport County, Richard Cheek Photographer)

Harold Brown Villa, Entrance Vestibule (Author's Collection, Aaron Usher III Photographer)

Harold Brown Villa, see page 101

Harold Brown Villa, Hall (Author's Collection, Aaron Usher III Photographer)

Harold Brown Villa, Library (Author's Collection, Aaron Usher III Photographer)

Harold Brown Villa, Dining Room (Author's Collection, Aaron Usher III Photographer)

Harold Brown Villa, Drawing Room (Author's Collection, Aaron Usher III Photographer)

Harbour Court, Entrance Façade (Photo Richard Cheek for Sotheby's International Realty)

Harbour Court, see page 223

Miramar, Ocean Terrace (Courtesy of the Preservation Society of Newport County)

Miramar, see page 272

Miramar, Parterre Gardens (Author's Collection, Edward Van Altena Photographer)

Miramar, Dining Room Detail (Courtesy of the Preservation Society of Newport County)

Miramar, Boudoir (Courtesy of the Preservation Society of Newport County)

Shamrock Cliff, Porte-cochère (Author's Collection, Edward Van Altena Photographer)

Terre Mare, Entrance Façade (Courtesy Lila Delman Real Estate, Jed Wilcox Photographer)

Shamrock Cliff, see page 120; Terre Mare, see page 345

Terre Mare, Entrance Hall (Courtesy Lila Delman Real Estate, Jed Wilcox Photographer)

Terre Mare, Living Room (Courtesy Lila Delman Real Estate, Jed Wilcox Photographer)

Terre Mare, Dining Room (Courtesy Lila Delman Real Estate, Jed Wilcox Photographer)

Horse Show at the Casino (Author's Collection)

NEWPORT VILLAS

NEWPORT VILLAS

THE REVIVAL STYLES, 1885–1935

MICHAEL C. KATHRENS

FLOORPLANS BY RICHARD C. MARCHAND

W. W. NORTON & COMPANY

NEW YORK • LONDON

For information about permission to reproduce selections from this book, write to
Permissions, W. W. Norton & Company, Inc., 500 Fifth Avenue, New York, NY 10110

For information about special discounts for bulk purchases, please contact
W. W. Norton Special Sales at specialsales@wwnorton.com or 800-233-4830

Manufacturing by Pimlico Book Company
Book design by Jonathan D. Lippincott
Production manager: Leeann Graham

Library of Congress Cataloging-in-Publication Data
Kathrens, Michael C.
    Newport villas : the revival styles, 1885-1935 / Michael C. Kathrens.
        p. cm.
    Includes bibliographical references and index.
    ISBN 978-0-393-73270-2 (hardcover)
1. Mansions—Rhode Island—Newport. 2. Architecture, Domestic—Rhode
Island—Newport. 3. Architecture and society—Rhode Island—Newport. 4.
Newport (R.I.)—Buildings, structures, etc. I. Title.
    NA7238.N67K38 2009
    728.809745'7—dc22

                                                                2008018249

ISBN 13: 978-0-393-73270-2

W. W. Norton & Company, Inc., 500 Fifth Avenue, New York, N.Y. 10110
www.wwnorton.com

W. W. Norton & Company Ltd., Castle House, 75/76 Wells Street, London W1T 3QT

1 2 3 4 5 6 7 8 9 0

CONTENTS

ACKNOWLEDGMENTS

No work of an historical nature can be produced without the help of many voices. I wish to acknowledge gratefully those institutions and individuals who had a hand in creating this volume. Their work and dedication to the project made the journey both easier and more enjoyable.

American Academy of Arts and Letters: Kathy Keinholz, Archivist

Avery Library, Columbia University: Janet Parks

Belcourt Castle: Donald and Harle Tinney

Boston Public Library: Janice H. Chadbourne, Curator of Fine Arts

Brown University, John Nicholas Brown Center: Ron. M. Potvin, Assistant Director and Curator

Historic New England: Lorna Condon, Curator of Library and Archive; Sally Hinkle, Library Assistant

Lenox Library Association: Denis Lesieur, Executive Director and Amy Lafave, Reference Librarian

Metropolitan Museum of Art: Print Study Room Staff

Newport Historical Society: Bertram Lippincott III, Librarian and Genealogist; Megan Delaney, Registrar

Newport Restoration Foundation: Bruce MacLeish, Director of Collections

New York Public Library: Thomas Lisanti

Philadelphia Museum of Art: Holly Frisbee

Preservation Society of Newport County: Paul Miller, Curator; John Tschirch, Architectural Historian; Charles Burns, Associate Curator; Andrea Carneiro, Communications Manager

Redwood Library and Athenaeum: Lisa C. Long, Ezra Stiles Special Collections Librarian

Salve Regina University: Joan Bartram, Collection Development Librarian, McKillop Library; Robert Snell Director of Facilities Management

Smithsonian Institution: Joyce Connolly, Museum Specialist

Rhode Island Historical Society: J. D. Kay

W. W. Norton & Company: Nancy Green and
    Vani Kannan

James Amodeo, editing and technical support
Matthew Kohl, editing and technical support
Richard C. Marchand, floor plans
Richard Cheek, Ira Kerns, Aaron Usher III, Jed
    Wilcox, photography

James A. Abbott
John Amodeo and Brian De Lorenzo
Laurence Cutler
Beth Daugherty
Angela Fischer

Ronald Lee Fleming
David Ford
Richard and Dee Gordon
James B. Garrison
Richard S. Jackson Jr.
Gilbert S. Kahn
Gary Lawrance
Paul Manno
William Morrison
Bettie Bearden Pardee
Frederick Platt
Glenn & Patricia Randall
Eileen Slocum
Kenneth Zarrilli and Joshua McKinney

INTRODUCTION

During the second half of the nineteenth century, wealthy Americans began developing a deep and abiding appreciation for the countryside, with its invigorating and healthful pursuits. The American plutocrat typically made his fortune in urban-based industry, hence he and his family sought periodic escape from the grime and frenzy associated with city living. This prompted an era of prodigious country-estate development in regions surrounding metropolitan areas. Some families wanted to go farther afield—particularly during the summer months of July and August when even suburban areas remained uncomfortably warm. In response, many found there way to Newport, Rhode Island.

Of all the seasonal resorts developed during this period, Newport was by far the most important. Other locales had equally beautiful scenery: Lenox, Massachusetts, had its verdant hills; Bar Harbor, Maine, its sparkling bay; and the eastern end of Long Island, New York, its miles of incomparable beaches; yet none of these ever acquired the social cachet of Newport. The wealthiest and most stylish families gravitated toward this tiny community located in Narragansett Bay. Although they enjoyed hearty outdoor activities such as tennis, horse riding, and sea bathing, this group also upheld the formal urban rituals associated with fashionable dress and entertaining. The estate areas of Newport became an arena for great display. All accoutrements were the best that money could buy, whether it was Parisian frocks, meticulously groomed thoroughbred horses, or meals prepared by imported French chefs. To properly mount their entertainments, Newport's elite built "cottages" that ranged in size from thirty to seventy rooms. The country's most accomplished architects designed these seaside villas, many of them rivaling the houses of European aristocrats.

This lavish lifestyle was emulated at other American resorts, but it never reached the same level of sophistication achieved in Newport—"The Queen of Resorts." For a period of about fifty years, Newport sat alone at the apex of American society, being the envy of those well-heeled multitudes trying to penetrate its elegant wrought-iron gates.

Sitting on the southern tip of Aquidneck Island, Newport juts out into the Atlantic Ocean, with its rocky and cliff-ringed mass having expansive views and salubrious air. The massive rock outcroppings found at areas such as Rough Point, Brenton Point, and the end of Ledge Road are visible signs of the retreat of glaciers during the Pleistocene period. From these elevated vantage points one can see limitless miles of sparkling ocean.

On the eastern edge of Newport, overlooking Easton's Beach, is the starting point for Cliff Walk, one of the nation's most important nature trails. It affords the visitor breathtaking water views on one side, while on the other is a spectacular array of private estates that have been developed over the preceding 150 years. Used by fishermen, Cliff Walk originated as a footpath to provide them access to the sea. In the last quarter of the nineteenth century, in spite of laws protecting this privilege, locals had to vigorously defend their right to retain accessibility as the surrounding landowners repeatedly tried, just as vigorously, to inhibit it. There are stories of stone walls being erected by wealthy summer colonists, which were then quickly dismantled and thrown into the sea by the populace—even when these walls were imbedded with shards of broken glass. Eventually, a truce was established, with estate owners taking responsibility for keeping the walk clean and serviceable as it runs along the edge of their property. As a result, today anyone can take this delightful excursion over what is probably one of the most dramatic walks of both natural and man-made scenery in the nation.

The natural landscape of Cliff Walk has remained virtually unaltered over the centuries, as opposed to the ephemeral nature of the houses that have overlooked it. Since they began being erected in the 1840s, the cottages of the summer colony have evolved, with the most dramatic architectural

Cliff Walk, c. 1870 (Author's Collection)

changes occurring between 1880 and the early 1930s. Many of these changes were the result of repercussions from the Civil War and the subsequent industrialization that followed. Contributing to this industrial expansion were the vast numbers of immigrants flocking to the United States to find a better life—all needing food, shelter, clothing, and transportation. Consequently, those who controlled the industries that produced these goods and services became immensely rich, with fortunes rivaling the leading financial powers of Europe. It was an era of unparalleled prosperity and growth for the nation, and Newport became a potent manifestation of its newly found financial might.

Newport was founded in 1639 by William Coddington, Jeremy Clarke, Thomas Hazard, William Brenton, John Coggeshall, Henry Bull, William Dyer, and Nicholas Easton—names still familiar today through the names of streets, land masses, and beaches. The town grew to be one of the most important commercial ports in North America. During the eighteenth century Newport became a bustling and prosperous community filled with impressively proportioned churches and fine residences. Quakers and Jews flocked to the city because of its religious tolerance, contributing to its diverse and vibrant urban tapestry. Local artisans who created furniture, silver, and clocks were famed for their quality work. Much of this prosperity derived from the molasses-rum-slave triangle that existed between Africa, the Caribbean, and the North American colonies. This aspect of the economy diminished over time and ended completely with the abolishment of the Newport slave trade in 1807.

The town's growth and the importance of its port ended abruptly with the onset of the American Revolution. During its three-year occupation by British troops, many important business leaders fled to find opportunities elsewhere. Despite the arrival of liberating troops in 1779, irrevocable damage had been inflicted on the city; Newport would never regain its stature as a leading commercial center.

As early as the 1720s, Newport began developing a summer colony principally populated by planters and merchants wishing to escape the stifling heat and disease associated with summers in the South. Initially, these visitors rented rooms in seasonal boardinghouses or leased entire houses from local families that were happy to vacate their dwellings temporarily for the sake of extra income. But it was not until the 1840s, with the advent of the steamship, that Newport began positioning itself as America's premier summer resort for the well-to-do.

By 1847 the Fall River Line had established regularly scheduled steamboat service from New York to Newport. Later, rail connections from Boston to Fall River, Massachusetts, made the trip faster for those coming from points north. As with other seaside towns in the mid nineteenth century, Newport developed a resort community that was centered on large seasonal hotels. Their chief design element featured wide verandas where guests could be advantageously seen promenading in fashionable attire. By 1850 there were numerous hotels catering to these summer visitors, with the social hubs centered at the Ocean House, the Bellevue House, and the Atlantic House.

At the same time that Newport's hotel culture was taking root, George Noble Jones of Savannah commissioned Richard Upjohn to design an elaborate cottage ornée (1841) in the Gothic Revival style. The Jones house was located on Bellevue Avenue, directly across from the Ocean House. A few years later Alexander Jackson Davis designed Malbone (1848–1849) on Tonomy Hill in a crenellated brownstone Gothic Revival mode. Competing with the developing Gothic vernacular was the Italianate Tuscan villa type exemplified by the Edward King house of 1847 and the French mansard-roof approach championed by architect Seth Bradford at Chateau-sur-Mer for the Wetmore family in 1852. While these styles represented only a handful of houses, they did

The Ocean House Hotel (Author's Collection)

Kingscote (Library of Congress)

reflect the growing elaborateness of the seasonal lifestyle in Newport.

The burgeoning summer colony began designating homes as "cottages"—a reference to the small satellite structures erected on the grounds of several of the seasonal hotels. Also, the cottage appellation differentiated these structures from houses that were occupied throughout the year, which were identified as villas. Over the following decades these designations became increasingly interchangeable, with ultimately no differentiation being made between them.

Unquestionably, the single most important individual in the development of Newport as a

Malbone (Library of Congress)

Chateau-sur-Mer (Library of Congress)

resort was Alfred Smith, a onetime tailor who became the town's leading real estate developer. Born in 1809 on a small farm in neighboring Middletown, Rhode Island, he later apprenticed as a tailor at the local Quaker firm of Isaac Gould & Son. Smith was later employed as a cloth-cutter in Providence before moving to New York as a tailor for the firm of Wheeler & Co. By the time he reached the age of thirty, he had saved an astonishing $20,000 with which he returned to Newport to begin a career in real estate. Smith grasped that the scenic beauty of the outlying areas surrounding Newport would continue to draw ever larger numbers of summer residents. He also foresaw that many of these visitors would be discontent lodging at hotels but instead would want the privacy and elevated social status associated with having one's own seasonal cottage.

Returning to Newport in 1844, Smith acquired land on Mt. Vernon Street, where he built a house for his bride, Anne Maria Talbot, the daughter of a local sea captain. Nine years earlier he consummated his first major real estate transaction in the city by persuading William Beach Lawrence, a prominent New York lawyer and statesman, to invest $12,000 in a sixty-acre oceanfront farm at Ochre Point. The property was bordered by Narragansett Avenue to the north and what would become Lawrence Avenue to the west, with ocean-facing cliffs to the east and south. In the two decades preceding his death in 1881, Lawrence began subdividing the property, selling large oceanfront parcels to Pierre Lorillard and his cousin Catherine Lorillard Wolfe. Under Alfred Smith's direction Ochre Point eventually evolved into the social epicenter of the summer colony, with houses for prominent New York and Philadelphia families predominating. To access this area required the creation of Ochre Point Avenue, which neatly bisects it from east to west.

In 1845, Smith formed a syndicate to buy three hundred acres north of Bath Road in what would become the Kay Street–Catherine Street–Old Beach Road neighborhood. He planned streets and created generous-sized housing lots from what had previously been undeveloped farm and grazing lands. Smith also envisioned development south of Ochre Point, pushing Bellevue Avenue to Rough Point, and then extending it west to "Bailey's farm beach." After convincing the town council, as well as the thirty affected property owners, Smith was able to initiate construction of the fifty-foot-wide Bellevue Avenue extension in 1852.

The last major component of the resort's development was the creation of a continuous drive that began at the southern edge of Newport Harbor and continued along the waterfront past Castle Hill and Brenton's Point, ultimately connecting with the far end of the newly extended Bellevue Avenue. In 1857, Smith convinced Edward King to purchase the Harrison farm just south of the harbor front and then deed enough land to create Harrison and Wellington Avenues, which replaced the rutted country road that led to Fort Adams and Castle Hill. With this accomplished, Smith was able to create a scenic oceanfront drive that connected Wellington Avenue to the southern end of Bellevue Avenue at Bailey's Beach, using Ocean Avenue, Ridge Road, Harrison Avenue, and Halidon Avenue. These plans were delayed by the Civil War, but to ensure completion of "The Ocean Drive," Smith personally paid for the last link: a stone causeway over the creek that ran from Almy's Pond to Bailey's Beach—thus opening the drive we still encounter today.

With these elements in place Smith began reaping his reward. The tax records of 1852 list only about a dozen houses for seasonal occupancy; but a little over two decades later, the number had skyrocketed to five hundred. Alfred Smith's combined real estate sales eventually stood at a phenomenal $21 million, from which he received a hefty commission from each transaction.

As Smith envisioned, the creation of the Bellevue Avenue extension and Ocean Drive led to the demise of the fashionable resort hotels. There was now a growing emphasis on the individual cottage—either owned or rented—and less on the communal nature of hotel society. Newport's hotels, like the Fillmore, Seaview House, and Bellevue House, began to slowly disappear. The Atlantic House was converted for use by the United States Naval Academy before being demolished in 1877, while the Ocean House met its end by fire in 1895.

With the arrival of the well-healed cottagers, there was an influx of artists and intellectuals. Many, like Henry James, were the children of colony families, while others depended on the patronage of the affluent summer families for their artistic careers. Included in this distinguished group (centered

John Noble Alsop Griswold House, Entrance Detail (Author's Collection)

within the Kay–Catherine–Old Beach Road district) were essayist and poet Thomas Gold Appleton, singer Charlotte Cushman, artist John La Farge, and the founder of the Massachusetts Institute of Technology, William Barton Rogers. Intellectual and philosophical societies, such as the Newport Historical Society, formed in 1854, and the Town and Country Club, founded in 1871 (although not formally named until three years later by Julia Ward Howe), flourished in this environment. Among the latter's diverse membership were architect Richard Morris Hunt, poet Emma Lazarus, scientist Alexander Agassiz, artist John La Farge, and financier Henry G. Marquand. Other noted artists who frequented Newport during these years included painter William Morris Hunt, marine artist William Trost Richards, sculptor

Richard S. Greenough, and portraitist Howard Gardiner Cushing—all but one the progeny of a well-connected Newport family. After its founding in 1912, the Art Association of Newport increasingly became the hub of Newport's artistic life, particularly after it moved into a permanent home: the recently acquired Bellevue Avenue estate of the late John Noble Alsop Griswold, a China trade and railroad magnate.

The Griswold house, which had been designed by Richard Morris Hunt in 1862, was one of the earliest Modern Gothic, or Stick Style, houses to be erected in Newport. Although the vernacular's architectural development was North American in nature, the idiom had many similarities to nineteenth-century seasonal villas in fashionable watering places like Deauville, France.

This asymmetrical architectural form incorporated an applied, nonstructural, decorative half-timbering to its elevations that often resembled those found on Swiss chalets.

The Stick Style remained the major architectural force in Newport until the end of the 1870s, with only the Queen Anne Revival presenting any significant competition. The latter style was developed in England during the 1860s under architects such as Richard Norman Shaw. He and other practitioners wanted to revive the texture and massing of Elizabethan and Jacobean models that were then overlaid with abundant Renaissance decorative detailing. A notable example of the Queen Anne vernacular is the 1875 William Watts Sherman house on Shepard Avenue designed by Henry Hobson Richardson.

Beginning in the early 1880s, Newport experienced an important new American architectural development. Known as the Shingle Style, it synthesized the organic shapes of the Queen Anne Revival with the American Victorian vernacular. They were then sheathed in shingles and articulated with Colonial Revival detailing in window and door surrounds. Asian elements were added, redo-

lent of Newport's China trade past. The Isaac Bell Jr. house of 1883, for example, features bamboo-style columns supporting veranda roofs, while a gilded dragon canopy guards the entranceway. The New York firm that designed the Bell house—McKim, Mead & White—became the leading exponent of the Shingle Style in Newport. The firm's villa Ochre Point, completed in 1884 for Robert Goelet, is the largest of the Shingle Style houses. It represents the magnified scale required by the aggrandizing social aspirations found within the summer colony and the growing affluence of its members. While the ocean façade of the house succeeds due to its well-organized and multifaceted design, the entrance elevation with its more severe articulation is barren and flat in appearance. Ultimately, the Shingle Style was unsuitable for houses of this size, so a new architectural paradigm was needed.

During the 1876 United States Centennial celebration a renewed interest in America's architectural history created a market for houses based on Colonial precedent. Unlike the Shingle Style that used Colonial elements in unique ways, the Colonial Revival movement was more closely allied to original period proportion and massing—often

William Watts Sherman Villa (Library of Congress)

with an academic precision based on scholarly research. In 1886, McKim, Mead & White completed a house on Annandale Road for New York financier H. A. C. Taylor. It was built on a scale rarely attempted during the Colonial period, but executed with such finesse that it seems neither cumbersome nor overwhelming. The firm incorporated delicate Palladian details, giving the house a fluidity and openness that seem quintessentially appropriate for a summer retreat.

THE EUROPEAN REVIVAL MOVEMENT

The Colonial Revival was a short-lived movement, which was soon replaced with a strongly European

Isaac Bell, Jr. Villa (Library of Congress)

Ochre Point (Author's Collection)

Henry Augustus Coit Taylor Villa (Author's Collection)

architectural perspective. Historicist revivalism began flourishing in Europe during the mid nineteenth century but did not arrive on American shores until the 1880s—and even then it took another decade before it moved to the forefront. The final push to establish its preeminence came with the neoclassical-inspired World's Columbian Exposition of 1893, held in Chicago. The White City, as it became known, caught the attention of the nation—particularly the artistic and architectural communities—inspiring a return to classical forms. New upper-class residential projects now became closely allied stylistically and sociologically with the centuries-old European great-house tradition and the formal way of life it embodied. America would now create its own unique interpretation of the architectural idiom.

Although the American tradition did not begin to establish itself firmly until the late nineteenth century, there were two important precursors to be found in Newport. The first was erected in the early 1850s for New York banker Delancey Kane and his wife, a member of the Astor family. In 1849, Kane began acquiring land at Bath Road and Rhode Island Avenue overlooking Easton's Beach. He

then had architect Detlef Lienau design a substantial brick and brownstone residence called Beach Cliffe to place on it. The house was based on a nineteenth-century Dutch interpretation of French seventeenth-century domestic architecture. Although eclectic in nature the Kane residence (unfortunately demolished) was the first to be built in the European manner and scale.

It would take another twenty years before the experiment was attempted again, this time in an eighteenth-century French Classical Revival house on Narragansett Avenue for Colonel George R. Fearing of New York. According to George Champlin Mason, the architect who supervised its erection, he adapted the plans from those of a house located on the outskirts of Geneva. The Orchard, as the Fearing house is known, has a slate roof and walls veneered with beige-colored Milwaukee brick, with limestone quoins and window surrounds. It was completed in May of 1874.

By far the most important architect of the historicist period, and the best remembered today, is Richard Morris Hunt. In the late 1880s and '90s he designed a group of houses in Newport that eclipsed in sumptuousness and scale all that had come

Beach Cliffe (George Champlin Mason, *Newport & Its Cottages*)

The Orchard (George Champlin Mason, *Newport & Its Cottages*)

before. These works included Ochre Court for Ogden Goelet, Marble House for William K. Vanderbilt (both begun in 1888), Belcourt for Oliver Hazard Perry Belmont (designed in 1891), and The Breakers for Cornelius Vanderbilt II (begun in 1893). Hunt is considered by many to be the father of American architecture because he helped to establish it as a profession by creating set fees and by making architectural contracts legally binding. He was also the first American to graduate from the École des Beaux-Arts in Paris, the world's leading architectural school in the nineteenth century. Hunt's remarkable houses from this period defined Newport at the end of the century and, in many ways, still do so today.

Following Hunt's death in 1895, other important architects such as Thomas Hastings, John Russell Pope, and Horace Trumbauer stepped in to fill the void. The essence of the European Revival movement in Newport is centered on the brilliant designs of these American architectural authors. It is their deft handling of historical European proportion and detailing, while at the same time successfully melding and incorporating the innovative technological advancements of the modern era, which allowed them to create such enduring masterpieces. These architects had the advantage of being able to cull though centuries of architectural design elements, choosing only the best from any vernacular, and incorporating them within a new composition. A talented architect working in Newport during this period was able to eliminate many of the missteps that are often associated with a new and developing vernacular and to create a wholly satisfying composition that speaks of the fully developed form. Helping these practitioners in creating suitably elaborate interior spaces were leading decorators. These included Vernon of Newport and high-powered New York decorators like William Baumgarten and Ogden Codman. Others chose decorating firms of international repute, such as the Parisian based firm of Jules Allard et Fils and White Allom & Company of London.

Although the architect was responsible for creating a cogent and serviceable plan, after its completion it was the household staff that was expected to keep it operating smoothly. To run and maintain a Newport cottage efficiently required a minimum staff of ten, and depending on the size of the house and the number of family members in residence, this number could easily double. Included in the list would be a butler, a housekeeper, a cook, a laundress, and two maids who toiled within the house itself, while a coachman, groom, and chauffeur took charge of the carriage house and the family's transportation needs. Added to the roster was at least one gardener who tended to the grounds and gardens. In houses with younger children, there would be a governess, who was often supplemented with

the employment of a trained nurse. In larger establishments, there were often two to four footmen to serve meals and keep the front of the house running smoothly, as well as additional maids, laundresses, grooms, coachmen, and gardeners. The master of the house would need a valet and his wife a lady's maid to handle their personal grooming and wardrobe needs. In the kitchen, in addition to the chef, there might also be a sous-chef, a pastry chef, and a scullery maid. The volume of labor expected from these servants was enormous, with the laundresses alone expected to handle upwards of five hundred pieces of laundry a week. The cost of running one of the larger houses for a single season could easily exceed a $100,000 when factoring in entertaining expenses and seasonal clothing allowances.

Even though Newport villas commonly sit on only two to ten acres of land, there remains a spaciousness and sense of seclusion. This is largely attributable to the skill of the many notable landscaping firms that were hired to transform what had principally been undeveloped farmland into verdant Elysian Fields. Houses were often positioned near the center of the property to allow for lawns all around, often with flower beds and formal gardens immediately adjacent. Exceptions occurred when the house was placed to one side of the site to allow for a longer view off the principal garden façade, which had the effect of making the estate appear larger than it actually was. Newport's estates and their gardens exhibited a timelessness that transcended both time and place, and put them on a par with Old World gardens that had taken centuries to develop. Around the grounds were plantings of rare specimen trees such as Norway spruce, Chinese ginkgoes, Japanese cypress, and European lindens. The different varieties of beech trees that thrived in the ocean air and grew to enormous proportions, however, were the most spectacular.

There is a long-held popular belief that these lavish cottages were used only during the eight-week-long summer season and then boarded up for the remainder of the year. It is true that Newport's high season began in early July and ended with the Newport Horse Show, held during the first week in September, but many families arrived earlier—often in April and May, and stayed until late fall. There were even a few hardy colonists who continued to entertain through the Thanksgiving and Christmas holidays before departing. Granted, these events were never on the grand scale of functions held during the high season, but life continued in many of these houses for most of the year—particularly for families who did not own suburban country estates closer to their primary city residences. In his 1956 biographical work *Queen of the Golden Age*, Cornelius Vanderbilt IV paints a charming picture of crisp early fall days spent with his mother, renowned hostess Grace Wilson Vanderbilt. He recalls taking drives together in the country and visiting ancient cemeteries, things that she would not have had time to do during the height of the summer season. The slower pace exhibited during the off-seasons was more conducive to relaxation and normal family interaction.

Princely dwellings and the elaborate social functions held within them—both hallmarks of a Newport season—did not detract from the sporting and outdoor recreational activities that had originally brought these families to the shores of Rhode Island in the first place. Chief among these pursuits were boating activities that centered on sailing regattas and day excursions on luxuriously fitted motor yachts. Even yachtsmen who did not own a local villa generally made Newport a port-of-call during the season. J. P. Morgan entertained his many Newport friends and business associates aboard his 350-foot-long Corsair while it was anchored in the harbor.

Racing became formalized in Newport in 1872 with the advent of the Brenton Reef Cup Races sponsored by James Gordon Bennett, publisher of the *New York Herald*. For the Astor Cup Races a golden trophy (donated by John Jacob Astor III) was awarded to the winner. Solidifying its relationship with Newport in 1890, the New York Yacht Club opened a permanent station that for many years became the principal center for boating activities in Newport. In 1928, the Ida Lewis Yacht Club was formed utilizing the Lime Rock Lighthouse structure in Newport Harbor that for many years was operated by the legendary Ms. Lewis, who is credited with saving many lives on Narragansett Bay.

Equally important was sea bathing, which was

Yachts in Newport Harbor (Author's Collection)

Casino Courtyard (Author's Collection)

done by early summer colonists at Easton's Beach. With the development of the resort came the arrival of hordes of middle-class tourists, thus the summer colony sought a private beach to escape the prying eyes of the hoi polloi. Chartered as the Spouting Rock Beach Association, it is more familiarly known as Bailey's Beach because of the family that had owned the surrounding farmland in the nineteenth century. Alfred Smith thought of the idea for the club, and incorporated it into his development plans by including a cabana at Bailey's Beach with the purchase of a building lot on either Bellevue Avenue or Ochre Point. Despite the beach's small size and rocky sand, having a cabana at Bailey's is still considered the bellwether of social success in Newport.

For tennis enthusiasts there was the Newport Casino, founded by James Gordon Bennett, Jr., who summered at Stone Villa directly across the street. Reputedly, the reason Bennett established the Casino was in response to a censure he received from the board of governors at the Newport Reading Room, the preeminent men's club in town. This occurred after he asked a visiting English polo

player to ride his horse up the front steps and into the lobby of the clubhouse. For revenge, he elected to form his own male preserve to eclipse the Reading Room. Although there may be some truth to the story, the finished clubhouse (executed in the Shingle Style between 1879 and 1881 by McKim, Mead & White) was designed for activities that included both sexes. The facility not only included tennis courts, but also a restaurant, café, and theater. During the season, bands played every morning while gentlemen in morning coats and ladies in silk organdy gowns strolled on the verandas and watched the more athletically inclined play tennis. During the Casino's inaugural year, the United States Lawn Tennis Association was established and held its first Men's Singles Championship there. The club also became the venue for the horse show held annually during the first week of September.

Prominent colonists such as John Jacob Astor, Theodore Havemeyer, and Cornelius II, Frederick, and William K. Vanderbilt founded the Newport Golf Club (later known as the Newport Country Club) in 1894. One of the oldest courses in the

The Casino Entrance on Bellevue Avenue (Author's Collection)

Coaching Party at the Newport Country Club (Author's Collection)

country; it was one of only five American clubs that participated in the establishment of the United States Golf Association. Opening in 1895, the club's premier event of the season was hosting the first U.S. Open competition, as well as the first U.S. Amateur Championship. The elegant clubhouse was designed by Whitney Warren as a wooden interpretation of a seventeenth-century French Baroque design.

Fisherman had the Graves Point Fishing Club and the Newport Fishing Club, both of which limited their membership to fewer than fifteen. Even more exclusive was the Newport Clambake Club, where it was rumored that admission was through bloodline inheritance only. Another sporting association prominent during this period was the Westchester Polo Club, which staged competitions between its members and visiting teams.

One of the chief pastimes in Newport during the late 1890s was the automobile. Oliver Belmont is said to be the first to import a French machine to his villa Belcourt in 1897. Soon others followed his lead and "bubbles" began appearing all over the fashionable end of town. In 1899, there was an automobile race held at Belcourt that transformed the grounds into an obstacle course filled with dummies representing "horses, dogs, nurses, children, maids, policemen and other obstacles." The drivers were expected to maneuver around these figures without knocking them down. Adding gaiety to the event were the flowers that completely encased the automobiles from wheel to dome. Of the eighteen or so participants, only Colonel Jack Astor managed to run the course without inflicting heavy casualties among the "pedestrians."

The summer colony had many sporting options that would keep them out in the fresh air. Even the indolent took the air during the daily afternoon drive along Bellevue Avenue and Ocean Drive in handsomely turned out carriages with meticulously groomed horses that were driven by coachmen in livery. As with most activities during the season,

this outing was a highly ritualized event that was tightly choreographed. The first time you passed an acquaintance you bowed; the second time you smiled; and if you had the misfortune to pass someone for a third time, you both turned away.

The more strenuous sporting options available to the Newport colonist were predominately male activities, where women's participation was generally limited to the role of spectator. Conversely, in the social arena of balls, receptions, musicales, and dinners, Newport was strictly matriarchal in nature, with a handful of important hostesses holding sway over the entire colony. During the 1870s and '80s, Caroline Schermerhorn Astor (the wife of William Backhouse Astor, Jr.) became the ultimate social arbiter at her villa Beechwood (1853). She ruled Newport with the help of Ward McAllister, who created the term "The 400"—the number of people who could be comfortably accommodated in Mrs. Astor's New York ballroom. McAllister later fell from grace and was replaced by an impecunious but affable young Baltimorean named Henry "Harry" Symes Lehr, who became known throughout America for his high-pitched

Beechwood (Redwood Library and Athenaeum, Newport, Rhode Island)

Beaulieu (Author's Collection)

laugh and wry humor. Mrs. Astor, with the help of her two successive "court chamberlains," ruled both New York and Newport society with an iron hand that was softly gloved in royal-blue velvet (this particular shade being the color of the Astor livery). After suffering a debilitating stroke in 1905, Caroline was forced to retire from active social life. Her position was filled by the "Great Triumvirate" of Alva Belmont, Theresa Fair Oelrichs, and Mamie Fish. Each of these formidable ladies kept a vigilant eye on Newport social activities, but as the years passed, there was a loosening of the old social order, with a pronounced emphasis on amusement rather than on the strict social forms so admired by Mrs. Astor.

Newport not only looked to Europe for architectural inspiration, but also welcomed and embraced royalty and aristocratic visitors during the high season. Chief among these was the Grand Duke Boris of Russia who, after attending Grace Vanderbilt's "Fête of Roses" at Beaulieu during August of 1902, commented: "I have never even dreamt of such luxury as I have seen in Newport. . . . Such an outpouring of riches! It is like walking on gold." Others included Prince Wilhelm of Sweden, Marquis Boni de Castellane, and the English Dukes of Marlborough and Roxburghe—the last two actively pursuing local heiresses to wed. Adding to the international flavor were the diplomatic missions of Germany, Russia, and Spain that graced the Newport season in the decades leading up to World War I.

While one might assume that the Great Depression of the 1930s put an end to the frivolity of the Newport season, the truth is quite the opposite. Newport remained a haven for families of wealth and position who continued to enjoy the seclusion the island afforded, which also insulated them from many of the worst aspects of the Depression. Here families could continue to live lives of conspicuous consumption without raising the ire of their less fortunate citizenry. In the national consciousness, Newport continued to retain its position as America's social Mecca. In the

1939 film *The Women*, based on Clare Booth Luce's Broadway play of the same name, a character entitled the Countess DeLave is worried that she will not be able to make a "success of Buck at Newport" when speaking of her singing-cowboy boyfriend to fellow Reno divorcées.

The golden summers of the 1930s were the end of an era. The colony could no longer shield itself from the modernizing world beyond Bellevue Avenue. The quickening pace of life spelled doom for the studied and ritualized pace of old-line Newport. By the following decade many of the progeny of prominent colony families moved to other resorts, leaving many cottages deserted. Those that remained often opted for smaller houses, which were more economical to maintain. Some even elected to live in apartments that had been carved out of subdivided cottages.

At the end of World War II this trend continued and intensified, with many cottages falling victim to vandals and arsonists. Newport was becoming an anachronism for a way of life that was swiftly disappearing from the American landscape. The 1950s saw the demise of great hostesses such as Grace Vanderbilt and Florence Twombly, and the closing of their respective cottages, Beaulieu and Vinland. But the death knell for the well-run Newport cottage, with its requisite staff of plentiful servants, came in 1969 with the death of Margaret Louise (Daisy) Bruguière (the former Mrs. James Laurens Van Alen.) The closing of her cottage Wakehurst, and the dispersal of the Van Alen collection of fine and decorative art pieces, signaled the end of the great-house era in Newport.

In the ensuing years many Newport houses were lost. Some, like Chetwode and Beacon Hill House, were destroyed by fire. Others, like Villa Rosa, Rockhurst, and Stoneacre, were lost through neglect or razed to minimize a tax burden (undeveloped land is taxed at a lower rate).

Despite these highly significant losses, Newport has managed to retain much of its architectural distinction. The survival of the Newport of Bellevue Avenue can largely be attributed to the 1962 actions of Katherine Urquhart Warren, a founder of the Preservation Society of Newport County. In what the *New York Times* described as "The Battle of The Elms," Mrs. Warren and other members of the summer colony raised over $100,000 to save the Berwind estate, The Elms, from imminent destruction by a commercial developer. Mrs. Warren and her allies essentially reversed the movement toward wholesale residential destruction in the area. In saving the neighborhood for themselves and their own descendants, they were also able to protect this precious architectural heritage for all Americans.

Today, Newport families tend to be avid preservationists who want to be good stewards of their properties, protecting their architectural integrity for posterity. Most of them have a thorough knowledge of the history of their homes, often keeping files with information assiduously gathered over the years. Many of them seem to understand that they are but one in a series of owners, and that there is an obligation to protect and preserve these remarkable structures for future generations. The Preservation Society of Newport County has been instrumental in saving many of the larger villas from extinction. In addition, the Newport Historical Society, the Redwood Library and Athenaeum, as well as the Newport Restoration Foundation have also done a tremendous job of categorizing, interpreting, and preserving archival information on these houses for future generations.

NEWPORT VILLAS

WAKEHURST

JAMES J. VAN ALEN

Charles Eamer Kempe and Dudley Newton, 1884–1887

Although Richard Morris Hunt is credited with bringing the large-scale historicist house to Newport in his residences for the Goelet and Vanderbilt families, Wakehurst actually predates the completion of any of them by over four years. Not merely historical in nature, Wakehurst's entrance façade is an exact replica of an Elizabethan manor house. James J. Van Alen, who commissioned this American version, was a devoted Anglophile who spent much of each year at his English estate Rushton Hall. Born in 1846, Van Alen was the son of James H. Van Alen, a financier, railroad man, and Civil War general. Long associated with the resort, the senior Van Alen occupied a cottage called The Grange on Ochre Point Avenue.

The general's only child, James J. Van Alen, was a colorful character whose exploits were often reported in the press. According to his grandson William Van Alen, James ran away at the age of fifteen to become a drummer in the Civil War. Surviving this adventure, he went on to become known for his physical prowess. When in Newport, he daily swam the three-quarters of a mile from the mainland to Gooseberry Island. Even at the age of sixty-two he was still able to tackle the two-mile distance between Bailey's Beach and the Gooseberry Island Club—arriving there a bit winded but ready for lunch. As a noted sportsman, he hunted wild game in Africa and annually fished for salmon on the Grand Cascapedia in Canada. A ladies man of great appeal, he once had to defend himself from an alienation-of-affection lawsuit brought on by a disgruntled husband. Withal, his greatest strength may have been the connoisseur's eye he developed over the years and the remarkable collection of fine and decorative art pieces that he acquired throughout his adult life. It was this eye, coupled with

Entrance Gates (Courtesy of the Lenox Library Association, Edwin Hale Lincoln Collection)

Entrance Façade (Courtesy of the Preservation Society of Newport County)

Entrance Detail (Library of Congress, Gottscho-Schleissner Collection)

a sustained purist vision, which enabled him to create a remarkable residence such as Wakehurst.

In 1875, Van Alen eloped with Emily Astor, the eldest daughter of William Backhouse Astor and Caroline Schermerhorn Astor, then the leader of New York society—much to the consternation of the bride's family. Despite the animosity between the two families, the marriage seems to have been happy, but tragically short-lived because of Emily's premature death at the age of twenty-eight. To console his son, the general gave him the northern half of his Ochre Point property, telling him to build whatever type of house he wanted. Having already spent many years in England in which he had developed a strong affinity for its longstanding social rituals, Van Alen turned to Englishman Charles Eamer Kempe to draw up plans for a new house. These plans are based on Wakehurst Place, the Elizabethan manor house in Sussex, England, which had been completed by the Culpeper family in 1590. Kempe, who was a renowned stained-glass artist and scholar, as well as an architect, developed plans for a substantial structure that measures 60 by 111 feet and has over forty rooms. Concurrent with the design process, Kempe searched for period interior architectural elements that would complete the Tudor ambience that Van Alen admired. A year and a half later Kempe turned the plans over to local Newport architect Dudley Newton for execution. Construction began in 1884 and was completed three years later.

The early English Renaissance–style entrance front of Wakehurst, like its prototype, presents an undulating rhythm of gabled projections and shadowed indentations. The mass of the smooth Indiana limestone walls is broken by stone-mullioned leaded windows, while the third-floor dormers break from the lower wall planes and are capped, like the neighboring gables, with ball-topped finials. The whole is roofed in thick slabs of slate that are seamed and crested with lead and copper, while stone-clad chimneystacks visually break up the mass. The projection found in the central position of the elevation has an entrance door capped with early English Renaissance detailing that frames the home's erection dates. Added height is given to the structure by placing it on a raised earthen terrace that is punctuated by sets of symmetrically placed stone steps. The northern and southern façades have similar fenestrations, but the latter has an adjacent stone-paved terrace that was covered with a green-and-white-striped canvas awning during the season. While this was a favorite retreat for the family on warm summer afternoons, it also served to augment the square footage of the public rooms of the house for large social functions. Because of the way the land slopes to the west, a lower-level service court is created on this side of the house that was purposely kept well below the sight lines of the first-floor apartments. It is here that access is provided to the kitchen, scullery, laundry, servants' hall, and other staff-related facilities.

The entrance vestibule to the house measures approximately 8 feet square and has walls embellished with unusual wrought-iron bell pulls that are 5 and 6 feet long. This space opens onto a 65-foot-long paneled hall that spans the front of the house. Directly ahead is a 25-by-20-foot extension containing the staircase, which is bathed in light coming through the large mullioned stained-glass windows. The south wing of the house contains the library and the dining room, which both face the previously mentioned terrace and a sunken garden. The eighteenth-century–style library utilizes designs borrowed from Robert Adam. The cream-colored room has a blue and white Wedgwood plaque set into the mantelpiece, with a large mirror set into the wall above it. Next door, the dining room, with oak paneling taken from a house in Bruges, Belgium, has its upper walls adorned with a hand-tooled leather wall covering, which is surmounted by an oak coffered ceiling whose divisions are filled with stucco insets painted with decorative arabesques. At the opposite end of the house is a smoking room or den whose paneling originally graced the London home of Lady Fitzherbert.

The ballroom fills the entire first floor of the

Garden Façade (Redwood Library and Athenaeum, Newport, Rhode Island)

South Terrace (Library of Congress, Gottscho-Schleissner Collection)

Children's Garden Party (Redwood Library and Athenaeum, Newport, Rhode Island)

Main Hall (Library of Congress, Gottscho-Schleissner Collection)

Staircase (Library of Congress, Gottscho-Schleissner Collection)

Library (Library of Congress, Gottscho-Schleissner Collection)

north wing. It originally measured 21 by 57 feet, and has walls delineated with carved oaken wainscoting and pilasters, topped by a plaster frieze of wreaths that supports a richly decorated ceiling of the same material that is lightly washed in gold. The house was piped for gas, although electricity was later introduced. Even so, the dining room and great drawing room continued to be illuminated only with candles. Before retiring each night, Van Alen made sure that all the gaslights in the house had been extinguished. The nightly ritual concluded as he lit his way to bed using a brass candlestick "of which there were several on a tray in the front hall each evening."

Upstairs, the second floor has six bedrooms, all adapted from original period English models, with many sheathed in oak paneling and having elaborate plaster ceilings. Much of the decoration on this level was executed by the Boston firm of Page &

Littlefield, and compares favorably with the ground-floor reception rooms executed by the London firm of Battiscombe & Harris. All bedrooms have fireplaces and canopied beds, and are furnished with works of art and furniture in keeping with the rooms' intended decorative period—but with modern additions such as good reading lamps and dressing tables. Adhering to late-nineteenth-century English custom, there were only two bathrooms, one located at either end of the main corridor at the top of the stairs.

Ernest Bowditch laid out the grounds of Wakehurst in an English design of pastoral vistas framed by specimen trees such as weeping beeches, Atlas cedars, oaks, maples, and London plane trees. The house, sited very close to the northern perimeter of the property, allows for extensive lawns to the south. To give the illusion of greater space, Bowditch laid out the drive in a large U-shape, so

Dining Room (Library of Congress, Gottscho-Schleissner Collection)

that visitors experience a great expanse of lawn before swinging back around to the house that has been hidden behind a screen of trees and shrubs. Because of this clever layout one is not initially aware of how close the house actually sits to the Spanish hammered-iron entrance gates located at the northeast corner of the property. A sunken formal garden immediately adjacent to the south façade of the house was originally designed by Ogden Codman and included a wooden trelliswork wall in the French eighteenth-century taste on its western boundary. This garden was later redone by Portuguese landscape designer Frank P. Mendes.

The Wakehurst acreage was later expanded southward to Shepard Avenue after Van Alen demolished The Grange after his father's death. On a portion of this property he had a carriage house erected in the same style as the house. Designed by Newton in 1888, it was completed the following year. On adjacent property the family developed produce gardens as well as orchards, the latter decorated with classical statuary. A gardener's cottage, eleven greenhouses, and a separate house for the family chef were situated at the edges of these gardens. At the beginning of the twentieth century the grounds and gardens of Wakehurst were maintained by a staff of seven. Surrounding the thirteen-and-a-half-acre estate was a 7-foot-high stone wall capped by a 9-inch stone coping.

Soon after its completion Van Alen discovered that his reception rooms were not large enough. To correct the situation he decided to have the western wall of the structure, except for the portion enclosing the grand staircase, moved out 12.5 feet. This allowed for an expanded dining room and butler's pantry at the southern end of the house, while at the opposite end the den and ballroom also received additional square footage. This was accom-

Den (Library of Congress, Gottscho-Schleissner Collection)

plished by duplicating the exterior fenestration and by matching the interior finishes to the original. In the ballroom a partially enclosed alcove was created that could be used for quiet conversation during receptions, or it could be filled with musicians for balls. On the floor above, three bedrooms were enlarged, while the southwestern chamber also received its own bathroom.

At Van Alen's death in 1923 the house passed to his son James Laurens Van Alen and his wife, the former Margaret Louise (Daisy) Post. Four years later the younger Van Alen died of Bright's disease—leaving Wakehurst to his widow. Daisy was a niece through marriage of Frederick Vanderbilt, and after his death in June of 1938, she inherited one-quarter of his $76 million fortune. This, coupled with the Van Alen millions, enabled her to carry on in the grand manner and live a life of great luxury.

In 1948, Daisy surprised her friends by marrying Louis S. Bruguière, a noted yachtsman and art connoisseur. Bruguière was the grandson of Peder Sather, who had established the Sather Bank, later the San Francisco National Bank. His mother had built Castlewood on the opposite side of town earlier in the century. Louis died six years later, leaving Daisy alone in regal splendor. Well into the 1960s she continued to employ a staff of twenty-three to care for the house and grounds. As she herself put it, Wakehurst "is the last [estate] in Newport to be run properly."

After her death in 1969 an auction was held that stripped the house of close to a hundred years of Van Alen accumulations. Fortunately, all is not lost, because the house, grounds, and superb interior finishes substantially survive. Salve Regina College (now University) purchased Wakehurst in 1975 for $200,000 and currently uses it as a student center.

Ballroom (Library of Congress, Gottscho-Schleissner Collection)

Bedroom (Courtesy of the Lenox Library Association, Edwin Hale Lincoln Collection)

Bedroom (Courtesy of the Lenox Library Association, Edwin Hale Lincoln Collection)

Bedroom (Courtesy of the Lenox Library Association , Edwin Hale Lincoln Collection)

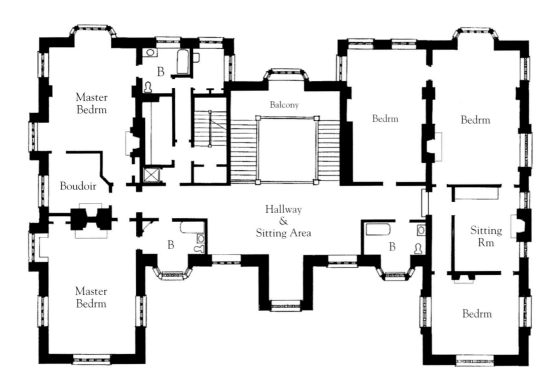

Master
Bedrm

B

Boudoir

Master
Bedrm

Balcony

Hallway
&
Sitting Area

B

B

Bedrm

Bedrm

Sitting
Rm

Bedrm

Second Floor

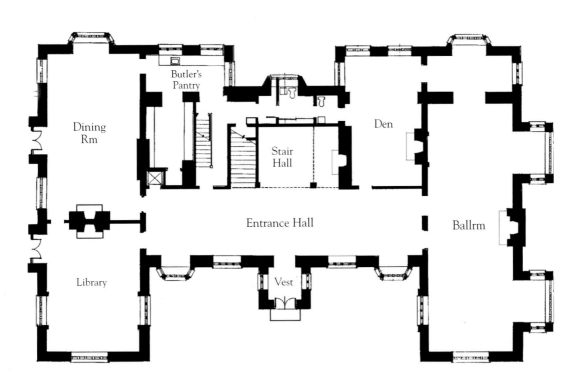

Butler's
Pantry

Dining
Rm

Den

Stair
Hall

Entrance Hall

Ballrm

Library

Vest

First Floor

OCHRE COURT

OGDEN GOELET

Richard Morris Hunt, 1888–1893

Ogden Goelet had a fortune based in New York real estate. He and his brother, next to the Astor family, were the largest landowners in the city. Of French Huguenot decent, the Goelets had been prospering on this side of the Atlantic since the early eighteenth century when Jean Goelet married the daughter of Jan Canon, a wealthy merchant. Jean's descendants acquired huge swaths of Manhattan real estate in the late eighteenth and early nineteenth centuries, whose value increased exponentially as the city grew and expanded. In 1861 the family fortune was estimated at $6,000,000, but a little over a decade later it rose to $13,000,000. In 1879, brothers Peter and Robert Goelet died, leaving the bulk of the estate to Robert's two sons, Ogden and Robert.

In 1877, two years before receiving his inheritance, Ogden married Mary Reta (May) Wilson. May's father, Richard T. Wilson, was a southern businessman who reputedly went to England with Confederate funds with which to purchase war supplies. After the cessation of hostilities he returned to this country with several hundred thousand dollars to invest. Some saw him as an astute businessman, while others labeled Wilson a disreputable war profiteer. Instead of returning to the war-ravaged South, he settled in New York, where he excelled at banking and investing. The Wilsons were a physically attractive family who, with determination and great charm, quickly carved a niche for themselves within the social hierarchy of the city. They astounded social chroniclers of the day by their many advantageous matrimonial alliances with the Astor, Vanderbilt, and Goelet families. With impeccable social connections and an ample fortune, the young Goelets cut a wide swath through

Entrance Gates (Author's Collection)

Entrance Façade (Author's Collection)

Ocean Façade (Author's Collection)

international social circles. In 1884 they moved into a red brick and stone mansion at 608 Fifth Avenue. Four years later they would be looking to Richard Morris Hunt to provide an appropriate seasonal retreat in Newport.

The property is entered on Ochre Point Avenue through wrought-iron gates set within a highly ornamental framework. Within them the visitor finds a short and straight tree-lined drive that leads to a graveled forecourt and the looming façade of the house. Surrounding two sides of this courtyard are balustrades terminating in stone plinths capped with stone and bronze dual lamp standards, which frame both the entrance drive and a secondary drive to the north. To the south the balustrade is pierced by a Gothic stone screen with a fountain at its base. A broad porte-cochère, with arched openings and a pierced Gothic parapet, projects from the entrance pavilion of the

structure and is the most prominent feature in this multifaceted elevation. Above the entrance a stained-glass window is bracketed by small grilled doors, which access the roof. Higher up is an arched double window that breaks through the cornice and is surmounted by a pedimented and pinnacled dormer. Breaking the wall plane and adding much-needed decoration are two rectangular bas-relief panels of early Renaissance design. A high slate-covered and copper-crested roof punctuated with soaring stone chimneys surmounts the entire composition.

The ocean façade of Ochre Court is more inviting, with wide arch-topped stone-mullioned windows piercing the wall planes. Situated between balancing projections is a ground level loggia, which provides much-needed shadows to help break up the mass visually. Above this, a Gothic-styled balustrade guards a series of three identical tripartite windows

Northeastern View (Author's Collection)

Hall and Staircase (Author's Collection)

Great Hall (Author's Collection)

that are bracketed by small pedimented windows at either end. Above the cornice line is another balustrade, which fronts the base of three copper-sheathed canopied dormers. A portion of Ochre Court's estimated construction cost of nearly $4,000,000 went into having it wired for electricity, the first house in Newport to be so equipped.

The Olmsted Brothers were responsible for the grounds and gardens. Many of the larger trees ringing the perimeter of the property may already have been in place, as the planting lists attached to this commission in the Olmsted records indicate only

perennials for the flower gardens, large numbers of flowering shrubs, wildflowers, rhododendron, roses, and flowering trees. All of which were chosen to be at their blooming peak during the height of the season. The most formal element of the design was the placement of a colorful parterre garden on the upper eastern terrace, while the lower terrace sweeps forward to a stone balustrade that edges Cliff Walk. So as not to crowd the site, the brick stable and carriage-house complex was erected on a separate piece of property located at Lawrence and Leroy Avenues.

Wooden entrance doors open onto a stone-sheathed vestibule, which in turn leads to a small open hall located beneath the grand staircase landing. After ascending a few steps, the visitor is at the base of the main staircase that climbs at right angles to the floor above. The walls here are entirely sheathed in Caen stone from France, while a railing of the same material is carved in an elaborate cherub and dolphin motif. On the landing is placed a large fifteenth-century stained-glass window, formerly in the Spitzer Collection but originally coming from the Carmelite church at Boppard-am-Rhein, Germany.

The staircase hall opens to the largest space in the house, a three-story marble-floored great hall that has lower walls covered in carved Caen stone, while the two upper levels are encircled by elaborately carved oak galleries. A fireplace on the southern wall is surmounted by the Goelet coat-of-arms, represented by a helmet and shield decorated

with a cygnet. Below it, the Latin inscription reads "Ex Candore Decus," which translates "From Sincerity, Honor." On the ceiling is an oil painting entitled *The Banquet of the Gods*, which depicts Zeus entertaining gods and goddesses.

To the right of the hall, at the front of the house, is found a ballroom executed in a Rococo Louis XV style, with cream and gilded boiserie surmounted by a ceiling cove of frolicking cherubs. On the ceiling is a canvas depicting Tannhauser and Venus entitled *L'Amour des Dieux*. In the southeast corner of the room an arch supported by gilded women carrying sheaths of cattails leads to a shallow musician's alcove, which in turn accesses a small marble-clad conservatory on its western side. East of the ballroom, and facing the sea, is a drawing room in the Louis XVI style with boiserie delineated by fluted Ionic pilasters. The arched window openings in the drawing room have carved floral

Dining Room (Author's Collection)

ornamentation, while illumination for the room is provided by gilt bronze sconces in a lily motif and by a large bronze and crystal chandelier hanging from a central ceiling medallion.

On the opposite side of the great hall are four additional entertainment rooms. The library is sheathed in oak Régence-style boiserie with carved decorative details highlighted in gold. The two bronze chandeliers have unusual crystal drops in the shape of pears and grape clusters. Farther north in the dining room, mirrored sliding door panels reflect the sumptuousness of the oak paneling in the Louis XIV taste, while a deep-orange-marble double hearth embellished with a gilt bronze masque of Bacchus provides the principal architectural feature. Set within the central panel of a fully developed plaster ceiling design is a canvas representing Daphne, Apollo's first love, turning into a laurel tree to escape his advances. Across a small hallway is the family dining room, which has ivory-colored walls and a deep-rose-colored mantle of African marble. Inset within the boiserie are paintings in the style of François Boucher that represent the natural elements, fire, wind, and water. Next door is Ogden Goelet's study, which has crimson-silk-covered walls with oak linenfold wainscoting. The framing around the doors is elaborately carved with early Renaissance details. A sumptuously carved stone mantelpiece that was made circa 1571 for the Salle des Séances of the Tribunal des Grands Jours in the Prévôt of Saint-Mihiel in Lorraine originally stood on the south wall. A coffered ceiling is supported by a deep frieze delineated by carved brackets that frame paintings of Renaissance nobility and their coat-of-arms.

While the grand staircase only rises to the second floor, adjacent to it is a secondary staircase, framed by elaborate brushed-steel gates and grilles, that connects all three family and guest levels. The private apartments on the second and third floors are almost as elaborately executed as are the principal rooms below, most of them executed in the Louis XV and XVI styles with intricately carved *boiserie* and marble fireplaces. The southern end of the second level was reserved for the master and mistress of the house. Ogden had an ocean-facing

Library (Author's Collection)

Ballroom (Author's Collection)

bedroom in the Francis I style, while his wife's adjoining suite consists of a Louis XVI–style bedroom and an oval Rococo boudoir. Each has its own bathroom, while the five chambers on the northern half of the floor were expected to share but a single bath, which is located near the entrance to the service wing. A similar arrangement is found on the floor above, except for the additional space gained above the grand staircase that is filled with an English Arts and Crafts–style billiard room.

Ochre Court was ready for occupancy as early as 1893, although work continued on the interiors for two more years. It seems that there was never a large housewarming function because of the family's many European social commitments. After experiencing a period of declining health in the early part of 1897, Ogden fell victim to a fatal stroke in August of the same year while on his yacht the *Mayflower* at Cowes for the Royal Regatta. Upon hearing of his illness, the Prince of Wales sent his personal physi-

cian to attend. It was a fashionable ending to a life by then primarily devoted to fashionable pursuits.

In 1900, after a three-year period of mourning, Ochre Court was finally ready for a formal opening. The occasion being celebrated was the long-delayed American debut of Goelet's daughter May. "In appointments, decoration, and display it was not only the most notable entertainment this season, but of several seasons," the *New York Times* gushed. "Curiosity to see the villa, the anticipatory statements, regarding the decorations, favors, &c., and the prominence the hostess and her daughter have attained in English society, made invitations for this evening greatly in demand, and few who received these invitations were absent."

This was the first of many such events held at Ochre Court, several with an aristocratic pedigree. Highlights included entertaining Duke Franz Josef of Bavaria in 1910, and the 1902 Royal visit of Grand Duke Boris of Russia, an uncle of the Czar.

But May's biggest coup was hosting the Scottish Duke of Roxburghe in 1903, which culminated in the engagement of the Duke to her daughter.

In the years leading up to World War I, May Goelet began absenting herself from the Newport season, preferring to stay in Europe. Writing to her sister Grace from the Ritz in Paris during the spring of 1913, she explains her reasons:

> I hope to sail about June 25th but, aside from the joy and happiness of being near you, I am not looking forward to my return or summer at Newport. It will mean such a lot of trouble and endless domestic worries, running that big establishment—just a housekeeper for the 27 servants, the 8 coachmen and grooms and 12 gardeners. I feel Ogden intended Ochre Court as a home for his children as well as for me, so I hope to gain some sense of pleasure in fulfilling what I believe to have been his wish.

Following World War I, her son Robert frequently occupied the house, with his mother rarely making an appearance. In 1929, May died in New York at a suite at the Savoy Hotel. By the early 1940s, Robert was echoing his mother's sentiments in regard to the headache and expense involved in maintaining Ochre Court. He soon purchased the more manageable Bellevue Avenue estate Champ Soleil.

In 1945 he offered Ochre Court as a headquarters for the United Nations if they relocated to Newport. After these plans failed, Goelet donated Ochre Court to the Roman Catholic bishop of Providence in 1947, who then presented it to the Sisters of Mercy. Within the year the sisters had converted the structure into Salve Regina College. Over the years the institution, which has now grown into a much-respected university, has done an outstanding job of keeping Ochre Court and its grounds in pristine condition, and by allowing an interested public to visit the building when its schedule permits.

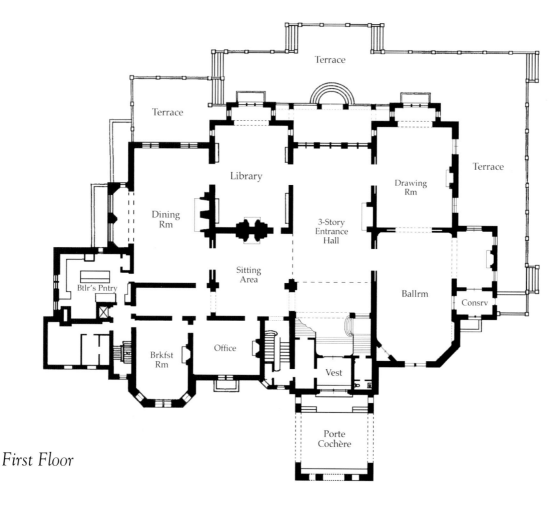

First Floor

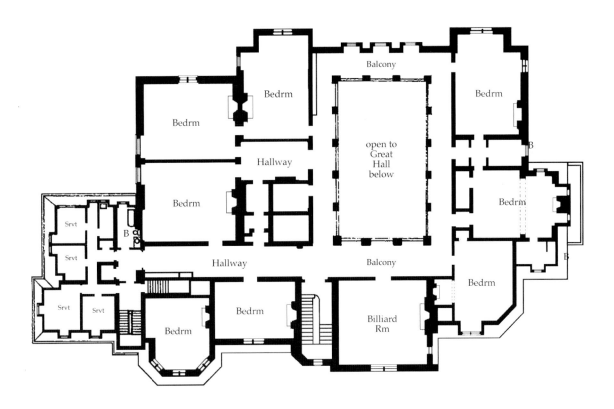

Third Floor

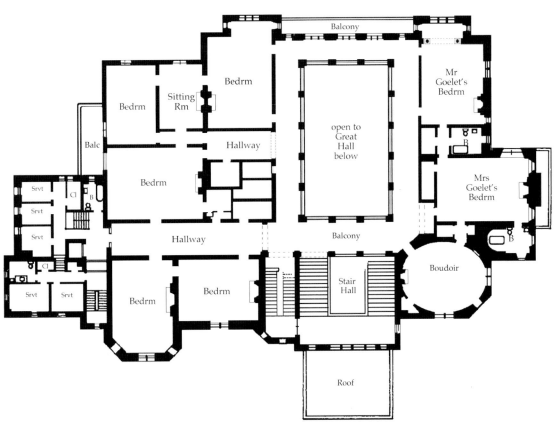

Second Floor

ROUGH POINT

FREDERICK W. VANDERBILT

Peabody & Stearns, 1887–1889; Horace Trumbauer, 1922–1923

Of the many notable branches of the prolific Vanderbilt family, the third generation is the best remembered. Their entertainments, yachts, and homes were the talk of two continents, while their foibles were fodder for the international press. It was only natural that the family joined Newport's summer colony, with four members of this generation purchasing and developing impressive waterfront estates between the late 1880s and 1910. Frederick William Vanderbilt, the youngest of the four, purchased the William W. Tucker estate in 1887 and the adjoining Jacob Dunnell property the following year. The combined purchases created an estate of just under ten acres. The enviable site held sweeping views of the Atlantic Ocean from its lofty position overlooking the crashing waves at Rough Point.

Frederick Law Olmsted was brought in to tame the rugged landscape. The awkward site has a deep gorge running inland, close to where the new house was projected to stand. To keep the curious along Cliff Walk at bay, an arched stone bridge was constructed to span the chasm at its outer reaches. To avoid crowding the site, the carriage-house complex was placed on a separate parcel of land on Lakeview Avenue. Olmsted placed the principal entrance gates north of the house so that arriving visitors would turn into the estate and be immediately confronted by an unobstructed view of the water. On the other side of the house, the undulating grassy surfaces were punctuated with minimal plantings placed amid natural stone outcroppings.

Into this open and rugged terrain the architectural firm of Peabody & Stearns placed an English manor house. Although it had many Cotswold elements, it probably relates more closely to the late-nineteenth-century Arts and Crafts Movement

Ocean Façade (Redwood Library and Athenaeum, Newport, Rhode Island)

Entrance Façade (Redwood Library and Athenaeum, Newport, Rhode Island)

Ocean Façade c. 1923 (Newport Historical Society, Henry O. Havemeyer Collection)

espoused by the early works of Charles F. A. Voysey and Edwin Lutyens. The 170-foot-long structure seemed to ramble over its site, with the clear intention of allowing the dramatic natural scenery to take center stage. Sheathed in rough granite with red limestone trim, the house personified strength and permanence. The basic shape of the structure was linear, with gabled projections and a dogleg service wing attached at its southern end. In the rear a large two-story bay was flanked by mullioned windows and gabled projections that had single-story covered piazzas.

Typical of the era, Rough Point, like many of its Shingle Style contemporaries, had a floor plan centered on a two-story living hall. This space had ceiling-high windows facing the water, and a balcony encircling much of the upper half of the other three sides. The walls in the hall were paneled in oak and topped by a coordinating beamed ceiling that extended up through the roof. To one side of the hall were placed the billiard and dining rooms. In the other direction were found the drawing room and library. Upstairs there were five bedrooms, a housekeeper's room, and four staff rooms, with additional staff accommodations being located in the attic.

Even though Frederick Vanderbilt's wife Lulu, the former Louise Anthony Torrance, enjoyed entertaining, her shy husband did not care for the frenetic pace of socializing in Newport. The couple only spent a few seasons at Rough Point before moving to the less hectic summer environment of Bar Harbor, Maine. For the next twelve seasons the house was leased to a series of social luminaries, until it was finally sold to William B. Leeds, the "Tin Plate King," in December of 1906. Leeds was thought to have paid in the neighborhood of $800,000 for the property. He and his beautiful wife, Nonnie (Nancy) Stewart Leeds, had ambitious plans for Newport entertaining, calling in John Russell Pope to complete plans for Rough Point's aggrandizement.

This project was abruptly halted in 1907, when at the age of forty-six Leeds was felled by the first of a series of strokes that would eventually lead to his death in June of the following year. After a period of mourning his widow elected to travel. Nancy enjoyed socializing with European aristocrats, finally marrying Prince Christopher of Greece in 1920. In October of 1922, Princess Anastasia of Greece (as Nancy was then addressed) sold Rough Point to the tobacco and utilities magnate James B. Duke and

Staircase (Newport Restoration Foundation, Newport, Rhode Island)

Morning Room (Newport Restoration Foundation, Newport, Rhode Island)

his spouse Nanaline Holt Inman Duke. After pur-chasing Rough Point, the Dukes decided it needed a major renovation and enlargement to make the thirty-year-old structure habitable.

Horace Trumbauer, who had already received the commission for several projects for the family, including their New York mansion at 78th Street and Fifth Avenue and the entire campus of Duke University, was called in to make needed changes to the Newport estate. The architect's work at Rough Point is comprehensive but so subtle in character that many were not aware of the changes until inside. Aside from the most obvious addi-tion—the ballroom/music room wing at the north-ern end of the house—the entire entrance front of the multifaceted elevation was brought forward to

include a larger drawing room, a ladies' reception room, a separate entrance foyer, and an enlarged grand staircase. In the southern section, service rooms were eliminated at the front of the house, which allowed the dining room to run through the entire depth of the structure.

The most imposing area is the enlarged great hall, which was created from the Vanderbilt living hall. Originally, only two-thirds of the space rose through the second floor, but Trumbauer elimi-nated the second-floor rooms and galleries above it to create a space of greater volume. The decorative wooden roof rafters of the Vanderbilt living hall were eliminated and replaced with a flat strapwork ceiling that rises only to the height of the second-floor ceiling. The original living room and its adja-

Doris Duke's Bedroom (Newport Restoration Foundation, Newport, Rhode Island)

cent library were combined to create a Georgian-style drawing room. Adjacent to the drawing room, facing the sea, is an enclosed loggia. The 36-by-56-foot ballroom is embellished with pale green paneling highlighted by lightly gilded details. At the other end of the house is a Tudor-style paneled morning room and the enlarged dining room. These rooms were executed in period styles by the London-based firm of White Allom & Company, the acclaimed firm that redecorated Buckingham Palace for Edward VII after the death of Queen Victoria.

These improvements cost Duke over $650,000. Unfortunately, he was not able to enjoy the splendors of his new abode for long, succumbing to pneumonia at his New York home in October 1925. Rough Point was left in trust to his daughter Doris, with lifetime occupancy granted to his widow. Doris Duke first began seasonally occupying the house during the 1950s. She also began augmenting her parents' fine and decorative art collection with an eclectic mix of Asian and European items. Being an accomplished pianist, she transformed the ballroom into a music room for recitals by covering the walls with eighteenth-century floral Chinese wallpaper.

Doris Duke died in 1993, leaving Rough Point and its collection to the Newport Restoration Foundation, a preservation organization she founded in 1968 to save the city's crumbling eighteenth-century structures. The foundation has opened Rough Point to the public so that all can now enjoy the beauty that both man and nature have created on this dramatic oceanfront promontory.

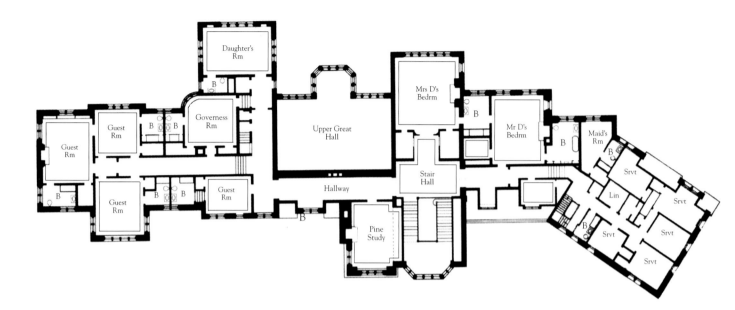

Second Floor

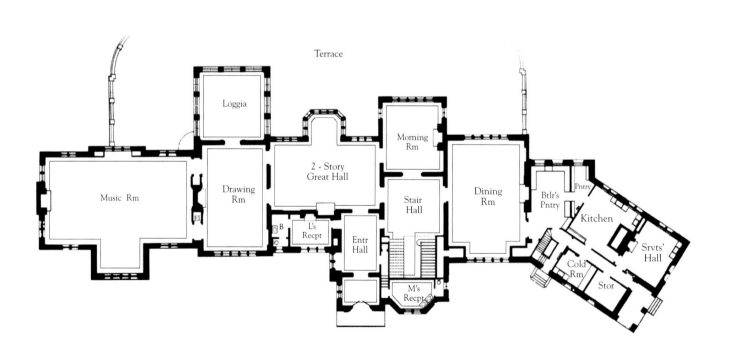

First Floor

BEACON ROCK

EDWIN D. MORGAN III

McKim, Mead & White, 1888–1891

The rocky peninsula known as Beacon Rock is bounded by Brenton's Cove and Newport Harbor. Its impressive stony visage was a romantic sight loved by nineteenth-century artists and writers. The massiveness of its stone formation was best captured by John Frederick Kensett's 1864 painting Marine View of Beacon Rock, Newport Harbor, which depicts the shear face of the Brenton's Cove elevation springing almost perpendicularly from calm harbor waters. In 1889 this view was forever altered when dynamite blasting removed the top of the mass in order to create a level platform on which to build. The newly created construction site and the mainland were divided by a chasm that was traversed by the erection of a 200-foot-long causeway, whose massive stone arches resemble a Roman aqueduct.

Two years before blasting commenced, Beacon Rock was purchased by Edward Dennison Morgan III, a grandson of New York governor E. D. Morgan, Sr., a long-standing summer colonist in Newport. The younger Morgan had been christened Alfred Waterman Morgan at birth, but in 1879, after the death of his father, Edwin. D. Morgan, Jr., his grandfather asked the twenty-three-year-old to change his name to ensure its survival into the twentieth century.

Morgan purchased Beacon Rock soon after his marriage to Elizabeth Mary Mora, his second wife. Design work began in 1888, with construction commencing the following year and continuing well into 1891. Charles Follen McKim would be the partner in charge, while Stanford White would be responsible for the interior work. The project cost Morgan $228,338.

Drawings in the collection of the New-York Historical Society show that the

Entrance Façade (Redwood Library and Athenaeum, Newport, Rhode Island)

Harbor Façade (Author's Collection)

Oblique View (Author's Collection)

Morgan house's original design was more organic in feeling, and much akin to the firm's Shingle Style work. Because it was intended to be of coursed quarry-faced ashlar construction, Beacon Rock is even more closely attuned to the firm's Edgehill (1887–88), the George Gordon King house on Harrison Avenue. Because of the linear space constraints imposed by the narrow site, McKim added large, forward-projecting wings to either end of the mass, creating a three-sided entrance court. Early drawings show large round turrets at the forward end of each wing.

Midway through the Morgan project McKim became immersed in plans for the World's Columbian Exposition, which was to be held in Chicago in 1893. Along with other architectural luminaries such as Daniel H. Burnham, Richard Morris Hunt, Robert Swain Peabody and George Brown Post, McKim created what became known as the White City, considered the country's first major foray into the classical architectural revival style.

The exposition's form derived from ancient Greek and Roman precedent, as filtered through the lens of both the Italian Renaissance and the French neoclassical movement. The influence of this project effected McKim's other work, including the Morgan project, resulting in radical alterations of Beacon Rock's exterior to reflect this nascent design philosophy.

Beacon Rock's finished form was an amalgam of classical detailing overlaying an organic superstructure, which resulted in strongly contrasting fronts. The façade facing the water remained substantially as originally planned, except for the enveloping colonnade surrounding a large focal turret. Even here the columns, although hinting of classical inspiration, were of the same rough granite as the body of the house. In contrast, the entrance front was now of Greek derivation—appearing almost as an ancient acropolis with its pedimented temples surrounded by marble Ionic columns. But on closer inspection, one sees that the classical detailing of

Hall (Author's Collection)

the entrance court overlays rough stone walls that are painted white to minimize the textural and aesthetic differences.

An engaging floor plan within exhibits the brilliance of an architectural firm just reaching the pinnacle of its creative powers. McKim was able to seamlessly integrate oval, hexagonal and bowed spaces into a coherent and comfortably livable plan. The exuberant detailing of the principal entertaining rooms is typical of the 1890s. A rectangular entrance hall is framed by detached Corinthian columns. At the far end is a stone chimneypiece in the Italian Renaissance style, and to the right is a set of doors leading into the dining room. The hall floor is terrazzo; the ceiling is coffered, with each section filled with multiple cross beams. To the left are two sets of doors, the first leads to an oval reception room and the next accesses the service wing. The opposite side of the entrance hall is left open to allow a full view of the staircase with its ornate iron balustrade. Angled out of the far end of the staircase hall is the entrance to

a sunken drawing room. Sheathed in richly molded paneling, the living room boasts a Renaissance-style fireplace, and windows with sweeping views of the harbor. The adjacent hexagonally shaped dining room is also paneled, this time richly articulated with Corinthian pilasters. An arch framing the fireplace is entirely filled with marble that matches the projecting classical mantel within.

A mezzanine level located in the eastern wing of the house, which is accessed from the main staircase landing, holds the master bedroom suite. It consists of two bedrooms and two baths, plus a shared sitting room. Mrs. Morgan has a small dressing room directly adjacent to her room, while her husband's much larger dressing room is located on the second floor above the living room. An additional six bedrooms are located on the second floor, along with three additional baths and two dressing rooms.

In 1921, Morgan sold Beacon Rock to Captain Marion Eppley and began summering in Windsor, Vermont. Eppley was a retired naval captain as well

Dining Room (Author's Collection)

Staircase (Author's Collection)

as a noted scientist. Mrs. Eppley, the former Ethelberta Pyne Russell, was the great-granddaughter of Moses Taylor, the New York merchant and president of the National City Bank. Soon after the couple took possession of Beacon Rock, they initiated significant alterations to the home's interiors. Most of Stanford White's 1890s exuberant Beaux-Arts detailing was replaced with a pared-down version of the English Georgian vernacular.

The Eppleys occupied the house until 1942, when New York's Seventh Regiment commandeered it for use an antiaircraft facility during World War II. A year before Mrs. Eppley's death in 1952, the estate was sold to Felix de Weldon of Washington, D.C. De Weldon, an artist, is best known for his United States Marine Corps Memorial sculpture depicting the flag raising at Iwo Jima. In 1996, Beacon Rock was purchased by attorney Brian R. Cunha, who recently completed a substantial renovation.

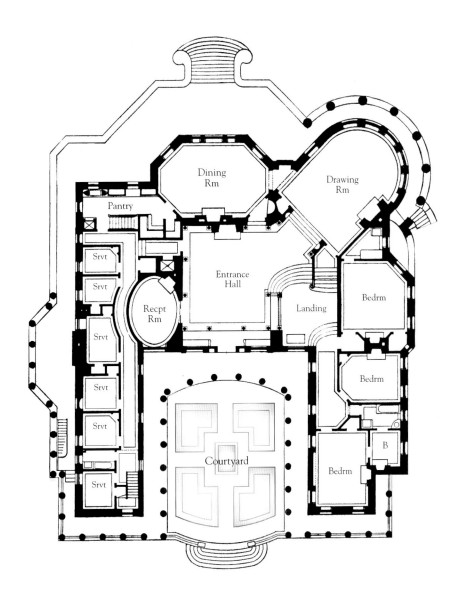

Dining Rm

Drawing Rm

Pantry

Srvt

Srvt

Recpt Rm

Entrance Hall

Landing

Bedrm

Srvt

Srvt

Bedrm

Srvt

Courtyard

B

Bedrm

Srvt

First Floor

MARBLE HOUSE

WILLIAM KISSAM VANDERBILT

Richard Morris Hunt, 1889–1892

In 1888, William Kissam Vanderbilt decided to build a summer house in Newport as a fortieth-birthday present for his wife, the former Alva Erskine Smith. Vanderbilt contacted Richard Morris Hunt, who had previously designed the family's New York City house, and reputedly asked him to build "the very best living accommodations that money could provide." Alva, as she had done with the New York project, would carefully supervise the design and construction process from beginning to end. She made important alterations to the design that contributed greatly to its success, all under the watchful and knowledgeable eye of Hunt. Alva became so emotionally attached to the house that she considered it "like a fourth child."

For over a year she and Hunt worked on the plans before finally breaking ground in the late summer of 1889. For the next three years she tried to keep prying eyes away by erecting high wooden walls around the site. It was said that she wanted only foreign-speaking workers because they were less likely to communicate with reporters. Alva was only partially successful in her quest for secrecy because the house was erected only steps away from busy Bellevue Avenue, but when completed Marble House would dazzle all.

The gleaming white Tuckahoe marble façade—with sculpted elements in the more easily carved Carrara marble—was so beautifully proportioned and the carvings so masterfully executed that the house brought American architecture to a new level of refinement. Adele Sloane, a niece of Mr. Vanderbilt's, opined that "no description can possibly give one an idea of how marvelously beautiful it is. It is far ahead of any palace I have ever seen abroad, far ahead of any I have ever dreamed of." This was a feeling

House Seen Through Entrance Gate (Courtesy of the Preservation Society of Newport County)

Entrance Façade (Redwood Library and Athenaeum, Newport, Rhode Island)

shared by many at the time. Although often compared to the Petit Trianon at Versailles, it has none of the lightness and elegant refinement attributed to Ange-Jacques Gabriel's masterpiece. Marble House is the complete antithesis, exhibiting a massiveness and bravura that is the architectural embodiment of nascent American imperialism.

The entrance façade faces west and has a central portico supported by four Corinthian columns. As on all elevations, the linear mass is divided by Corinthian pilasters that support a full entablature and a deep cornice—held aloft by modillions—which in turn supports a roof balustrade. The structure faces semicircular balustraded ramps, which rise gently to the base of the first-floor level. At the four corners of each ramp stone plinths support bronze lampstands that are illuminated by five opalescent glass globes. Fronting the portico, the stone balustrade gives way to ornate bronze fencing that overlooks a pool with three carved mascarons shooting water onto its surface. Within the portico, the ground floor is pierced by an intricately mod-

eled bronzed and glass grille that is centered by a set of entrance doors, each 6 feet wide. Designed by Hunt and executed by the John Williams Bronze Foundry in New York, the ten-ton screen was publicly exhibited before being shipped to Newport for installation. Directly above it is a decorative bas-relief panel depicting classical figures, which separates the grille from the three casement windows found above.

Facing the water, the east façade has wings that project from the central mass at either end. While these wings continue the fenestration found on the front of the house, the elevation between them has significant differences. Here the windows of the first and second floors are treated as one, with only a short run of balusters demarcating a division of levels. The second-story windows have arched tops and are set lower in the wall because they begin at the landing level of the staircase within. The additional space left above is filled with floral swags in relief, while the spandrels have carved figures representing the signs of the Zodiac.

Ocean Façade (Redwood Library and Athenaeum, Newport, Rhode Island))

Gothic Room (Courtesy of the Preservation Society of Newport County)

Inside, a 30-foot-wide entrance hall is entirely walled and floored in yellow Sienna marble from Italy, which brings with it a golden luminosity. To the right is a bronze wall fountain embellished with faux water flows made of crystal that is surmounted by a Venetian mirror. Around the hall are positioned sets of doors with gilded frames enriched with nautically themed hardware, which support clear beveled-glass panes. In the center of the hall, a stairwell rises 40 feet to a ceiling canvas depicting gods and cherubs playfully disporting themselves among the clouds. From the center of this canvas hangs a large, gilt-bronze lantern embellished with flying putti. The marble ramps of the staircase have a Vitruvian wave border, while the bronze railing is embellished with gilded trophy plaques and Apollo sunbursts.

On the staircase landing are two windows that are capped by gilded frames holding commemorative plaques. Hunt's bas-relief image is placed over one, while the other is surmounted with the image of Louis XIV's chief architect, Jules Hardouin-Mansart. Perched on a wall bracket between the windows is a copy of a seventeenth-century bust of

Louis XIV by Bernini. At the sides of the landing are beveled-glass sets of doors that access a study for Mr. Vanderbilt and a boudoir for his wife. In the upper hall the dado and surrounds are of Sienna marble, but wall planes are painted in trompe l'oeil to match.

The principal entertainment rooms are equally as lavish, with the Gold Room being the most imposing. Here decorative carved panels, supplied by decorator Jules Allard, depicting sea mythology are affixed to the walls on either side of a fleur-de-pêche marble fireplace. The panels are gilded with three different shades of gold leaf to enhance detailing. Seated atop the ends of the fireplace are life-size bronze figures depicting youth and old age, which are connected by swags of the same material to a central classical mask. Above this is a terrestrial globe made of transparent glass, which marks the time by revolving around an inner sphere that represents the universe. In the center of the ceiling is an allegorical canvas framed by gilded plasterwork and white stucco panels with painted gold wreaths placed at each corner. Hanging from either end of the canvas is a gilded bronze chandelier whose numerous branches are held aloft by a circle of trumpet-blowing putti.

Across the hall, the dining room is inspired by the Salon d'Hercule at Versailles, except that in France the room was veneered in polychrome marble, while in Newport pink Numidian marble was used exclusively. The richness of the stonework makes a strong contrast with the gilt-bronze wall trophies and light fixtures. Pilasters with bronze bases and modified Corinthian capitals encircle the room and support a full entablature with a cornice supported by carved marble brackets. Surrounding a rectangular mythological ceiling painting are gilded three-dimensional hunting elements, such as boar and stag heads. Above the fireplace—adding royal luster—is a portrait depicting Louis XIV as a young man,

which is now attributed to the French painter Henri Testelin (1616–1695).

A transverse hall located at the back of the entrance hall leads to the two remaining reception rooms of the house. At the south end of the corridor lies the Gothic Room. It was designed to house a collection of religious artifacts purchased in 1889 from the Émile Gavet Collection. The lower walls of the room are covered with carved Gothic paneling, while above hangs crimson silk damask. To enhance the ecclesiastical mood set by the artwork, the window embrasures were covered with period panels of stained-glass that were backlit to bring out their jewel-like tones. The ceiling-high chimneypiece is a replica of one found in the fifteenth-century house of Jacques Coeur in Bourges, France. The room is covered by

Boudoir (Courtesy of the Preservation Society of Newport County)

an elaborately ribbed tracery ceiling inset with painted foliate canvas panels, which is supported by corner struts and centered by a Gothic finial.

At the opposite side of the house is a Rococo-style library, with richly carved Louis XV–style walnut paneling and apple-green silk insets, the latter replaced later with solid wooden panels. An ebullient pink-and-blue-coved ceiling has gilded trim and allegorical paintings depicting the arts and sciences. Built-in glazed bookcases in the Louis XV–style flank a gray marble fireplace that has a garlanded mirror above.

At the top of the staircase is William Vanderbilt's bedroom, finished in a subdued Louis XVI manner with silk-covered walls and a marble fireplace. The largest and most opulently appointed bedroom was of course Alva's, which was located next door to that of her husband. Executed in the Rococo style, it has an ornate plaster ceiling and heliotrope-colored silk-damask-covered walls and furniture. A central ceiling painting depicts Athena, the goddess of war. The four windows are surmounted by carved wooden pelmets centered by female masks, with a cherub on either side grasping floral festoons. Wall panels and a mirrored overmantel frame a fleur-de-pêche marble fireplace that supports at each end almost life-size bronze figures holding aloft gilded candelabra.

The Vanderbilt's only daughter, Consuelo, had a bedroom facing the sea from the southeast corner of the house. The English Tudor–style room with its dark wainscoting and heavy canopied four-poster bed is hardly the choice of a teenage girl; instead it suited her mother's ambitions. She enveloped Consuelo in surroundings suitable for an English peeress—betraying Alva's ultimate goal for her. Next door was a small dressing room and an additional bedroom. The principal guest suite consists of a large bedroom, with a small adjoining sitting room, each with elaborately molded plaster ceilings and carved marble fireplaces. Behind this suite is an oak-paneled hallway that leads to three bedrooms, probably used by the Vanderbilt's two sons and their live-in tutor.

The housewarming—a combined dinner and musicale—took place on August 18, 1892. Guests were asked to wait at the Bellevue Avenue gates, with the house shrouded in darkness. When they were assembled, the entire house and grounds were illuminated at once, giving all a spectacular introduction to Marble House. The New York Times reported that "the grand portico was a blaze of light and liveried attendants were on hand from carriage to cloakroom." Dinner was served at numerous tables, each with gold-plated cutlery and a centerpiece shaped in the form of miniature lakes filled with night-blooming lilies.

The couple had only two seasons in the cottage before their acrimonious divorce in March of 1895. Within months of the decree, Alva was dazzling Newport society with her houseguest, the ninth Duke of Marlborough. The season would climax on August 28 with a ball for four hundred guests, announcing the debut of Consuelo. The Duke proposed shortly thereafter, with the wedding being set for the following November. Within two months of her daughter's wedding, Alva herself married Oliver H. P. Belmont, the son of August Belmont, the American representative of the European Rothschild banking interests. Subsequently, Alva closed Marble House—except for its superior laundry facilities—and began summering at her husband's villa, Belcourt, just down the avenue.

After Oliver's death in 1908, Alva returned to Marble House, continuing her lavish entertainments and interspersing them with suffragette events—a cause she passionately embraced. In 1912, she asked the firm of Hunt & Hunt, sons of the deceased Richard Morris Hunt, to design a teahouse that would sit just above the crashing breakers on the cliffs. "The Chinese House" was completed in time for the 1914 season. As the world was at the precipice of war, Alva was preparing to give "the most beautiful ball I have ever given."

After attending preball dinners at other cottages, invitees began assembling at Marble House for the Chinese Ball. Alva received them in the Gold Room in the guise of a Chinese empress, while her daughter appeared in a black velvet and

Chinese Teahouse (Author's Collection)

Guests at Chinese Ball (Courtesy of the International Tennis Hall of Fame & Museum, Newport, Rhode Island)

gold costume as Lady Chang—consort to the Emperor. To enhance the historical illusion, Alva had her staff outfitted in costumes duplicating those worn by servants in the imperial household. The grounds and terraces were brilliantly illuminated with Chinese lanterns interspersed among yellow and red flowers, while thousands of twinkling electric lights illuminated trees and shrubbery. Hidden lights bathed the new teahouse in a magical glow. In a grove of trees to the side of the property was a large marquee where supper was served at small tables set amid bowers filled with red and yellow blossoms and Chinese lilies. The dancing began at midnight in the Gold Room and the entrance hall, with an orchestra stationed at the head of the staircase. The Seventh Band from Fort Adams offered additional music from its location near the teahouse.

In 1923, Alva moved to France to be near her daughter, leaving Marble House dark and shuttered. Nine years later she parted with her "fourth child," selling it to Chicago financier Frederick H. Prince for only $100,000—a fraction of the reputed $11,000,000 spent on its construction. Mr. Prince and his family occupied the house until his death thirty-one years later. The new owners made few changes, mostly limited to updating bathrooms and service facilities. The second-floor corridor in the north wing was reconfigured so that an elevator could be installed. Another change was the combining of two small dressing rooms and an adjacent bedroom to create a larger bedroom decorated in an incongruous American Federal style.

Marble House was purchased by the Preservation Society of Newport County in 1962, with funds provided by Alva's younger son Harold, while the original furnishings were donated by the Frederick H. Prince Trust. Today this seminal piece of American architecture and its equally outstanding decorative art collection is now open to the public as a house museum, looking much as it did when the Vanderbilts were in residence.

Second Floor

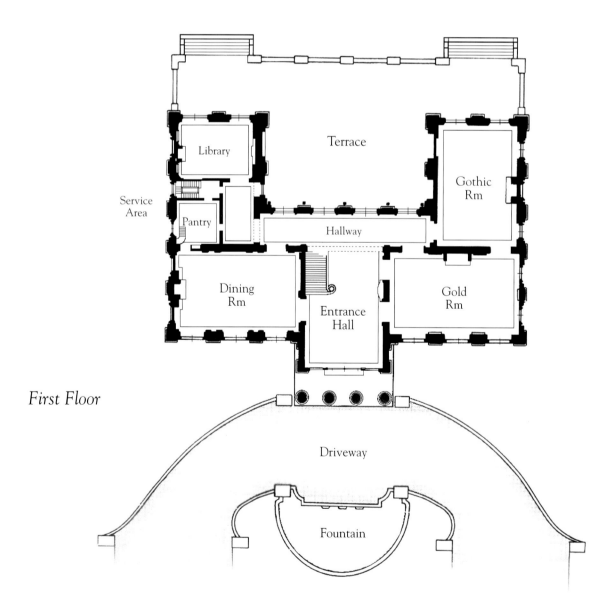

First Floor

BELCOURT

O. H. P. BELMONT

Richard Morris Hunt, 1891–1894

Alterations: John Russell Pope, 1907; Horace Trumbauer, c. 1915

A most singular house," opined Julia Ward Howe after an initial tour of Belcourt. Another visitor described it as "a palatial stable with an incidental apartment and an incidental ballroom," a description that would have delighted its owner, who was a devoted horseman; he had designed his cottage to house his horses in as much luxury as he expected for himself. Only at Belcourt could one be driven by carriage directly into the house and alight near the bottom of a staircase that led to grand reception rooms above. A bachelor at the time of its construction, Belmont also craved privacy, so he placed the house far away from Bellevue Avenue, setting the house behind a forest of trees. Designed by Richard Morris Hunt, it had fifty rooms and its erection reputedly cost in the neighborhood of $3 million.

Oliver Hazard Perry Belmont, the man who brought this unique architectural vision into reality, was the son of August Belmont, the American representative of the European Rothschild banking interests. His mother, Caroline Slidell Perry, was the daughter of Commodore Matthew Calbraith Perry, who negotiated a treaty that opened trade between Japan and the United States. At his father's request Oliver attempted a career in the family business, but banking bored him and he soon left. Later he attended the Naval Academy at Annapolis, where he graduated in 1880. After serving two years in the navy, he resigned his commission and entered his father's firm in what would ultimately be another failed attempt at banking. Later he pursued a successful career in politics. From 1901 to 1906 he served in Congress as a representative of New York's 13th District. In December of 1882, Belmont married Sallie Whiting of New York but separated within months of the ceremony.

North Façade (Author's Collection)

Aerial View (© John T. Hopf)

In 1891, Oliver hired Richard Morris Hunt to draw up plans for a villa located on a three-acre site bordered by Bellevue Avenue, Ledge Road, and Lakeview Avenue. The architect designed the structure to resemble a Louis XIII hunting lodge, with details reminiscent of the original structure found at the core of the Palace of Versailles. The bulk of Belcourt sits on a 4-foot-thick slab of concrete, while the stucco-covered brick and granite walls are 42 inches thick in places. The main body of the house runs parallel to Lakeview Avenue near the corner of Ledge Road. It has two stories, which are capped by a slate-covered Mansard roof pierced by stone and brick-trimmed dormer windows at each end. The dormers that run atop the long central portion of this façade are oval in shape and have lead-and-copper-sheathed frames. Below these, at the second-floor level, are a series round-topped French doors set within brick and stone frames, which are guarded by wrought-iron balconies incorporating a nautical shell motif. Highly-studded paired windows run along the central mass of the first story, while projecting pavilions found at either end contain a set of wrought-iron and glass carriageway doors that originally formed the principal entrance to the house. Around the corner on the western façade is a single-story vestibule extension with a prominent set of wooden doors that could be used as an entrance by the occasional visitor that arrived on foot. Next to this entrance is placed a bayed projection, with a gracefully shaped angled roof.

On the southern side of the house a three-sided extension creates a courtyard within. Belmont's horses were housed on the ground floor, while his thirty servants were lodged above. The brick and

Courtyard (Author's Collection)

Second Floor Loggia (Author's Collection)

half-timbered courtyard was designed as a paddock. A second-floor loggia was created so Belmont and his guests could watch the horses being exercised below. The stable is 180 feet long and 20 feet wide, and could accommodate up to thirty horses. In this space are four box stalls, each 12 by 12 feet, and twenty-six straight stalls that measured 9 by 5 feet. A centrally-positioned marble trough was installed to water the horses. Durable Belgian blocks paved the corridors, while the stalls themselves were paved with yellow brick. The horses were accoutred in the finest linen, emblazoned with the Belmont crest. The walls of the stable were adorned with cream-and-maroon-colored tiles that matched the Belmont racing colors.

The first floor of Belcourt was devoted almost exclusively to horses and carriages, but upstairs the luxurious appointments were suitable for a scion of a wealthy American family. At the top of a carved wooden staircase, based on one found at the Maison Cluny in Paris, is a paneled hallway leading to the principal rooms of the house. Corinthian columns circle the oval dining room, supporting an intricately decorated domed ceiling. Above the full cornice and entablature are concealed lights that illuminate the ceiling detail. This was one of the first attempts at indirect lighting in the country and was reputedly designed by Thomas Alva Edison. The walls between the columns, plus the sliding door and window shutters, are covered in paned mirrors that create an enchantingly luminous setting for dining. Belmont, fearing for the safety of his horses in case of fire, had a separate building constructed to house his kitchen. Because of this, all food was carried into the house, and since there was no butler's pantry, serving tables were placed in the adjacent hallway to expedite meals.

Next to the dining room is a paneled salon executed in a French Renaissance Revival style, embellished with a ceiling-high stone fireplace and delicate overdoor bas-relief panels executed in white plaster. A 75-foot-long two-story French Gothic ballroom displays a vaulted ceiling punctuated by stained-glass trefoil-shaped windows on one side and balancing openings on the opposite side for a musicians' gallery. A series of ogee-arched stained-glass windows on the north side of the room let in diffused lighting during the day, which enhanced the museumlike atmosphere for the display of Belmont's collection of antique armor. At one end of the room is a Gothic organ console balanced at the opposite end by a stone fireplace surmounted by a fanciful castle. On either side of this fireplace, doors lead to the owner's French Gothic bedroom and bath. There were originally no guest accommodations.

Belmont married Alva Vanderbilt on January 11, 1896, less than a year after her divorce from William K. Vanderbilt. Although receiving Marble House in the divorce settlement, she and Oliver decided to summer at Belcourt. As a wedding gift, Oliver deeded Alva Belcourt, along with his horse-breeding farm in neighboring Middletown. The firm of Hunt & Hunt was called in to add a bedroom, sheathed in eighteenth-century French boiserie, and a bath, for Alva. Additionally, a third-floor suite of rooms was created for her

Second Floor Hall (Author's Collection)

Dining Room (Author's Collection)

younger son Harold Vanderbilt that was accessed from the musician's gallery. With the ascendancy of the automobile over the horse-drawn carriage, Belmont chose to have John Russell Pope convert the ground-floor carriage house into a gala reception area in 1907.

On June 10, 1908, Belmont succumbed to septic poisoning following an operation for appendicitis. After his death Alva returned to Marble House and put Belcourt on the market. Oliver's older brother Perry purchased the house in 1915 and asked Horace Trumbauer to update the twenty-year-old house. The architect's work principally involved the creation of additional entertaining rooms on the first floor. This was accomplished by sacrificing key elements of his brother's original carriageway entrances. A reception room replaced the west entrance, while the adjoining entrance hall was enlarged, the latter necessitating the turning of the staircase in a 90-degree angle. A Tudor-style library

was inserted into the western perimeter of what was once the paddock, which was now transformed into a garden court. At the opposite end of the courtyard, a new Palladian-style entrance was created that provides access to the east lawn and gardens. Sometime after 1917, the third-floor addition was removed and Hunt's original roof design restored.

In the early 1930s, Perry and his wife Jessie experienced financial setbacks and found Belcourt too costly to maintain. They put it on the market and began summering at a smaller villa called Elm Lodge on Old Beach Road. Around 1932, Alva repurchased Belcourt, allowing her brother-in-law to avoid foreclosure. In 1940, after regaining title to the property, Perry Belmont sold it to George H. Waterman, who used Belcourt to house his carriage and vintage-automobile museum. Later it was considered as a venue for the Newport Jazz Festival by Louis Lorillard, but his horrified neighbors quickly quashed the proposal.

Ballroom (Author's Collection)

Entrance Hall c. 1917 (Author's Collection)

In October of 1956, Belcourt was purchased by Mr. and Mrs. Harold P. Tinney. With the help of their son Donald and his wife Harle, the family operated the house as a museum that is called Belcourt Castle. Over the years it has been altered to fit the Tinney family's growing collection of fine and decorative art, although always respecting the architectural integrity of the Hunt, Pope, and Trumbauer work.

New Courtyard Entrance (Author's Collection)

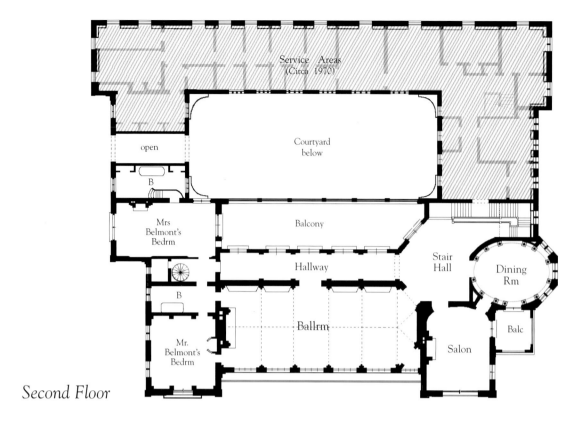

Second Floor

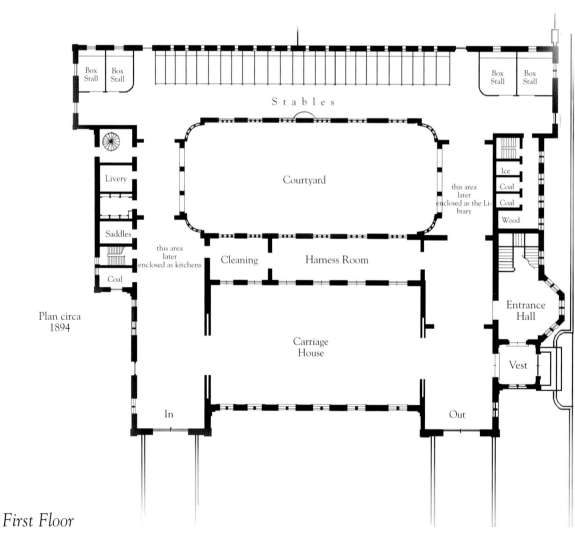

Plan circa
1894

First Floor

HAROLD BROWN VILLA

HAROLD BROWN

Dudley Newton, 1893-1894

Harold Brown was born on Christmas Eve in 1863. His parents, John Carter Brown, a noted bibliophile and philanthropist of the prominent Providence, Rhode Island, family, and Sophia Augusta Brown, were both longtime summer residents of Newport. In 1888, Harold and his older brother John Nicholas Brown began a business partnership, establishing the real estate and mortgage company of J.N. & H. Brown, although John Nicolas was the more active partner, with Harold spending much of his time pursuing his interests in the arts and the Episcopal Church.

In 1892, Harold married Georgette Wetmore Sherman, the daughter of William Watts Sherman and Anne Wetmore. Anne was the daughter of William Shepard Wetmore, who had built Chateau-sur-Mer, the Bellevue Avenue cottage designed in 1852 by Seth C. Bradford and substantially enlarged by Richard Morris Hunt in the 1870s. Following Anne's death, her husband married Harold's sister Sophia, making Sherman simultaneously both a father-in-law and a brother-in-law.

The year following his marriage, Brown purchased the Burns estate, immediately adjacent to his parents' Bellevue Avenue home. He then asked Dudley Newton to develop plans for a summer villa in a baronial style that would be sheathed in rough-cut granite. In February of 1894 the contractor Robert Curry guaranteed to have the house completed by November 1 of the same year, exclusive of the interior finish of the principal entertaining rooms. Curry was given a budget of $10,764 for the project. Because of the relative narrowness of the property, the architect sited the house on an east-west axis, with the entrance porte-cochère being placed on the narrow east end, while extending the mass of the structure westward from it. The building's asymmetrically

Entrance Façade (Gary Lawrance Collection)

South Façade (Author's Collection)

placed bay windows, doors, and gabled extensions seem to exemplify a nineteenth-century Scottish baronial taste. In keeping with the seasonal aspect of the house, there was a south-facing paved terrace and an enclosed conservatory on the opposite side of the house.

To ensure privacy the house was placed near the western edge of the property, far away from Bellevue Avenue. Another reason for placing the house so far back was that nearly half of the eventual Bellevue Avenue frontage was, until the 1920s, occupied by a small villa owned by the Benjamin Hazard estate. The Olmsted Brothers filled this forward expanse of lawn with a forest of specimen beech, maple, oak, and butternut trees so that the house became practically invisible from the avenue. Adding color throughout the growing season were masses of rhododendrons, azaleas, and lilacs. Winding through the estate were gravel paths that passed by multihued rose gardens and beds bursting with

colorful annuals and perennials such as lavender, petunias, columbines, pansies, and lilies. In the northwest corner of the property, a granite wall pierced by a roofed gateway led to Mrs. Brown's private garden, a secluded spot that remained in full bloom throughout the summer.

While the exterior of the house is rough and stylistically untamed, its principal interiors are executed within the strict classical formality of the French Empire. While on their honeymoon, the Browns began collecting art and decorative art pieces from the Napoleonic era, which they continued to do through the 1890s. Wanting to create an appropriate environment in which to house these pieces, Brown engaged Ogden Codman because of his expertise in the field of the French decorative arts. Combining superb architectural detailing with the appropriate light fixtures, door hardware, and drapery fabrics, Codman created an enveloping Empire ambience that was elegant but also extremely livable.

North Façade (Author's Collection)

Codman restructured Newton's asymmetrical floor plan to create balanced and well-proportioned spaces, in which symmetry is paramount. The massive wooden doors off the porte-cochère give access to an open vestibule with a short flight of steps that lead up to a paneled entrance gallery, whose linear divisions are marked by Ionic pilasters. To the right are doors leading to a small reception room with an accompanying lavatory, and to a secondary staircase leading up to a master suite. In the well of this staircase is placed a hydraulically powered elevator. At the far end of the gallery is a set of doors that lead into the principal hall. Here, the marbleized walls are in a rich golden color, while encircling Ionic columns and Doric pilasters are executed in a dark green marble, with capitals of light gray granite. A fireplace niche is to the left; providing balance on the opposite wall is a broad rectangular-shaped bay window. At the far end of the hall is a gracefully curved staircase, with a delicate Empire railing.

Recesses on either side of the hall fireplace lead to the drawing room, library, and dining room. The drawing room, located in the southeast corner of the house, has gray-green walls that are articulated by decorative pilasters enriched with classically inspired detailing. A marble mantelpiece, glass-fronted built-in vitrines, and mirrored wall panels add texture and a sense of drama to the space. The adjacent library has similar decorative detailing, this time in shades of cream; but its chief glory are the mahogany bookshelves found at each end of the room. Here the polished woodwork is embellished by gilt-bronze mounts that, in combination with the richly hued leather-bound books, create a subdued but richly-hued effect. Above the marble fireplace is a built-in mirror, while on either side

family portraits hang above freestanding mahogany bookcases. A set of doors at the western end of the room leads to the dining room. This room has walls painted cream, with their decorative detailing highlighted in dark green. To ensure a symmetrical appearance, Codman visually turned the southern end of the dining room into an alcove, which he framed with fluted columns and pilasters with Ionic capitals. Between the windows and below a mirrored trumeau is a green marble mantelpiece embellished with gilded mounts. Three sets of false doors are incorporated into the design to maintain symmetry.

While in Europe in the spring of 1900, Harold Brown received a cable telling of the fatal illness of his brother. Upon hearing the news, he hurriedly sailed home on the White Star liner *Oceanic*, his wife traveling on a later vessel. While aboard the ship he became desperately ill himself, with doctors being summoned to meet the boat on its arrival in New York. Brown and his attending physicians were then taken to his mother's suite at the Hotel Netherland, where he died two days later.

Harold's widow continued to occupy the house until her own death sixty years later. The house and its furnishings were inherited by her niece Eileen S. S. Gillespie Slocum, the daughter of Georgette's sister Mrs. Lawrence Lewis Gillespie. Eileen's late husband John Jermain Slocum was a distinguished diplomat and scholar, whose important collection of James Joyce material is now ensconced in the Beinecke Rare Book and Manuscript Library at Yale University. Today the Harold Brown Villa is the only Bellevue Avenue house still inhabited by descendents of its original occupants.

Mrs. Slocum died in July 2008.

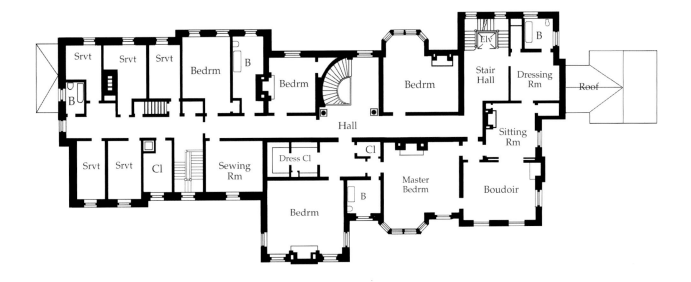

Second Floor

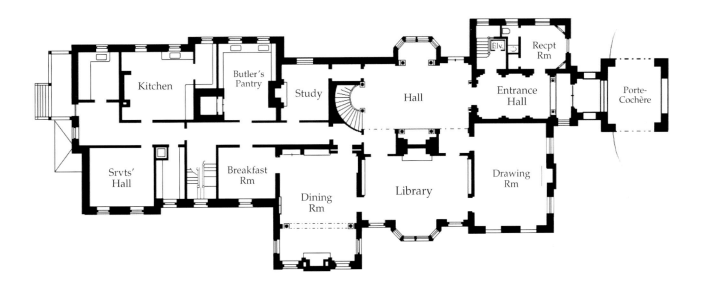

First Floor

THE BREAKERS

CORNELIUS VANDERBILT II

Richard Morris Hunt, 1893-1895

The Vanderbilt family's association with this enviable oceanfront spot dates to 1885, when Cornelius Vanderbilt II purchased the eleven-acre site from Pierre Lorillard for $400,000. Lorillard, whose family fortune was derived from tobacco, had purchased the undeveloped farmland in 1877, subsequently commissioning the Boston firm of Peabody & Stearns to design a substantial brick and shingle Queen Anne–style house for the location. Tiring of the pace of the Newport social scene, Lorillard soon departed to develop the resort of Tuxedo Park, New York.

Immediately following the acquisition, Vanderbilt asked Peabody & Stearns to return and make improvements. These renovations included: a wing on the north side of the house that held a new dining room; an enlarged carriage house with adjacent greenhouses; and a children's playhouse that was based on an almshouse in Guilford, England. When the work was completed, Mr. Vanderbilt, his wife Alice Claypoole Gwynne Vanderbilt, and their six children occupied one of the finest cottages in Newport.

On a chilly day in November of 1892, with the house furnaces stoked, the family—now in mourning over the loss of eldest son William Henry Vanderbilt II—was enjoying the tranquility of Newport out of season. While entertaining Edith and Teddy Wharton, a wisp of smoke was seen rising from the roof. Within an hour the house was engulfed in flames. By the following morning only charred chimneystacks remained standing.

Undaunted, Cornelius commissioned Richard Morris Hunt to develop plans for a larger house for the site. Hunt's original French Gothic–style proposal was rejected

The Original Breakers (Author's Collection)

West Entrance Gates (Author's Collection)

because it was too similar in appearance to Ochre Court, a house that the architect had recently completed for Ogden Goelet just down the street. A second proposal in the Italian Renaissance style based on Genoese *palazzi* was accepted by Vanderbilt. Because of the efficiency and speed of Hunt's draftsmen, construction could begin within only four months of the fire. Considering the scope and complexity of the design, it is remarkable that the structure was completed in just a little over two years.

The new Breakers has a reinforced steel I-beam frame partitioned with brick inner walls, while the exterior is veneered in sumptuously articulated carved limestone. With over seventy rooms, it has a main block measuring 250 by 150 feet, plus the addition of a separate kitchen wing extending from its northwest corner. There are two basement levels, three principal floors, and an attic. Vanderbilt originally wanted only a two-story house with staff accommodations in the attic but was soon persuaded by the architect that a full three stories was needed to effectively convey the desired effect. Aside from aesthetic reasons, the additional floor was also necessary to accommodate the numerous bedroom suites required for all seven family members. Another consideration for its final size was the need for extensive service areas, which eventually consumed almost a third of the total square footage of the structure.

The east, or ocean, façade is the most successful. Projecting wings at either end of the elevation rise up through the third-floor level and bracket loggias placed at the first and second-story levels. A triple arcade on the ground-story loggia is surmounted by a doubled arcade above, which is then, in turn, capped by a balustrade. The fenestration on both of the projections utilizes a Palladian window effect with the dividing members bracketed by Corinthian pilasters on the first two floors. The attic-story windows are placed within the entabla-

Entrance Façade (Author's Collection)

Ocean Façade (Author's Collection)

South Façade (Author's Collection)

Great Hall (Author's Collection)

ture, between paired and tripled consoles that support a full cornice. Adding color to the composition is a multihued roof made of different shades of red and yellow clay tiles.

The tripartite design of the south elevation has a two-story, centrally positioned, five-bay projection that is augmented on the first two stories by a semicircular extension. The elevation is unified by the use of a first-floor loggia at either end, whose roofs are supported by paired columns, although the western loggia is enclosed to create a sunny interior alcove. Joining these two elements, and visually uniting the composition, is a half-circle pergola that fronts the central semicircular extension. Around the corner, the entrance façade is articulated with richly executed sculptural detailing. Like the southern elevation, Hunt uses a central projecting pavilion, this time augmented by a substantial

ground-floor porte-cochère. The north façade is the least successful, principally because the projecting kitchen wing robs it of symmetry.

One enters the structure through a set of towering oak doors that are each over a foot thick. They open to a stone-clad vestibule, with an ornate set of metal and glass doors on the opposite wall. This second set of doors accesses a Caen-stone-sheathed hallway, with steps at its midpoint leading up to the floor level of the principal reception rooms. On either side of this hallway are balancing entrances to the gentlemen's and ladies' reception rooms—each with an adjoining coat closet and lavatory. Even here, in these relatively unimportant spaces designed for guests to pass through quickly, the decorative finish is exceptional. The men's area is richly paneled in natural oak and has a ruddy-colored marble fireplace. The ladies' room is even more

Dining Room (Author's Collection)

Billiard Room (Author's Collection)

handsomely accoutred; the antique boiserie lining its walls was originally created in 1778 for the Hôtel Mégret de Sérilly in Paris and is embellished with richly carved and gilded classical allegorical figures representing the arts.

The floor plan of the house is centered on a square, marble-paved great hall. In Italy this would have been an open courtyard, but in deference to the harsher New England climate, Hunt had it covered with a 45-foot-high ceiling painted with a cloud-swept sky. The tripartite design of the walls are covered with Caen stone and inset with polychrome marbles placed within decorative frames. Surrounding the space are richly executed Corinthian pilasters sitting on high plinths. Between these pilasters are velvet-draped arched openings on the first floor, with galleries encircling three sides of the floor above.

On the east elevation plate-glass windows on both levels open onto ocean-facing loggias. The

Library (Author's Collection)

lower loggia has a vaulted and intricately detailed mosaic ceiling, while the flat ceiling on the second-floor loggia is painted to depict classically inspired fabric being stretched by cords, creating an ancient Roman sunshade effect. The central opening on the north side of the great hall contains a marble staircase, embellished with a bronze and wrought-iron railing, which splits at an initial landing before it ascends to a second landing, where it makes a final turn before reaching the second floor. The staircase is bathed in a soft filtered light coming through a stained-glass skylight. On the opposite side of the great hall is a stone fireplace sculpted by Karl Bitter. Overhead are four immense Second Empire–style chandeliers with opalescent globes, while additional illumination is provided by torchères that encircle the space.

A Circassian walnut–paneled library has insets of tooled Spanish leather and a coffered ceiling. It boasts a sixteenth-century French stone chimney-piece with an inscription that, loosely translated, reads, "Little do I care for riches, and do not miss them, since only cleverness prevails in the end." The billiard room has walls of pale gray-green Cippolino marble, with alabaster being liberally used for the carved decorative trimmings. Polychrome marbles are used to represent the colors of billiard balls in the detailing, while overhead a metal chandelier hangs from a classically inspired mosaic ceiling. On the floor, mosaic was again used, this time with an oak-leaf and acorn motif that represents the Vanderbilt family symbols of strength and longevity.

While Hunt was responsible for the three pre-

First Floor Loggia (Author's Collection)

viously mentioned spaces, he turned over the decoration of the other principal rooms on the first floor to Jules Allard. These rooms—walls, floors, and ceilings—were created in France, then dismantled, each section then being shipped in sealed tin cases to the United States. Accompanying workmen were sent to install them upon there arrival in Newport.

The music room, found in the central position on the south side of the house, was designed by Richard Bouwens van der Boijen under Allard's direction. Here, the splendor of the gray, silver, and gold boiserie is enhanced by a blue Campan marble fireplace with gilt-bronze mounts. Overhead, a coffered ceiling has painted inserts of Renaissance classical imagery. The dining room, which was also designed by Van der Boijens, is even more elaborate. This space is 58 by 42 feet and over two stories

in height. Encircling the room, and supporting a full entablature along with a projecting cornice, are twelve monolithic columns of deep red alabaster, which are capped by gilded bronze Corinthian capitals. Niches set within ceiling vaults display oval windows, faced with decorative ironwork, framed by life-size plaster figures. In the center of the ceiling is a large canvas, *Aurora at Dawn*. Next door is a more moderately scaled family dining room decorated with Louis XV boiserie. An ocean-facing morning room is finished as a simpler and less opulent version of the music room.

With enormous sums being spent on the first-floor rooms, it is surprising that Vanderbilt contracted the second- and third-floor rooms to a then relatively unknown designer named Ogden Codman. He espoused a new design ethic based on eighteenth-century proportion and classical detail-

Music Room (Author's Collection)

Butler's Pantry (Library of Congress)

ing. Except for the late-seventeenth-century design for Mr. Vanderbilt's bedroom, Codman limited his work to the Louis XV and Louis XVI periods. The second floor has six bedrooms and four dressing rooms, plus a nursery and governess's room. Surprisingly, there were originally only four bathrooms on this level, but the master bath does have a tub carved from a solid block of marble.

It is only on the third floor that the immense scale of the house becomes easily apparent. Although the rooms on this level are ample in size, the number of spaces almost doubles from that found on the floor below. Ceiling heights are also lower, giving these rooms a cozier aspect. A transverse hall that runs in a north-south axis bisects the plan. This intersects with a similar corridor spanning the east-west axis of the southern wing of the structure. Arranged along these halls are family and guest bedrooms, many paneled in fine woods and all executed in Codman's signature French eighteenth-century taste. From the center of the principal cor-

ridor are steps leading up to a rectangular platform that rises above the ceiling of the great hall below. On the east side of the platform are doors leading to three guest chambers. Around the rest of the floor are six additional bedroom suites. The northern wing of the third floor has a housekeeper's suite and eleven staff bedrooms, while on the floor above there are fifteen additional staff rooms, as well as water tanks and general storage areas.

Although the family arrived at the beginning of the 1895 season, the official housewarming did not take place until August 14, when a coming-out ball was given for Vanderbilt's elder daughter Gertrude. Anticipated by the entire colony, the three hundred invited guests were all anxious to see the home's many splendors. It was one of the major events of the season. The family received in the great hall, while music was provided by Mullaly's Orchestra and Sherry's Hungarian Band—both brought up from New York for the occasion. The *New York Herald* noted that "supper was served on

Second Floor Staircase Hall *(Author's Collection)*

Third Floor Bedroom Rendering (The Metropolitan Museum of Art, Gift of the Estate of Ogden Codman, 1951 [51.644.73(21)] Copy Photograph © The Metropolitan Museum of Art)

Third Floor Bath Rendering (The Metropolitan Museum of Art, Gift of the Estate of Ogden Codman, 1951 [51.644.74(4)] Copy Photograph © The Metropolitan Museum of Art)

innumerable small tables that were brought in as if by magic, each with its silver ornaments and pink shaded lamps. . . ." At midnight, Gertrude and Lispenard Stewart led a "spirited" cotillion.

The Breakers had little time to be used for large-scale social gatherings because Cornelius suffered a paralytic stroke in July of the following year. He made a slow and painful recovery, and by September of 1899 he seemed well enough to return to New York from Newport to attend a board meeting of the New York Central Railroad. He died of a massive cerebral hemorrhage the night before the meeting was to take place.

The Breakers was bequeathed to his widow. At Alice's death in 1934 the house went to her daughter Gladys, now Countess László Széchenyi. In 1948, Gladys leased the house to the Preservation Society of Newport County for the nominal sum of $1 a year, reserving the third floor for herself and her family. The Society opened the house to a curious public in order to raise funds for their programs. Generously, Gladys continued to pay taxes and all maintenance costs on the structure so that the Society could reap a greater benefit. Her heirs continued with this arrangement after her death in 1965, except that now the Society was expected to pay all taxes and maintenance costs. Seven years later the organization was able to negotiate an outright purchase of the house, while the original furnishings were donated by the heirs in yearly increments over the following decades. Today the Breakers is the most visited site in the state of Rhode Island, and continues to be a tangible manifestation of the American Renaissance and its most illustrious family.

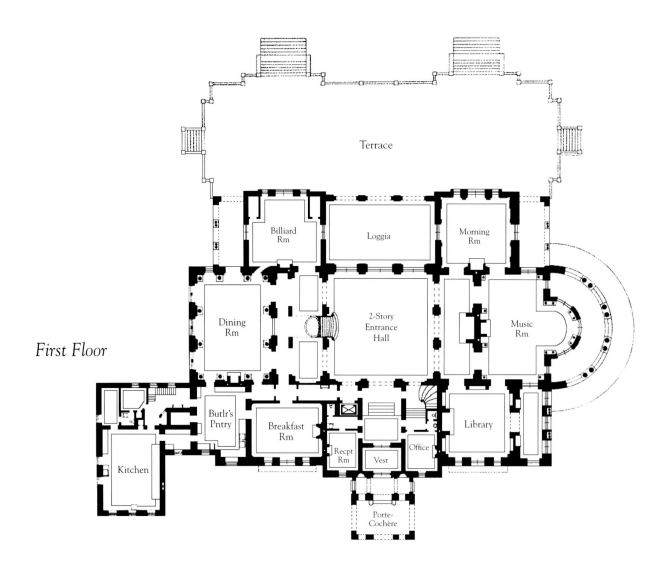

First Floor

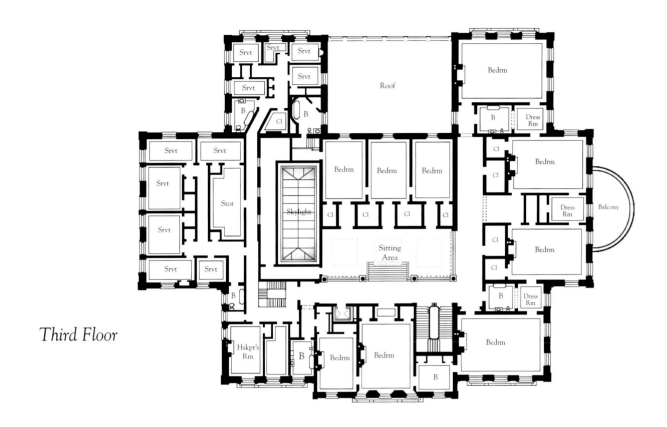

Third Floor

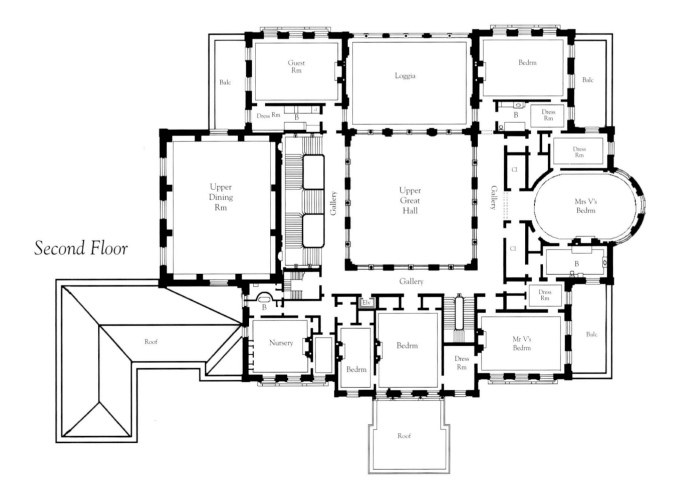

Second Floor

SHAMROCK CLIFF

GAUN MCROBERT HUTTON

Peabody & Stearns, 1894–1895

After passing Brenton Reef and entering Narragansett Bay, one is immediately confronted with a series of houses that are quite different from the more elaborate houses along Bellevue Avenue. Each has a rugged countenance, with little of the classical detailing that evokes the elegance associated with houses on the Avenue. On their elevated windswept sites, they act as architectural sentinels guarding the entrance to Newport Harbor. Beginning at Brenton's Point with the now-demolished Theodore M. Davis estate (The Reef), and continuing through to the shingled Auchincloss cottage (Hammersmith Farm) adjacent to Fort Adams, these houses collectively represent a panoply of architectural styles, each set within sprawling manicured lawns.

In the midst of this stands Shamrock Cliff, the home of Gaun McRobert Hutton and his wife, the former Celeste Winans. Mrs. Hutton was the granddaughter of Baltimore railroad magnate and financier Ross Winans. Her father, Thomas Winans, along with her uncle William, traveled to Russia in 1843 to develop the St. Petersburg-Moscow railroad for Nicholas I. With this and other railroad engineering projects, Thomas acquired a fortune of $10 million by the time he was thirty. The family's association with Newport began in 1861, when Thomas purchased a narrow strip of waterfront property near Castle Hill. There he erected a wooden cottage, with a squat tower and a mansard roof, which was named Bleak House.

At the time of her father's death in June of 1878, Celeste inherited a considerable portion of his estate. In 1883, while visiting family friends in Russia, she was introduced to a vice consul at the American embassy in St. Petersburg by the name of Gaun Hut-

Gate Lodge (Redwood Library and Atheaeum, Newport, Rhode Island)

Entrance Façade (Newport Historical Society)

Tower Detail (Newport Historical Society)

ton. Born in Ballygrangey, Ireland, in 1848, Hutton immigrated to Baltimore when he was sixteen. He later joined the United States Foreign Service, receiving an assignment in Russia. He and Celeste would be married within months of their meeting.

The following year Gaun resigned his diplomatic post and retired. The couple initially spent summers at Bleak House with Celeste's brother Ross but soon began looking for a place of their own. Leasing the estate of the late Arthur Bronson

Water Façade (Newport Historical Society)

on neighboring Ridge Road for a few seasons, the couple purchased it in 1887. The first thing they did was to rename the estate Shamrock Cliff in deference to Mr. Hutton's homeland. The wooden Bronson cottage sat on a cliff overlooking the neighboring Agassiz estate at Castle Hill. Three years later Hutton had the cove at the base of his property dredged to accommodate steam launches and sailing vessels. At the same time, Hutton commissioned a new carriage-house complex to be erected.

By the 1890s, the family had expanded by three daughters—Lucette Marguerite, Elsie Celeste, and Una Louise—and one son named Reginald. The Bronson house was too small to fulfill the family's needs. In response, in 1893, Hutton began a building campaign by hiring Peabody & Stearns to design a new gatehouse of rough sandstone crowned by a bright multihued tile roof. The following year he directed the architects to replace the Bronson cottage with something considerably larger. To ensure uninterrupted water views for the improved estate, Hutton purchased adjacent property known as McCagg's Field in 1911.

A long, curving drive ascends at a gentle grade to the crest of the hill where the new house, an American interpretation of an Anglo-Irish castle, now stands. The drive proceeds through a porte-cochère that pierces the southeast wing of the house, and then passes on into a circular entrance court. Visually anchoring this end of the structure is a three-storied tower that has a shallow hipped roof, whose four sides meet at a decorative copper finial. On the courtyard side of the tower is an attached hexagonal-shaped extension with a crenellated top that exhibits staggered windows that announce a staircase within. A single-story columned porch located in the court is bracketed by three-story gabled extensions, while above the porch is a steeply sloped roof with two tiers of dormer windows. On the remainder of this façade, as well as on all three others, the first-floor windows are rectangular-topped, while those above are arched. Several of the latter are paired, with the windows separated by carved engaged columns. The projecting side wings of the house are set at 45-degree angles from the central mass, which help create a wind-protected entrance court and carriage turnaround. The northern service wing is visually subservient to the towered wing opposite, and on its far side has a sunken-walled service court.

The ocean façade is centered by a projecting half-circle extension, which on the first floor has a set of French doors that are bracketed by paired windows. Above this is an open loggia with four columns that support a conical roof. At either end of this elevation are placed single-story tile-floored verandas, each with a shallow roof supported by rectangular piers. Attached to the northern end of the elevation is a square three-story tower that expands at the attic level by a corbel table pierced with slits for the arrows of imaginary medieval bowmen.

The arrangements of the principal spaces within are aligned along a bisecting transverse hall that runs north-south through the central block. Facing the water are the principal reception rooms, which include the billiard room, the library, and the dining room. Across the hall is a centrally placed entrance loggia bordered by an office and the main staircase. South of the staircase is a reception area and a hall leading to the principal entrance vestibule found within the porte-cochère. On the far side of the porte-cochère is a short flight of exterior steps that lead up to a secondary entrance. Beyond it is a school room for the Hutton children.

With his family in attendance, Hutton died at Shamrock Cliff in July of 1916. His widow continued to summer in the house, although she became more socially reclusive. At her death the Newport property was inherited by her son and two surviving daughters. In 1929, her son built Ballygrangey House on a portion of the McCagg's Field site, while his sisters continued to occupy Shamrock Cliff. In 1957, the cottage was sold to developers. Over the next two decades it survived as an inn, a restaurant, and a disco before being converted to timeshare units. The Hutton cottage is now used as a hotel, seasonal restaurant, and as a venue for private parties and weddings.

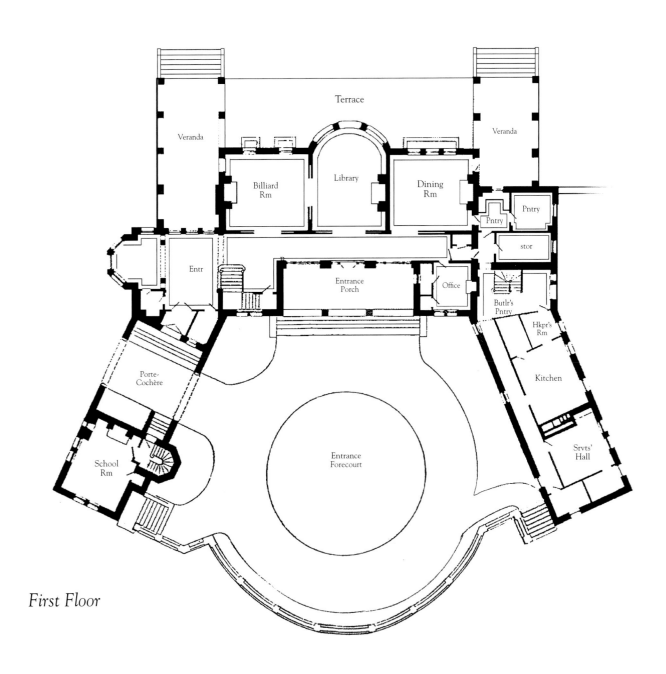

Terrace

Veranda

Veranda

Billiard
Rm

Library

Dining
Rm

Pntry

Pntry

stor

Entr

Entrance
Porch

Office

Butlr's
Pntry

Porte-
Cochère

Hkpr's
Rm

Kitchen

School
Rm

Entrance
Forecourt

Srvts'
Hall

First Floor

CROSSWAYS

STUYVESANT FISH

Dudley Newton, 1897–1898

Stuyvesant Fish descended from impeccable American lineage. His father Hamilton Fish was a onetime governor of New York, who later became secretary of State during the Grant administration. His grandfather Nicholas Fish, a leading Federalist politician, married Elizabeth Stuyvesant, a great-great granddaughter of one of New Amsterdam's founding fathers, Peter Stuyvesant. Also in the background were assorted Livingstons, Morrises, and Keans, all first families of the nation. Born in New York City on June 14, 1851, Stuyvesant Fish later became an executive of the Illinois Central Railroad, becoming its president from 1887 to 1906. Fish later turned to banking and investment interests.

Even with this exalted pedigree, Mr. Fish deferred social matters to his wife Mamie, whom he married on June 1, 1876. Marion (Mamie) Graves Anthon Fish was the daughter of William H. Anthon, a respected New York attorney. Famous for her quick and acerbic wit, she often had her friends convulsing in fits of laughter. Examples of Mamie's humor are legend. At the beginning of one Newport season she greeted her dining companions: "Well here you all are older faces and younger clothes." At another function Alice Drexel, complaining of her location at dinner, exclaimed, "I was so near the pantry that the waiters had to pass their dishes right over my head." "You certainly ought to be satisfied," retorted Mamie. "You not only had a dinner but a Passover too."

"Howdy-do, howdy-do" was her signature greeting to guests as she impatiently pushed new arrivals at Stuyvesant with a look of keen annoyance. A social innovator, she rebelled at the "three mortal hours" at table required by the typical eight-course

Entrance Façade (Courtesy of the Preservation Society of Newport County)

Hall (Author's Collection)

Hall Alcove (Courtesy of the Preservation Society of Newport County)

Dining Room (Courtesy of the Preservation Society of Newport County)

meal of the period. She liked having dinners served in less than an hour. A record was set at one meal when it was served in less than thirty minutes. Guests at that meal remembered having to hold the plate down with one hand while eating with the other in order to keep a footman from removing it.

In the spring of 1894, Stuyvesant began negotiations to purchase a 66,207-square-foot site on Ocean Avenue at Jeffrey Road. Because of its elevated position, it encompassed ocean views from Point Judith, Rhode Island, to Gay Head, Massachusetts. Fish was a shrewd negotiator, acquiring the property for only $11,000—a remarkable bargain at a time when other choice building sites were going for upward of $100,000. One of the reasons for the price may have been its rocky topography, which made it unfeasible to construct both a house

and a stable upon the site. Fish would have to acquire additional acreage before the project could commence. Unfortunately, the owner of the land immediately to the west initially asked what Fish felt was an exorbitant sum, so it took an additional three years of negotiations before the coveted land was obtained.

By November of 1897 construction finally commenced. Since everyone working on the project was locally based, including the architect Dudley Newton, the contractor R. W. Curry, and the interior decorating firm of Vernon, the house was actually ready for occupancy the following season. There are no European evocations here; Crossways is designed in the Colonial Revival style, which had already waned in fashionable circles. Fish, not being as wealthy as many of his fellow colonists, prob-

Library (Author's Collection)

Drawing Room (Author's Collection)

ably chose the wooden Colonial vernacular because it was cheaper to build.

Round stone entrance piers mark the entrance to the estate on Ocean Avenue. From them a short, curved, driveway leads up to a Colonial house built on a massive scale. In the center of the composition is placed a pedimented porte-cochère, supported by four Corinthian columns. A central mass measuring 61 by 46 feet is bracketed by matching wings of 26 by 45 feet. Extending from the latter are single-story 14-foot-wide verandas with roofs held aloft by Ionic columns. Alternate-size wooden blocks designed to appear as quoins mark the linear divisions, while shutters are used to break up the wall planes. A hipped roof is punctuated by red brick chimneys and is crowned by a widow's walk.

The rear of the house is less ordered, abandoning symmetry altogether. A basement-level service entrance is accessed from a gorge cut into a rock formation that embraces the rear of the house. To help facilitate large events, a ballroom designed by Joseph G. Williams was added to the northwestern corner of the house in 1913.

A set of wooden doors capped by a glazed fanlight opens to a vestibule containing two successive short flights of steps that lead up to an inner door. The latter is also topped by a fanlight, but is additionally embellished with side lights that have alternating circular and diamond-shaped panes of glass. The great hall found beyond rises up through to the roof, with open galleries running along the second-floor level. The hall, delineated by Ionic pilasters, is 43 feet long, with a depth of 22 feet, and is augmented by alcoves placed on either side of the entrance vestibule. These alcoves are fitted with comfortable divans and can be utilized as card-rooms, additional lounges, or dining areas for large parties. At the eastern end of the hall a broad opening leads into a 36-foot-long dining room. Here the trim and wainscoting is painted white, while above are sections covered in green silk damask. A scrolled broken pediment surmounts a wooden mantelpiece with a marble surround and a shelf supported by attached columns. At the opposite end of the house is the drawing room. This space has the most elaborate decorative program in the house, with walls completely paneled and decorated with classical detailing in the style of Robert Adam. The ceiling is divided into three oval sections, each with elaborate plasterwork that carries out the Adamesque theme. A library to the left of the main staircase has three-quarter-high bookcases, and walls covered with deep red hangings against which were hung family portraits. The second floor contains seven bedrooms that vary in size from 14 by 19 feet to 19 by 27 feet—all executed with simple American Colonial trim.

Ironically, the first major social function to be held at Crossways during its inaugural season was a barn dance that eschewed the house completely, as it was held in the stable. Two years later Mamie reinterpreted the same theme, but this time she moved the barnyard into the house with her guests attired as dairymaids and farmers. Atop the round stone gate piers that guard the entrance to the property were placed pumpkins carved into jack o' lanterns, each 12 feet in circumference. They were illuminated from within with calcium lighting that gave off an eerie glow. Between the gateway and the porte-cochère was a series of lantern-adorned arches, while the surrounding shrubs and trees were illuminated with hundreds of twinkling miniature lights that produced the effect of swarming fireflies. Scattered elsewhere around the grounds were haystacks, farm equipment, and teams of grazing oxen.

The porte-cochère was lined with shocks of wheat and corn, while the entrance vestibule was a bower of greens, wheat, and cattails. The main hall was wainscoted in 7-foot-high sheaves of wheat decorated with thousands of sunflowers and poppies. The space between the wheat sheaves and the ceiling was filled with farm implements and bushels of local produce, while suspended from the ceiling were garlands composed of greens, scarlet poppies, and sprays of winter wheat, all held aloft by ribbons of red and yellow. The adjacent drawing room was rimmed with palms and garlands that were inter-

Ballroom (Newport Historical Society)

twined with field poppies and cornflowers. Here, within a thatched-roofed enclosure, orchestra musicians performed behind a screen of plaited wheat. At midnight, a buffet supper was served in the dining room and adjacent veranda, which were both draped with fruit-laden vines to create a grape arbor effect. The table treatments consisted of a coarse sacking material covering adorned with centerpieces of fresh fruits, grains, and vegetables.

Mamie died of a cerebral hemorrhage in May 1915 while in the midst of making plans to open Crossways for the coming season. Her husband continued to occupy the house for a few more years, eventually putting it on the market in 1921. Stuyvesant died on April 11, 1923, before it was sold. In August of 1926, New York socialite Mrs. Morris de Peyster purchased it and occupied it seasonally until the 1940s, when it was converted into apartments.

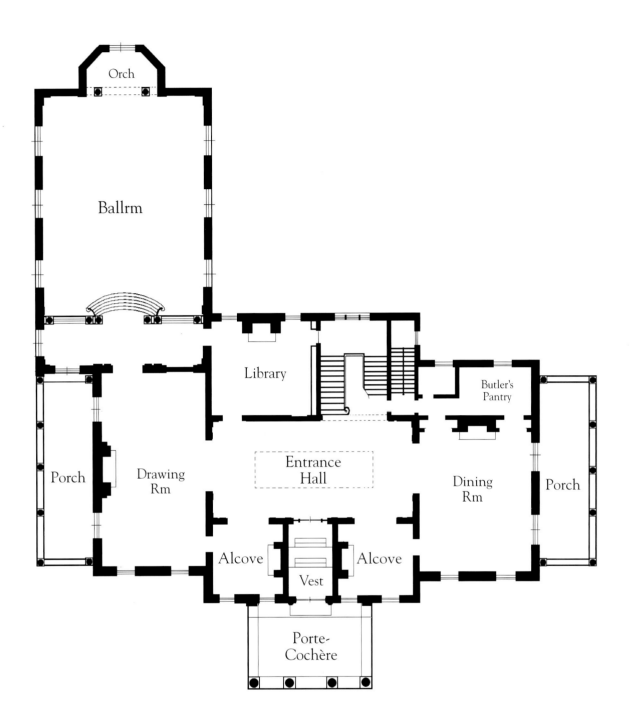

Orch

Ballrm

Library

Butler's
Pantry

Porch

Drawing
Rm

Entrance
Hall

Dining
Rm

Porch

Alcove

Alcove

Vest

Porte-
Cochère

First Floor

VILLA ROSA

E. ROLLINS MORSE

Ogden Codman, Jr., 1900–1901

Of Ogden Codman's five comprehensive residential Newport commissions, those not restricted to interior work alone, Villa Rosa is his most sophisticated and fully developed composition. The entrance façade of the house embodies the severest French Directoire style, while the garden elevation speaks of the more sophisticated presence of the eighteenth-century architect François-Joseph Bélanger and his Bagatelle pavilion erected in the Bois de Boulogne for the Comte d'Artois in 1777.

Villa Rosa was erected on a long but narrow piece of property on Bellevue Avenue that was bound on the north by Dixon Street and on the south by Narragansett Avenue. Three wooden houses—the Coles, Whiting, and Bryce cottages, all constructed in the mid-nineteenth century—were demolished to create the estate. Villa Rosa was not sited to face Bellevue Avenue, but rather to take advantage of the long north-south axis of the property. Also, to create longer vistas in the garden, the house was placed close to the quieter and less-traveled Dixon Street. On axis with the house at the southern end of the garden was a round open-air pavilion based on Marie Antoinette's Temple of Love at the Petit Trianon.

Constructed of stucco-over-concrete, Villa Rosa is painted a vibrant yellow with off-white trim. The entrance piers located on Bellevue Avenue lead, by way of a short allée, to a graveled courtyard. Straight ahead lay a wall whose principal feature consists of a centrally positioned decorative niche filled by a cascading fountain. On either side are small rectangular windows that are, in turn, bracketed by round-topped decorative trelliswork that replicates the scale of the fountain niche. Above a string-

Entrance Court (The Metropolitan Museum of Art, Gift of the Estate of Ogden Codman, 1951 [51.644.124(1)] Copy Photograph © The Metropolitan Museum of Art)

Garden Façade (Author's Collection)

Sculpture in Entrance Vestibule (The Metropolitan Museum of Art, Gift of the Estate of Ogden Codman, 1951 [51.644.145(18)] Copy Photograph © The Metropolitan Museum of Art)

course are found glazed rondels, which indicate the presence of a second story within what is, in actuality, a service wing.

On the south side of the court is the entrance façade. It is a three-story, simply massed, rectangle interrupted by a three-bay-wide two-story central projection. The latter feature is embellished at the first-floor level by a Doric arcade, whose columns separate arch-topped French doors. Above are symmetrically aligned casement windows, all sur-

Entrance Hall (The Metropolitan Museum of Art, Gift of the Estate of Ogden Codman, 1951 [51.644.124(2)] Copy Photograph © The Metropolitan Museum of Art)

mounted by an oculus-embellished pediment. The house is divided horizontally by a stringcourse located above the first-floor windows, a full entablature above the second-story windows, and an abbreviated cornice capped by a balustrade at the top of the house.

The garden elevation has a seamed copper-sheathed dome capping a centrally placed three-story rounded projection, which is interrupted by the cornice placed at the top of the second-story level. Above this division springs a continuing wall plane that has three small rectangular windows, while below it the first floor has three sets of round-topped French doors separated by rectangular decorative plaques designed as floral trophies. In place of windows at the second-floor level, there are five more of these decorative panels. Like Bélanger at Bagatelle, Codman utilized these decorative elements to front a domed ceiling within. At either side of this projection are symmetrically arranged casement windows on the top two floors, while the French doors below access paved terraces.

Inside, Codman designed a functional floor plan that unfolds in logical progressions. After stepping through a broad entrance foyer with large classical sculptures embellishing niches on both sides, the visitor enters a rectangular paneled entrance hall from which all the entertaining rooms emanate. On the left, in the front of the house, is the staircase hall, also paneled in white, with red plush covering the staircase's iron handrail. Next is the salon, whose white-painted paneling contrasts with the room's hangings and seating fabrics, done in shades of green. On axis with the front door is a circular domed ballroom. This is the first space in North America to utilize latticework as the principal decorative device. It precedes—by more than five years—Elsie de Wolfe's celebrated trelliswork room at the original Colony Club on Madison Avenue in New York. To the west is a dining room paneled in the Louis XVI style that is embellished with a white marble mantle and gilt-bronze sconces. A niche opposite the mantelpiece holds an aristocratic bust set on an oversized festooned

Salon (The Metropolitan Museum of Art, Gift of the Estate of Ogden Codman, 1951 [51.644.124(7)] Copy Photograph © The Metropolitan Museum of Art)

Ballroom (The Metropolitan Museum of Art, Gift of the Estate of Ogden Codman, 1951 [51.644.124(6)] Copy Photograph © The Metropolitan Museum of Art)

Dining Room (The Metropolitan Museum of Art, Gift of the Estate of Ogden Codman, 1951 [51.644.124(3)] Copy Photograph © The Metropolitan Museum of Art)

stand. An oak-paneled library found at the front of the house is also executed in the Louis XVI manner.

E. Rollins Morse was a prominent banker and investment broker who hailed from Boston, where he and his wife, Marion Steedman, were prominent in Back Bay social circles. Mrs. Morse's niece Marion, daughter of Dr. and Mrs. A. Lawrence Mason of Boston, was the wife of Richard T. Wilson, Jr. Two of Wilson's sisters were married to Cornelius Vanderbilt III and Ogden Goelet, while his brother was married to Carrie Astor, the youngest daughter of Caroline Astor. Through these familial connections, virtually all doors in Newport were open to them.

Typical of the elaborate entertainments given at Villa Rosa by the Morses was the lawn party and private amateur theatrical held on August 23, 1905.

For the event a vine-covered latticework theater was erected on the south end of the lawn. It was embellished with palms and classical marble busts. Guests performed "*Une danse anciènne*" to eighteenth-century music and readings of French poems. The play itself was a single-act comedy entitled *Le Baiser* by Théodore de Banville. After the performance four hundred guests were treated to tea and dancing in the theater structure, now magically transformed into a ballroom.

Within two years of this sumptuous event, Mr. Morse began experiencing financial setbacks, which eventually culminated in August of 1908 with attachments being placed on both his New York and Newport houses. Morse lost heavily in the financial panic of 1907, but it was also rumored that he had been living well beyond his means in order

Library (The Metropolitan Museum of Art, Gift of the Estate of Ogden Codman, 1951 [51.644.124(5)] Copy Photograph © The Metropolitan Museum of Art)

to emulate the lifestyle of his wife's wealthier relatives. He was able to hold on to the Newport property, but sold it in 1913 to James Ben Ali Haggin. Twenty-three years later Villa Rosa was purchased by William Henry and Emily Coddington Williams, who summered there for the following decade and a half. Finally, the estate was acquired by Edward A. McNulty, a Pawtucket, Rhode Island, road contractor, who added it to his portfolio of other investment properties in the state.

Although the house sat empty for several years, it remained in relatively good condition, suffering only minimal damage by youthful vandals. Villa Rosa's end came late in December of 1962, when it was demolished—in great haste—to protect the owner from incurring higher taxes during the following year. There seems to have been little attempt to salvage any interior or exterior decorative fittings. It is rumored that the crystal chandeliers and marble mantelpieces were still in place when the wrecking ball began pulverizing Ogden Codman's masterpiece into dust.

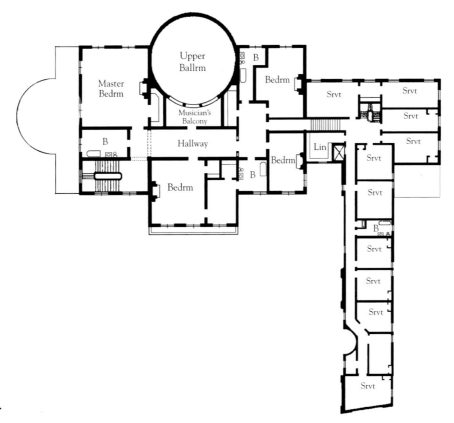

Second Floor

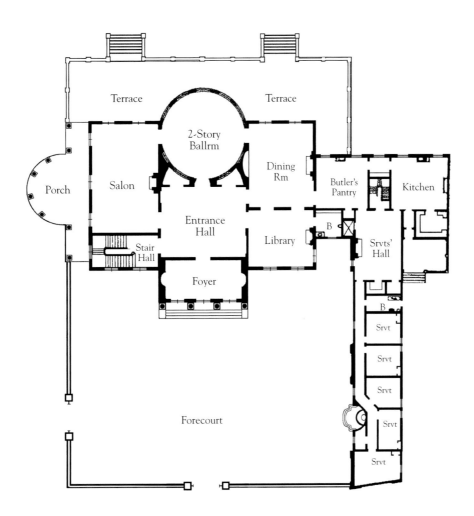

First Floor

HIGH TIDE

WILLIAM STARR MILLER

Warren & Wetmore, 1900

At the end of the nineteenth century William Starr Miller, a successful venture capitalist, purchased property that commands an elevated position overlooking Bailey's Beach near the beginning of Ocean Avenue. Here he commissioned the architect Whitney Warren to design High Tide—unsurprising since Warren was the brother of Mr. Miller's wife, the former Edith C. Warren. High Tide sits amid verdant sloping lawns accented with natural stone outcroppings. The structure is framed on three sides by water views, with the tranquil waters of Almy's Pond to the east, and limitless ocean vistas to the south and west.

High Tide is designed around a three-sided courtyard, whose sections visibly descend in mass and importance. Looking southward is the main body of the house, which contains the entertainment rooms on the lower level and the family's private accommodations on the floor above. Extending from the northeastern corner of this mass is a perpendicular wing devoted to service facilities, with guest accommodations tucked above. Sequentially, a second wing then projects westward from the far end of the first wing. This final segment of the tripartite arrangement is filled with staff bedrooms on the principal floor, and a stable and carriage house beneath—unusual because it physically attaches a stable to family living areas.

The principal mass of the structure is classical in inspiration, but was "provincialized" to adapt it to its rocky windswept site. This was accomplished by the use of minimal ornamentation in a design that is capped by a textured broken-pitch roof, whose lower level extends far out from the cream-colored-stucco wall planes. Because of this configuration there is no need for guttering at the roof's edge, allowing the rafters to

Ocean Façade (Richard & Dee Gordon Collection)

be exposed—giving the house a rustic appearance. Warren did not eschew all classical detailing, however; decorative elements such as the uncarved keystones above the first-floor openings and two stringcourses that wrap the façade help give the house definition and a hint of formal structuring. The principal elevation has a central rounded projection with a conical roof; but even here a subtle asymmetry is apparent, with three bays to the left and only two on the right. Inset within the second floor of the bayed projection is a decorative wooden framework, which has pilasters separating three windows that are fronted by a wooden balustrade. Towering above the composition are nine hooded chimneys that project from the slate roof.

The Millers turned over the major interior spaces to Ogden Codman for execution. Codman's design for High Tide exemplifies his decorative doc-

Ariel View (Richard & Dee Gordon Collection)

trine of simple classical forms utilized to create comfortable, yet elegant, spaces in which to live. An octagonal entrance hall has plaster walls embellished with Louis XVI moldings. The space was bright and airy, thanks to the large windows on the angled walls found on either side of the oak entrance doors. A molded frieze supports an acanthus-leaf cornice, while hanging from the center of the ceiling is an oversized gilded bronze lantern. An adjacent staircase hall has traditional wall moldings, and a wooden staircase is embellished with a wrought-iron balustrade in the Louis XVI style. A rectangular vestibule, extending from the south end of the entrance hall, accesses the three principal entertainment rooms of the house, all executed in the Louis XVI style. Straight ahead is a circular salon with mirrored wall and door panels, elaborated by scrolled keystones and floral swags. A gray marble mantel resonates with similar floral detailing. The adjacent drawing room has oak-paneled walls

articulated by arched divisions, surmounted by richly carved fluted and swaged cornice brackets. Further embellishing the room is a handsome chimneypiece of heavily veined black and white marble, inset with white marble floral bas-relief panels.

At the opposite end of the wing is an oval-shaped dining room. Here the walls are embellished with acanthus-leaf-detailed and beribboned brackets that support a bound-reed cornice. These brackets also become the capitals of simple boxed pilasters that envelop the room and give it definition. A baseboard that encircles the space has been marbleized to match the gray marble chimneypiece.

Family bedrooms are located above the reception rooms and consist of separate bedrooms for Mr. and Mrs. Miller, plus an extra room that was probably used as a boudoir for Mrs. Miller. A separate suite designed for the couple's only child, a daughter named Edith Starr Miller, completed this level. Two guest bedrooms are located in the central wing

Entrance Hall (Richard & Dee Gordon Collection)

Drawing Room (Richard & Dee Gordon Collection)

Dining Room (Richard & Dee Gordon Collection)

Dining Room Detail (Richard & Dee Gordon Collection)

Salon (Richard & Dee Gordon Collection)

of the house, and are accessed from the landing of the principal staircase.

In the mid-twentieth century significant changes were imposed on Warren's design. The round terrace off the dining room was covered and enclosed, while a similarly shaped covered veranda at the opposite end of the house was eliminated altogether. When the house became a year-round residence, it was discovered that winter winds barreled through the house every time the front door was opened. The problem was rectified by pushing out the original three-sided exterior entrance pavilion walls to create a rectangular-shaped enclosed vestibule, with a small office and a reception room filling the voids at either side. Unfortunately, this extension encroached so far into the entrance court that it became impossible for an automobile to make a circle within it. (The current owners have now converted the space into a walled garden court paved with Belgian blocks.) Other interior changes included the elimination of the staff bedrooms in the west wing, allowing for the creation of a self-contained apartment. At the same time, the kitchen was moved from the basement level to the first floor in a space originally allotted for staff bedrooms.

Miller continued to occupy the house until his death in 1935, and his widow until she died nine years later. High Tide sat empty for several seasons until after World War II, when it was purchased by Joseph Washington Frazer of the Kaiser-Frazer Corporation. In 1960 it was sold to developers who planned to convert it to a private club, but two years later the group went into foreclosure. It was later owned by Hickman Price, Jr., who sold it to Verner Z. Reed, Jr., in 1975. Reed, whose fortune derived from western mining interests, had a long history in Newport as the original owner of the estate Terre Mare. Mr. and Mrs. Reed continued to occupy High Tide through 1986, at the time of Mr. Reed's death. Later that same year it was purchased by real estate developer Richard H. Gordon and his wife Dee. The Gordons instigated a comprehensive renovation of the property, adding tennis courts, a putting green, and a swimming pool with an accompanying cabana that has been sensitively designed to blend architecturally with the house.

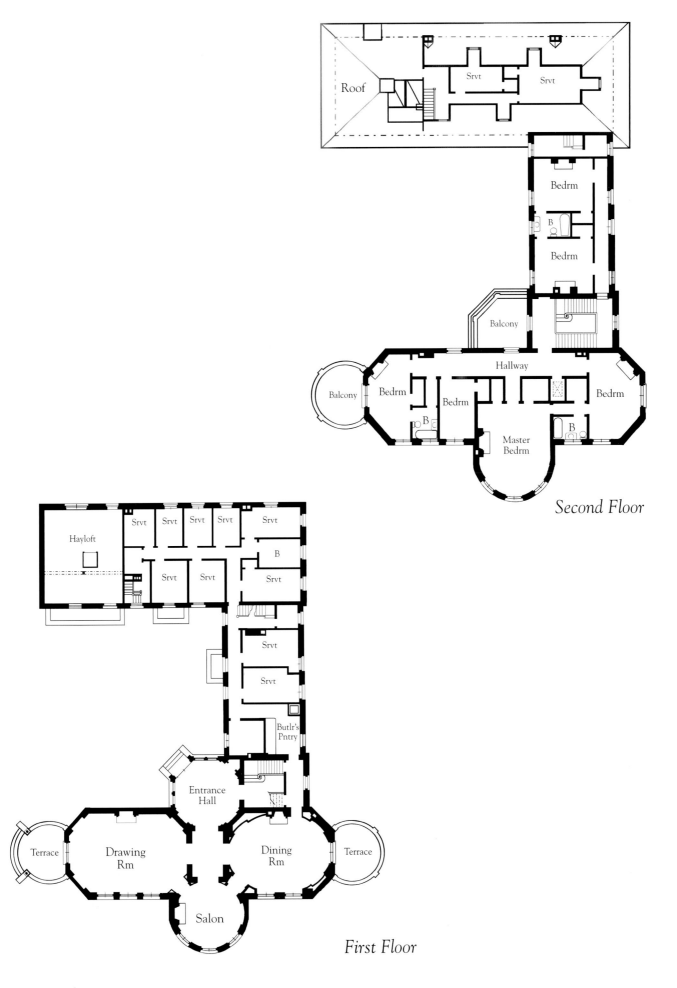

Roof

Srvt

Srvt

Bedrm

B

Bedrm

Balcony

Hallway

Balcony

Bedrm

Bedrm

Bedrm

B

Master
Bedrm

B

Second Floor

Hayloft

Srvt

Srvt

Srvt

Srvt

Srvt

B

Srvt

Srvt

Srvt

Srvt

Srvt

Butlr's
Pntry

Entrance
Hall

Terrace

Drawing
Rm

Dining
Rm

Terrace

Salon

First Floor

VERNON COURT

MRS. RICHARD A. GAMBRILL

Carrère & Hastings, 1899-1901

Mrs. Richard Gambrill was born Anna Van Nest, a descendant of Pieter Pietersen Van Nest who immigrated to New Amsterdam from Holland in 1647. Soon after his arrival in the new world, Pieter founded a dynasty of prosperous landowners and merchants. Anna's father, Alexander T. Van Nest, was a financial partner with the Blair family in developing the Delaware, Lackawanna & Western Railroad. On April 28, 1888, Anna married Richard Augustus Gambrill, a prominent New York attorney who began his career working in the office of traction magnate William Collins Whitney. By 1885 he had moved on to become senior management in the Evansville & Terre Haute Railroad. In 1890, Gambrill succumbed to bronchial pneumonia at the age of forty-one, leaving Anna widowed with a young son.

After emerging from mourning, Anna established herself as a prominent hostess in New York and Newport. By the late 1890s she had decided to erect a cottage in Newport that would compare favorably to other houses rising around hers. Thomas Hastings, of the firm of Carrère & Hastings, was selected because Anna's sister, Mrs. Giraud Foster, was simultaneously having the architect design Bellefontaine, her home in Lenox, Massachusetts.

Barr Ferree in *American Estates and Gardens* (1904) states that "Vernon Court has a starling beauty and daring originality . . . giving it the highest rank among the most notable houses in America." Based on seventeenth-century French-château models, Vernon Court has a rectangular mass topped by a steep hipped roof. Of masonry construction, the walls of the house are veneered in ivory-painted stucco. The eight rectangular chimneystacks emanating from the gray slate roof add verticality to the

Entrance Court (Author's Collection)

Garden Façade (Author's Collection)

Trellis Garden (Author's Collection)

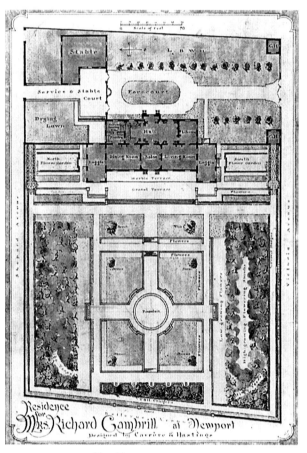

Plot Plan (Author's Collection)

composition, with each rising some 80 feet. The roof is pierced by symmetrically positioned hip-roofed dormers, with smaller decorative oeil-de-boeuf apertures aligned above. The two principal entrances to the structure have surrounds composed of paired columns on either side that support a full entablature and balustrade—a device adapted from the garden front of the Château de Haroue near Nancy, France. Ringing the first floor are French doors. The doors in the front of the house are pro-

Hall (Author's Collection)

tected by wrought-iron railings, while those in the rear open onto a broad marble-paved terrace. Above each is a decorative keystone and bas-relief panel, the latter reaching up to a stringcourse. The upper openings are also French doors, each having a shallow wrought-iron balcony that is floored by a projecting shelf supported by scrolled brackets.

Bordering the garden terrace, single-story loggias provide elegant transition areas between house and garden. Originally intended to be open-air spaces, these loggias were later enclosed with French doors embellished with elaborate trelliswork detailing. The arched openings of the loggia are highlighted with volute keystones, while the spandrels are filled with floral garlands. The piers between the openings contain ornate latticework capped by a decorative oval design. Parapet balustrades that surmount each loggia originally had corners embellished with playful cherub sculptures.

The firm of Wadley & Smythe is responsible for the estate's tightly controlled landscape. One enters the property through a high wrought-iron screen that is centered by a set of gates with elaborate detailing. At either side is placed a small gate lodge with an external wall pierced by an oval window draped by floral garlands. Atop these are oversized chimera that act as sentinels guarding the estate. A short, straight drive bordered by clipped maple trees leads to a graveled entrance court, with a central grass oval embellished with cherubcapped urns at either end. At the far end of the courtyard is a stucco-covered wall with two balancing sets of solid oak gates leading to a carriage house and service area.

The west side of the house has an even more ambitious program, with formal gardens set within geometrical settings filling every square inch of land, but so cleverly executed that it avoids any sense of crowding. At either end of the house are parterre gardens boarded by a loggia on one side and an elaborate trelliswork pergola with a domed end-pavilion on the other. The central garden, with its circular reflecting pool bordered with pink anemone, is an adaptation of the Pond Garden at

Hall Looking Toward Staircase (Author's Collection)

Petit Salon (Author's Collection)

Grand Salon (Author's Collection)

Dining Room (Author's Collection)

Library (General Research Division, The New York Public Library, Astor, Lenox and Tilden Foundation)

Hampton Court that Henry VIII built for Anne Boleyn. On either side of this square-shaped garden are lawns bordered by gravel paths edged with blue hydrangea. Along the perimeter of the site are strategically placed fern-leaf beech, copper beech, native oak, gingko, and plane trees, as well as boundary privet hedges that were later replaced by arborvitae.

Hastings created a floor plan designed to allow for large groups to flow easily through the first-floor rooms, onto the terrace, and into the gardens. The meticulously crafted interiors that fill Vernon Court were designed by the firm of Jules Allard et Fils. The Carrara-marble-paved entrance hall is sheathed in architecturally treated faux Caen stone walls and is embellished with faux brèche-violette Ionic columns that support a floral and leaf frieze capped by a modillion cornice. The east and west walls of the space have a tripartite design with sets of French doors bordering sculpture-filled niches capped with a shell motif. To the right an extension to the hall is reached via a flat arch supported by paired columns. Within this space is a staircase em-

bellished by a decorative wrought-iron railing, whose treads ascend in a graceful arc to the floor above. Across the hall, on axis with the front door of the house, is the petit salon, whose Louis XVI–style boiserie is painted a light mauve with off-white trim. The room also boasts a white Carrara marble fireplace with gilt-bronze mounts. The adjacent grand salon, executed in a robust Régence manner, is paneled in French walnut whose plaster entablature is painted and grained to match, with the carved detailing in both areas accented in gold leaf. The marble fireplace here is of brèche-dorée.

Located on the opposite side of the house, the dining room has off-white walls lined with fluted pilasters supporting a full entablature. On the room's long west wall is a marble serving console, while on the opposite wall is a fireplace of the same material but with the addition of gilt-bronze decorative mounts. The floor of the dining room is bordered by strips of alternating white and black marble that surround simple wooden flooring that was meant to be covered with a carpet. Opening off the dining room is the north loggia. The walls here were dec-

Loggia (Author's Collection)

orated with murals (now lost) of naturalistically painted fruits and flowers created by James Wall Finn of Tiffany Studios. Finn also created murals for the loggia at the opposite end of the house that depict vines growing over trelliswork, with playful putti cavorting among classical urns and exotic birds. These murals are adapted from those created for Pope Julius III at the Villa Giulia in Rome. A library located at the front of the house has Louis XVI–style boiserie painted a soft green. Subtle color is added to the library by a Connemara marble fireplace embellished with ormolu mounts.

After summering at Vernon Court for almost three decades, Anna died on March 23, 1928. Her son Richard Van Nest Gambrill and his wife, the former Edith D. Blair, inherited the Newport cottage. Edith, a member of the same family that Alexander Van Nest partnered with in the creation of his railroad fortune, had spent much of her life dwelling within Carrère & Hastings–designed houses. Her father, C. Ledyard Blair, had commissioned Blairsden, his country estate in Peapack, New Jersey, as well as a New York townhouse lo-

cated at 70th Street and Fifth Avenue, from the illustrious firm.

Vernon Court was purchased in 1956 by Lloyd Hatch, founder of the Hatch Preparatory School. It became Vernon Court Junior College, with the house being utilized as classrooms and administrative offices. After the school declared bankruptcy in 1972, the estate was purchased by the Buckingham Group, a local investment firm. During the 1980s an attempt to convert the house into condominiums failed. For a short time British entrepreneur and yachtsman Peter de Savary owned it, with the intent of turning it into a private club. William A. Perry acquired the house in the early 1990s, when the house went through a major restoration.

In 1998, New York art dealer Judy Goffman Cutler and her husband, architect Laurence Cutler, purchased Vernon Court to house their collection of art. After a substantial renovation, it has been opened as the National Museum of American Illustration. It houses an important collection, which includes works by Norman Rockwell, Maxfield Parrish, and Joseph C. Leyendecker.

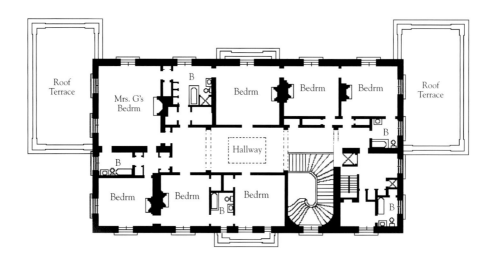

Second Floor

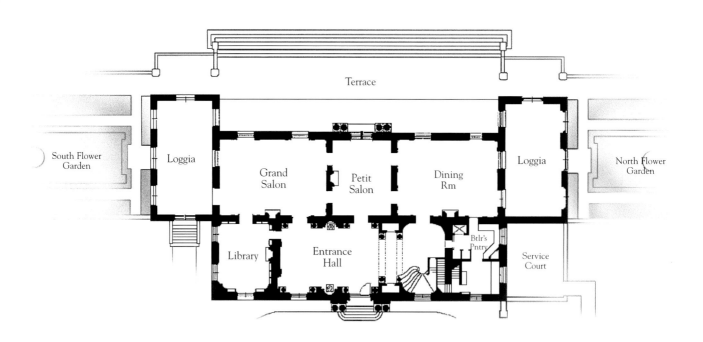

First Floor

THE ELMS

EDWARD JULIUS BERWIND

Horace Trumbauer, 1899-1901

Coal baron Edward Julius Berwind and his wife, the former Sarah Vesta Herminie Torrey, commissioned the Elms to replace a smaller wooden cottage that had originally been owned by the Merritt family. Berwind hailed from Philadelphia, but because of national and international business interests he found it necessary to move to New York. He left management of the Berwind-White Coal Mining Company headquarters in Philadelphia to three of his brothers—Charles, John, and Harry. The company, which became the world's leading supplier of bituminous coal, had been founded in 1874 by Berwind, his brother Charles, and Judge Allison White.

Inspiration for the Newport house was decided upon when decorator Jules Allard sold sculptural groupings to the Berwinds that had originally graced the façade of the Château d'Asnières, located just outside Paris. The château had been designed in 1750 by Jacques Hardouin-Mansart de Sagonne, a grandson of Jules Hardouin-Mansart. These pieces were by Guillaume Coustou the Younger and had been acquired by the decorator at a sale of the château's contents in 1896.

Berwind's architect, Horace Trumbauer, despite working within a limited framework, cleverly manipulated the elements to create something better proportioned than the original. The château had a pronounced horizontality that Trumbauer minimized by placing the Elms on raised terraces. To enhance the effect, he eliminated a bay at either end of the principal elevations, while at the same time scaling up all the components to create greater height. Although the central projection on the west façade that utilized the Coustou sculptures mimicked the original, there are fundamental dif-

Entrance Gates (Author's Collection)

ferences between the two. These differences include replacing a heavy escutcheon surround with a simpler triangular pediment and enhancing the French doors with undulating muntin that reflect a subtle wavelike appearance.

The entrance elevation to the house gave the architect more leeway, with its central projection creating an architectural tour de force, using elements borrowed from several sources. It contains three round-topped decorative glazed wrought-iron doors set within concave chamfering. These are separated by Corinthian columns backed by matching pilasters. Above each opening are carved classical masks set within shell and floral frames. Separating the first and second levels is an entablature that supports a balustrade with floral swagged urns embellished with flaming finials. Capping the house is a full cornice with carved brackets that support an 8-foot-high decorative blind parapet, the latter effectively shielding the attic level from view.

On either end of the structure are terraced extensions that help integrate indoor and outdoor activities through the use of multiple French doors. Steps located at the west ends of each platform access lower terraces and the gardens. The north terrace was used for outdoor dining. To shield the Berwinds from the service entrance directly below, the architect designed a unique circular vine-covered trellis, which springs from a central decorative device consisting of a limestone urn containing an artificial plant of oxidized copper leaves. When in full leaf, this created a canopy that could not be visually penetrated by those on the terrace above.

A faux-Caen-stone-clad entrance hall is centered by a short flight of marble steps that lead up to a similarly finished transverse hall. To either side, at the front of the house, are matching alcoves demarcated by purple breccia marble columns sitting on bronze bases and capped by gilded plaster Corinthian capitals. Most of the home's interiors are executed in eighteenth-century style, with two major exceptions. A library located at the southern end of the transverse hall is in the French Renaissance style. It has walnut paneling with upper wall surfaces covered in crimson silk damask. Above a

Merritt Cottage (Redwood Library and Athenaeum, Newport, Rhode Island)

Entrance Façade (Courtesy of the Preservation Society of Newport County)

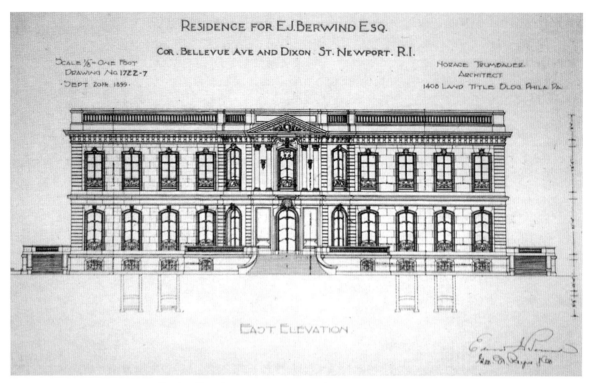

Garden Façade (Courtesy of the Preservation Society of Newport County)

Garden Allée (Gary Lawrance Collection)

Carriage House (Author's Collection)

Caen stone mantelpiece is an early terra-cotta cast of a Madonna and Child by Giovanni della Robbia. At the opposite end of the house, the dining room is executed in the Italian High Renaissance vernacular. Set within the elaborate oak paneling on opposite sides of the room are large canvases depicting events in the life of Scipio Africanus. Two additional paintings from this series were also purchased from Allard and are placed within gilded frames located on either side of the ballroom entrance in the hall. All four paintings were originally part of a decorative program in the great hall of the Ca' Corner in Venice. (Six smaller overdoor panels from the series were also acquired but were sold in a 1962 auction. Four of these have recently been returned to their 1901 positions.) The adjacent breakfast room returns to the eighteenth-century theme, with gilded-oak Louis XV—style boiserie framing black-lacquered chinoiserie panels. Lacking enough antique panels to fill all four spaces, Allard had a modern adaptation created to mimic the three antique panels.

A 40-by-50-foot ballroom is found on axis with the front door. It has handsome cream-and-ivory-colored Louis XV–style boiserie, with overdoor panels painted in grisaille. The north and south walls of the space each hold four sets of doors, with only one set in each pair being operational. This unusual arrangement is necessary to assure that symmetry is maintained within the space, while still allowing for properly positioned openings to adjacent rooms. The drawing room next door is completed in an amalgam of Louis XIV through Louis XVI detailing. The boiserie here is executed with classical imagery in shades of gray and white. The ceiling painting, attributed to Jacob De Witt, is an allegory representing dawn. Two sets of French doors on the south wall lead into a stone-sheathed conservatory whose wall treatment is meant to emulate the architectural detailing found on the exterior of the structure. At the east end of the conservatory are three rouge-royale marble basins. The two on either side are planters, while that in the central position is a fountain embellished with

Entrance Hall (Author's Collection)

bronze statues of Triton and Nereid seated on dolphins and sea horses.

In the main hall a divided staircase with Carrara marble treads and a finely executed iron and bronze balustrade seems to sweep toward the heavens, here represented by an antique cloud-swept ceiling painting taken from an Italian *palazzo*. A marble-floored second-story hall leads to seven bedrooms, six baths, plus a large sitting room overlooking the gardens. Except for Mr. Berwind's chamber, which is executed in a seventeenth-century motif, the rooms on this level are finished with French eighteenth-century-style paneling, marble mantelpieces, and gilt-bronze hardware.

The third floor contains eighteen staff bedrooms, two bathrooms, and a suite for the housekeeper. The staff also had access to a tiled roof promenade that entirely encircles this level behind the roof parapet. Filling the basement service areas are the kitchen, the servants' dining room, and laundry, drying, switchboard, silver, and refrigerator rooms. Beneath the steps leading from the ballroom to the gardens is placed a wine cellar.

Although the Elms seems to eschew the modern world, beneath the surface it actually incorporated all the latest technological developments such as electric service bells, ice-making machines, and the latest in fireproof construction. It was kept

Transverse Hall (Courtesy of the Preservation Society of Newport County)

Ballroom (Courtesy of the Preservation Society of Newport County)

Drawing Room (Courtesy of the Preservation Society of Newport County)

Conservatory (Courtesy of the Preservation Society of Newport County)

Dining Room (Courtesy of the Preservation Society of Newport County)

heated throughout the winter to protect the art and fragile textiles, even though the family rarely occupied it after September. Berwind may have made his money from coal, but he didn't want the dust and residue generated when depositing tons of it into his basement storage bins to create havoc on his surroundings. To keep soot from permeating the grounds, an underground tunnel was devised between the basement of the house and a loading entrance located outside of the perimeter wall on Dixon Street. Coal was lowered into coal bins mounted on narrow-gauge tracks, which led to storage areas adjacent to the basement furnaces.

The Berwinds would later ask Trumbauer to return to develop a formal sunken garden on newly acquired land on the western edge of the property. This garden—plus the twin teahouses and retaining wall facing it—added great elegance and refinement to the overall composition. The architect also

designed a Georgian-style superintendent's cottage and greenhouse network on an ancillary piece of property. His last addition to the estate came in 1911, when he was asked to design a new garage and carriage-house complex on the northwest corner of the estate. The finished complex was an enlarged version of the nineteenth-century carriage house at the Château du Barry in Louveciennes, France.

On the evening of August 30, 1901, the Berwinds officially opened the house with a ball for more than three hundred guests. According to the *New York Times*, "Previous entertainments of this season may have rivaled it in details, but none has been more artistic, none so largely attended, and none so conspicuous for lavish expenditure of money." Even a house on the scale of the Elms was not spacious enough to handle the crowd, so tents were placed on the lawn to house the overflow. The entrance hall to the house was transformed into a garden with rose trees in golden tubs judiciously placed throughout the entrance, the transverse hall, and the second-floor hallway. For the convenience of guests, several bedrooms had been converted to dressing rooms for the evening. Scattered among the first-floor rooms were tall vases filled with American Beauty roses, orchids, and lotus flowers. The west terrace was transformed into an orange grove, with its delicate fragrance drifting into the adjacent spaces, while the terraces at either end of the house were filled with towering palms, groups of orchids, and caladiums. On the lawn were large maple trees that had vines of red flowers intertwined through their branches.

For a midnight supper, the north terrace was enclosed with a framework festooned in pink and white fabric on which red and white roses were strung. The draped ceiling fabric covering the terrace was backed by electric lights that created a warm glow. Augmenting the north terrace with additional dining tables were the breakfast room, the dining room, and a marquee on the lawn. Each of the forty tables within these spaces was decorated with a candelabra surrounded by red and white roses. Music for the event was provided by Mullaly's Orchestra and Berger's Hungarian Band, while the cotillion was lead by Elisha Dyer, Jr., and Mrs. Berwind.

After Herminie's death in 1922, Berwind asked his unmarried sister Julia to become hostess at The Elms. When he died fourteen years later, he left life occupancy of the estate to her. Upon Julia's death at the age of ninety-five in 1961, a nephew inherited

Breakfast Room (Courtesy of the Preservation Society of Newport County)

Second Floor Sitting Room (Courtesy of the Preservation Society of Newport County)

the house. He auctioned the furnishings and sold the house to developers, who had plans to demolish it and develop the land. Alarmed, members of the Preservation Society of Newport County stepped in and purchased the house, knowing that if The Elms went, so went the rest of Bellevue Avenue. By borrowing from its members, as well as from museums in Boston and New York, the house was furnished and opened to an eager public in August of 1962. To mark The Elms's centenary in 2001, the Society completed extensive renovations of the house and its gardens, bringing them both back to there pre–World War I appearance.

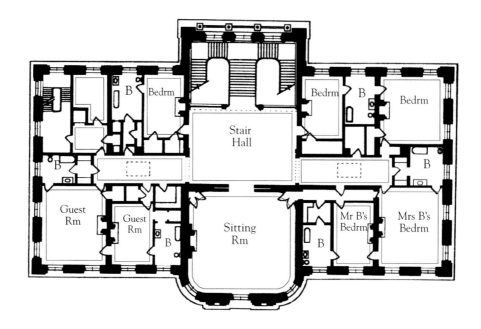

Second Floor

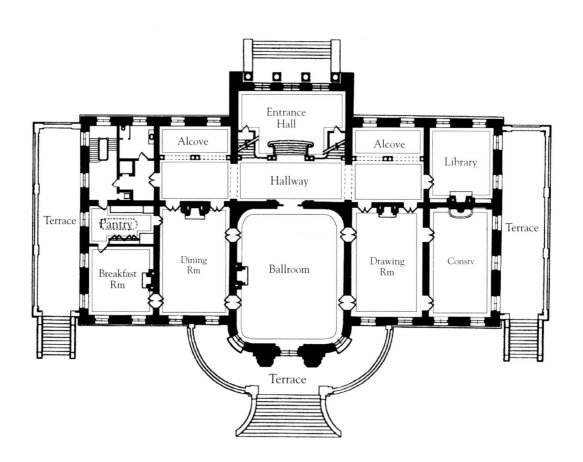

First Floor

ROSECLIFF

MRS. HERMANN OELRICHS

McKim, Mead & White, 1897-1902

The beautiful raven-haired Theresa (Tessie) Fair, and her equally lovely younger sister Virginia (Birdie) Fair, were both born in Nevada. They were two of the four children born to mining engineer James Graham Fair and his wife Theresa Rooney, an innkeeper's daughter. Fair would strike it rich as one of the four partners of the Comstock Lode, the country's largest silver deposit. Before its depletion in 1898, it offered up almost a half a billion dollars of the precious metal. The Fairs soon left Nevada, moving to the fashionable environs of Nob Hill in San Francisco. When nearing marriageable age, the sisters headed east to establish positions in both the New York and Newport social scenes. Each secured an advantageous marriage. Birdie married William Kissam Vanderbilt, Jr., allying herself with the fourth generation of the illustrious clan, while Tessie married Hermann Oelrichs, a great-grandson of Harrison Gray Otis, the Federalist statesman. The handsome and athletic Oelrichs was born in Baltimore and educated in Europe, then apprenticed at his father's shipping businesses in Bremen and London. Later he returned to the United States and became the American representative of the North German Lloyd Steamship Company.

At the time of her marriage in 1890, Tessie was given a million dollars from her father with which to start housekeeping. The following year the Oelrichs established themselves on Fifth Avenue with a mansion on the northeast corner of 57th Street that had originally been occupied by Mary Mason Jones, an aunt of the novelist Edith Wharton. James Fair died in 1894, leaving his fortune to be shared by his children. With part of this inheritance Tessie purchased the eleven-acre oceanfront estate of the late George Bancroft in Newport. Bancroft was a noted statesman and historian, and

Bancroft Cottage (Courtesy of the Preservation Society of Newport County)

Entrance Façade (Author's Collection)

Ocean Façade (Author's Collection)

a founder of the United States Naval Academy in Annapolis. The estate, with its comfortable wooden cottage, had been christened Rose Cliff because of its owner's famous rose gardens.

There was only one drawback to the property—it did not include a Bellevue Avenue frontage. Access to the house was restricted to a narrow easement driveway located at the southern edge of the Parkman estate that sat between the Oelrichs property and Bellevue Avenue. When enough additional land was acquired to create a wider and more formal drive, Tessie began dreaming of a villa that would rival those of other leading Newport hostesses.

Even with the inheritance of a substantial portion of her father's estate, Tessie still lacked the leviathan budget that Alva Vanderbilt had at her disposal to create Marble House just down the Avenue. What Alva created in marble and bronze, Tessie would have to accomplish in terra-cotta and plaster. Fortunately, she had a talented architect in Stanford White, who was capable of creating sumptuous effects without spending prodigious amounts. In the end, she inhabited a cottage comparable in scale to houses such as Marble House and The Elms, but she spent only $298,043 to do it.

The design process began in 1897, while construction began two years later and lasted until 1902. One reason for the prolonged construction period was that as soon as the structure was enclosed, the owner would expel the construction team each summer, utilizing the house in an unfinished state. This was accomplished by covering the bare walls and ceilings with fabrics, which were then augmented by banks of flowers during the Oelrichses entertainments. The design of the house was directly inspired by the Grand Trianon at Versailles, which had been executed by Jules Hardouin-Mansart in 1688 for Louis XIV. Ironically, the French king used Trianon as a place of retreat to get away from the formalities of court life, while its Newport interpretation was designed to frame a lifestyle of great display epitomized by large throngs attending formal and ritualized entertainments.

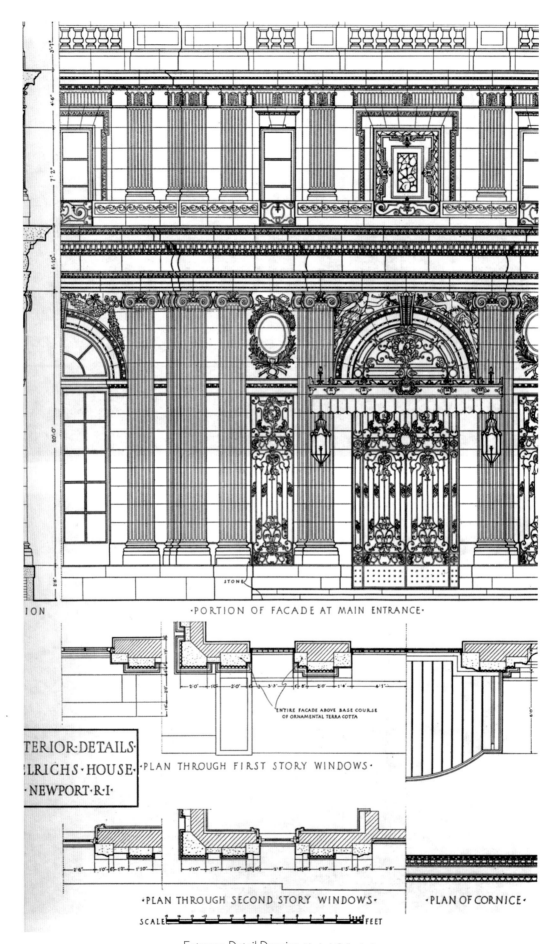

·PORTION OF FACADE AT MAIN ENTRANCE·

STONE

ENTIRE FACADE ABOVE BASE COURSE
OF ORNAMENTAL TERRA COTTA

·PLAN THROUGH FIRST STORY WINDOWS·

TERIOR·DETAILS·
LRICHS·HOUSE·
·NEWPORT·R·I·

·PLAN THROUGH SECOND STORY WINDOWS·   ·PLAN OF CORNICE·

SCALE ⊢⊣⊣⊣⊣⊣⊣⊣⊣⊣⊣⊣⊣ FEET

Entrance Detail Drawing (Author's Collection)

Entrance Hall (Courtesy of the Preservation Society of Newport County)

Sometime during the design process the name Rose Cliff was changed to the more compact "Rosecliff."

In his H-shaped plan, Stanford White retained Trianon's classical rhythm, defined by alternating windows and Ionic pilasters. By enclosing the open colonnaded "peristyle" found at Trianon, White created a centralized ballroom (living room on original plan) whose round-topped French doors open to a garden court on one side and a marble-paved terrace facing the ocean. Further deviating from Mansart's plan, White added a second floor to create a needed bedroom level, and placed a third floor for staff accommodations behind the roof balustrade. The most innovative aspect of the design was its use of material for the building's façade: previously terra-cotta had been used for decorative elements, but never before had such a large project been entirely veneered with it. Rosecliff revolutionized the use of terra-cotta in construction and opened the way for its use in high-rise monoliths such as the Woolworth tower in New York.

The house is symmetrical in appearance, but instead of placing the entrance in the central position, it was instead located at the end of the southern projection. It was arranged this way so that White could retain an unencumbered ballroom at the heart of his plan.

The entrance consists of a columned passageway that leads into a main hall whose principal focus is a heart-shaped staircase. The floors are marble, while the plaster walls are decorated with French eighteenth-century classical moldings and Ionic columns decorated with floral pendants. At the far side of the inner hall, on axis with the front door, is a broad set of doors leading to a salon decorated in the French Renaissance style. This space has decorative Corinthian-capped pilasters that support a richly coffered ceiling from which hang two enormous crystal chandeliers. In the central position of the southern wall of the room is a Gothic-style chimneypiece of Caen stone. The adjacent ballroom, one of the largest in Newport at some 80 feet in length, is encircled by fluted Corinthian pilasters that support a rococo plaster-

work ceiling decorated by a centrally placed cloud-swept ceiling painting. Surrounding this are smaller oval paintings depicting classical vases overflowing with flowers. At one end of the room is an alcove designed to hold a pipe organ console, which faces a marble fireplace at the opposite end. To the right of the fireplace is a door leading to a paneled billiard room, while on the left is a door accessing a marble-lined vestibule—complete with a splashing fountain—that leads to the dining room. The dining room is finished in the Louis XIV style with paneled walls and a marble chimneypiece.

McKim, Mead & White's original second-floor plan for Rosecliff shows nine bedrooms, although in actuality there were only seven, as one was used as a library for the master suite and another as a small sitting room for the principal guest suite. Most of these rooms are accessed from a long transverse hall that runs along the west side of the center section of the house and has windows overlooking the garden court below. The master bedroom suite is placed at the far, or north, end of the hall with Mr. Oelrichs's room facing the water and his wife's facing the front lawn.

Perhaps the most celebrated event mounted at Rosecliff was the famous Bal Blanc given on August 19, 1904. Ladies invited to the event were asked to dress all in white, while many of the male guests wore black formalwear with knee britches, white tie, and tails. Some male guests came in even more exotic costumes. Society's court jester Harry Lehr came dressed as a Louis XIV courtier in a white satin jacket with knee britches, while rhinestone buckles adorned his dancing pumps. Even the staff wore white livery specially made for the occasion. Floral decorations adorning the house were also all in white. Masses of hydrangeas and hollyhocks filled the entrance hall, while the ballroom was festooned with roses, orchids, and lilies-of-the-valley. The grounds of Rosecliff were illuminated by over 2,000 tiny lights, and swans gracefully glided in the pool off the terrace (which was ringed by masses of flowers that were laced with lights.) In addition, Mrs. Oelrichs had a mock fleet of white

Staircase (Author's Collection)

Salon (Author's Collection)

Ballroom (Living Room on Original Plan) (Author's Collection)

Billiard Room/Library (Author's Collection)

Dining Room (Author's Collection)

ships constructed and placed out on the water. These were illuminated to enhance an otherwise unadorned view of the ocean at night.

The mistress of Rosecliff ran a meticulous household without the use of a personal maid, social secretary, or housekeeper. She worked directly with Herbert, her butler of thirty years. Once when a maid said the marble floor in her entrance hall could not be made cleaner, Tessie got down on her hands and knees with a scrub brush to prove the girl wrong.

Hermann was caught in the 1906 San Francisco earthquake. Although he was not physically injured, he may have overextended himself in relief work, dying within the year. Tessie went into mourning, closing both her New York and Newport houses to all but her closest companions. In 1909 she even toyed with the idea of selling Rosecliff. On May 23, 1909, the *New York Times* mistakenly reported that the Newport house had been sold to

Thomas F. Walsh, the Colorado mine owner, for $250,000. Instead, Tessie retained ownership of Rosecliff and soon began resuming her hectic social schedule. In 1912, she was able to acquire the Parkman estate, finally giving her direct Bellevue Avenue frontage.

By the beginning of the 1920s, Tessie's health began to fail. In 1925 she was transported to Newport from New York by special train and withdrew into seclusion at Rosecliff. She would remain there for the rest of her life. When she died the following year at the age of fifty-seven, her son Hermann, Jr., had the funeral held in the dining room.

Hermann Jr. occupied the house until 1941, when he sold it for $21,000 and auctioned its furnishings for an additional $95,000. The purchaser was Anita Niesen, who gave it to her daughter, the noted singer Gertrude Niesen. The Niesens purchased many of the original furnishings at the Oelrichs auction, so they were able to open the house for the 1941 season. Unfortunately, when mother and daughter left that fall, they did not leave the house in the hands of a caretaker, so when the heater failed, the pipes burst, creating havoc with the interiors. The plaster ceilings collapsed, and the heart-shaped staircase became a frozen waterfall of ice. Besides an enormous amount of structural damage, the Niesens were also faced with an $800 water bill. Not being financially able to restore the house, the women decided to sell it. It was briefly acquired by Abraham Leighter—but quickly changed hands again, when in July of 1942 it was purchased by Ray Alan Van Clief for $30,000. Van Clief restored the damaged interiors and changed the name of the house to Oldcourt. It took almost three years to complete the work. Tragically, in 1945, Mr. Van Clief died in an automobile accident while on his way to Newport to open the house for his first season in the restored structure.

J. Edgar Monroe of New Orleans purchased the house in 1947 from Van Clief's widow Margaret and changed the name back to Rosecliff. For the next quarter century the Monroe family summered in the house. In 1971 the Monroes donated Rosecliff and its furnishings to the Preservation Society of Newport County, which maintains it as a house museum.

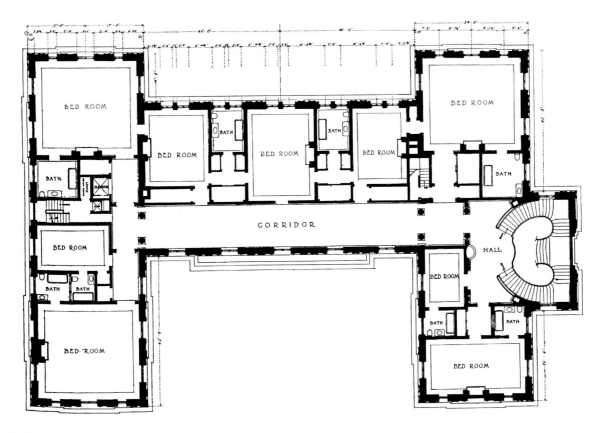

Second Floor

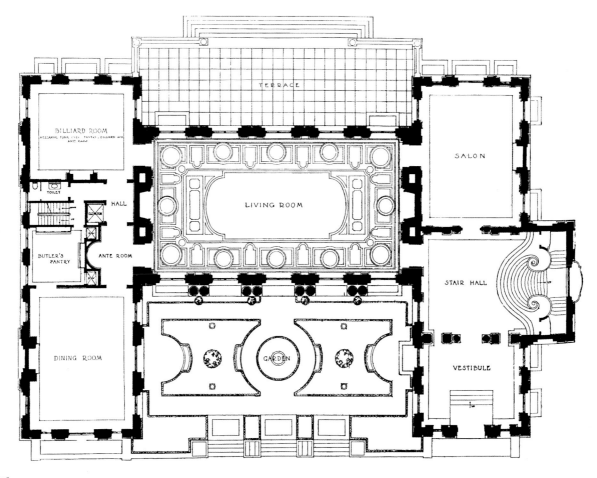

First Floor

HOPEDENE

Elizabeth Hope Gammell Slater was born in 1855. Her father, William Gammell, was a distinguished classics professor at Brown University, while her maternal grandfather was Robert Ives, a merchant prince of Rhode Island. Elizabeth eventually became the custodian of a fortune estimated at some $20 million dollars. In May of 1880 she married John Whipple Slater. Slater was the son of manufacturer William S. Slater, whose principal factories were located in the village of Slaterville, a few miles outside of Providence. With wealth and pedigree on both sides, it seemed a perfect match.

Alas, within a year of the marriage there were serious signs of trouble. Soon after the ceremony the bride began hearing rumors of John's many infidelities. In what was a daring move in an era when wives were expected to suffer in silence, Elizabeth decided she could not live under the same roof with him and asked John to stay away from their homes in Providence and Newport. He began hurling accusations of his own, declaring that she was frigid and that she refused to perform her "marriage duties." The Slater marriage became a major society scandal, whose details were much discussed in upper-class circles. On July 4, 1882, barely two years after their union, the Slaters experienced the humiliation of having the situation discussed in an article in the *New York Times*. After being publicly sanctioned in this way, the couple decided to cease open conflict and try to reconcile their differences privately. In an era when divorce was still anathema, they elected to live apart, with Mrs. Slater eventually moving to Washington, D.C., in 1895. She also dropped her husband's first name, although never actually divorcing him, and would thereafter become identified as Mrs. E. H. G. Slater.

Entrance Façade (Author's Collection)

West Façade (Author's Collection)

Petit Salon (The Metropolitan Museum of Art, Gift of the Estate of Ogden Codman, 1951 [51.644.127(1)] Copy Photograph © The Metropolitan Museum of Art)

Later, after receiving her inheritance, Elizabeth commissioned two substantial houses. In Washington she hired Horace Trumbauer to design a Louis XV–style home whose interiors were embellished by Jules Allard. At Newport she engaged Peabody & Stearns to design Hopedene, near the cottages of family relations on the cliffs overlooking Easton's Beach. Ogden Codman was responsible for the decoration of its major rooms. Construction on Hopedene commenced in 1899 and was completed in 1902. As one would expect, the principal entertaining rooms faced the water, but instead of placing the entrance on the opposite side of the house, giving it an east-west axis, Peabody & Stearns oriented it to the south. This enabled arriving guests to have sweeping ocean views from the balustraded forecourt.

When viewing Hopedene, one initially receives an impression of a red-brick Georgian Revival manor with a hipped slate roof, but upon closer inspection the strong Italian antecedents of the design reveal themselves. These can be seen in the arched windows of the first floor and in the richly modeled set of wooden entrance doors set within a stone surround surmounted by a glazed lunette. This lunette is supported by Ionic columns and a full entablature, creating a strong Florentine-inspired composition, which was originally covered by a barrel-shaped metal and glass marquee.

Sitting in the center of a marble-paved terrace on the east side of the structure is a single-story columned semicircular porch that was later topped by an enclosed second-floor sitting room. Both elements have since been replaced by a single-story so-

Salon (Author's Collection)

larium. The west elevation has also experienced changes. Originally, two balanced projecting wings embraced a recessed terrace whose central element consisted of a large Venetian window that was divided horizontally at the landing level of the principal staircase within. This terrace was covered by a striped canvas awning and filled with comfortable wicker furniture. This outdoor living area was later sacrificed to create a semicircular ballroom extension that is sheathed with a limestone façade in a severe neo-classical style.

At the roof level, the Italian influence evaporates completely and is replaced by American inventiveness. The overhang of the roof protects the second-story windows from the midday sun, much like the extended eaves found on Prairie Style houses of the American Midwest. This element is mimicked in the oversized attic dormers whose overhangs are supported by miniature wooden columns.

Hopedene is entered through a bilevel vestibule embellished with a coffered barrel ceiling and marble mosaic flooring. The main hall, paved in white marble, extends north to a shell-capped niche. The walls here are divided by Ionic pilasters on one side, with columns of the same order on the opposite side. The latter frame the grand staircase, with its *Directoire*-style wrought-iron railing. A set of doors located under the staircase landing was originally glazed, and opened to the west terrace. They now lead into the ballroom addition, whose walls are embellished with swagged Ionic pilasters in the Louis XVI manner.

The petit salon is paneled in the French Régence

Library (Author's Collection)

Dining Room (Author's Collection)

style with painted floral panels inset above the doors on the north and south sides of the room. Just south of this room is the grand salon, which is also conceived in the Régence taste. The veined white marble mantel that Codman placed in the room is still present today, but the elaborate overmantel mirror that was surmounted by a bas-relief panel depicting a classical urn framed by cavorting cherubs was eliminated many years ago by subsequent owners in an attempt to modernize the house.

At the opposite end of the house is the dining room, which was originally executed in a severe Louis XVI motif. The walls were encircled by Corinthian pilasters set upon high molded plinths. The lunettes located above the doorways were centered with decorative rondels framed with molded trim. A marble mantel, inset paintings, and a large arched mirror located above a marble console table completed the original design. Little but the mantelpiece remains. As a departure from the eighteenth-century-inspired decoration exhibited in the other major spaces on this level, Codman chose an earlier vernacular for the library. Here the varnished woodwork is evocative of a design at the Château de Blois, executed during the time of Francis I. The walls of the room hold richly detailed panels that support a heavily beamed ceiling.

Hopedene was later acquired by Mr. and Mrs. Charles C. Paterson. Mr. Paterson bequeathed the property to the Preservation Society of Newport County, who sold it to increase the Society's endowment. It has since had additional owners but has remained essentially unchanged, except for the updating of service areas. The combination of Hopedene's red brick façades, white stonework balustrades, and emerald-green lawns bordered by sculpted hedges still exhibit an aristocratic ambience that even by Newport standards is hard to rival.

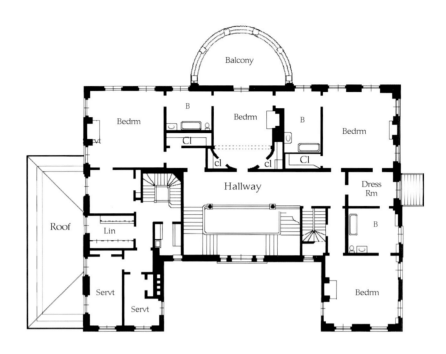

Second Floor

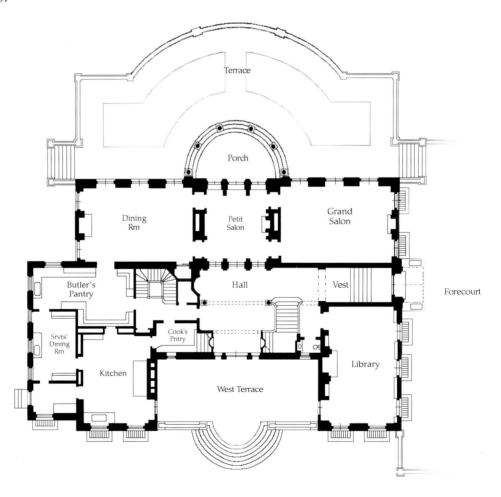

First Floor

CHETWODE

WILLIAM STORRS WELLS

Horace Trumbauer, 1900–1902

William Storrs Wells, president of the Fairbanks Company—a manufacturer of scales—and his wife, the former Annie Raynor, a daughter of James A. Raynor, president of the Erie Railroad, were high-profile socialites within the summer colony, and their Bellevue Avenue villa, Pansy Cottage, was always a center of activity during the season. As the nineteenth century ended, the Wellses hired Parisian decorator Jules Allard to revamp their home's interiors. This was accomplished with the help of French boiserie, eighteenth-century tapestries, and Renaissance mantelpieces. At the beginning of May in 1900, as finishing touches were being applied to the rooms and furniture was being placed in anticipation of a housewarming party to be held the following month, a fire began in the main salon that quickly grew to engulf the entire structure. At the time, the loss was estimated to be around $100,000.

Undaunted, the Wellses hired Horace Trumbauer to create plans for a new villa that was christened Chetwode when completed two years later. Chetwode was executed in the Louis XV style, but with a steel I-beam frame and all modern technological advances incorporated into its architectural fabric. The structure was veneered in buff brick that was delineated by an abundance of handsome limestone decorative trim. The shade of brick blended so seamlessly with the stonework that it compelled many to remember it in later years as a completely limestone structure.

The H-shaped plan was severely formal by definition, but the carved detailing makes it playfully ebullient in appearance. The decorative elements defining the entrance loggia, the eastern terrace, and the large rounded loggia extending from the

Garden Façade (Author's Collection)

west elevation give the design a lyrical quality that helps mitigate any severity in the classical design. Instead of being situated with an entrance facing Bellevue Avenue, which would have been the typical sequential approach, the Wellses directed their architect to follow the footprint of the earlier house, which had a southern entrance facing Ruggles Avenue. The western loggia was perhaps the most ingenious element of the design. It melds a modern unenclosed covered sitting area with an

Pansy Cottage (Courtesy of the Preservation Society of Newport County)

Entrance (Author's Collection)

otherwise traditional interpretation of the French eighteenth-century vernacular.

Enclosing the five-acre estate is an elaborate wrought-iron fence that sits upon a shallow granite foundation. This fencing gives way to brick and stone walls when needed to block service areas from view. A stone stable complex that predates the house, and an adjoining greenhouse, are located on the western edge of the property. Mrs. Wells had extensive gardens laid out around the house, which

Garden Façade (Newport Historical Society)

Southwest View (Courtesy of the International Tennis Hall of Fame & Museum, Newport, Rhode Island)

were later enhanced when John Russell Pope was asked to design a formal allée and reflecting pool on axis with the west portico.

The lavish interiors of Chetwode were designed by Jules Allard predominately in the Louis XV and XVI taste. The principal exception to this eighteenth-century theme is a two-story central great hall that was executed in an early French Renaissance manner. This space is entered through a screen of twisted Baroque columns that separates it from the entrance hall. Both it and the great hall have paneled wainscots topped by expanses of red silk damask brocade. At the far end of the space is a raised platform from which a spiral staircase ascends to the floor above. Encircling the two upper floors are balconies whose galleries are supported by beamed undersides. During daylight hours a centrally positioned skylight with tinted glass bathes the space in diffused light.

Surrounding the great hall are the principal entertainment rooms of the house. The morning room has cream and gold moldings with red damask curtains and wall coverings. A gilt-bronze chandelier has six coordinating wall lights, each embellished with Dresden porcelain flowers. A brèche-violette marble mantelpiece has decorative bronze mounts that coordinate with the gilt-bronze boar and stag andirons. Adjoining the morning room is a grand salon (or music room) that features a white and gold boiserie, with elements copied from the Bureau du Roi at Versailles. Next is the dining room, which is sheathed in natural oak with gilded trim and has a dark green marble chimneypiece embellished with gilt-bronze mounts. Special distinction is given to the room by the addition of the four antique Dutch floral and landscape paintings that encircle it.

Hall (Courtesy of the Preservation Society of Newport County)

Petit Salon (Newport Historical Society)

Located on the opposite side of the great hall is the Green Salon, later a billiard room, that is decorated as a masculine preserve, with dark oak paneling and green silk damask covered walls. An Italian Renaissance fireplace is set between the two windows on the north wall. The adjoining Petit salon is finished with another of Allard's handsome sets of gilded boiserie, this time in the Louis XVI mode. Here a neoclassical white and gray mantel supports a high gilt-framed round-topped mirror that, along with the room's mirrored door surfaces, enlarges the space visually. The last major space located on this level is called the library, despite its being curiously devoid of books. Like the dining room, its walls are encased in oak with accents picked out in gold.

On the second floor five bedrooms and a boudoir are arranged around the second-floor balconies overlooking the great hall. Except for Mr.

Wells's room, which is executed in the French Renaissance style, the bedrooms wear eighteenth-century dress. A master suite located on the west side of the house consists of two bedrooms, two baths, a dressing room for Mrs. Wells, and an adjoining room for a lady's maid. Somewhat unusually, the boudoir is situated on the opposite side of the house, thus making it more of a shared sitting room rather than a private domain for Mrs. Wells. On the third floor are chambers for the couple's two offspring—a son, J. Raynor Wells, and a daughter, later Mrs. Harry T. Peters—and two additional guest bedrooms. Completing this level are storage rooms and ten staff bedrooms.

Wells died in 1926, but his widow continued to summer at Chetwode until the beginning of the 1930s, when she leased the villa to A. J. Drexel Biddle, Jr. In 1934, a year before her death, Annie sold

Salon (Newport Historical Society)

Dining Room (© John T. Hopf)

Library Fireplace Detail (© John T. Hopf)

Mr. Wells Bedroom (Newport Historical Society)

the house to John Jacob Astor VI. Astor, who had just married his first wife, Ellen Tuck French, purchased the house fully furnished for a mere $150,000. When Astor sold the property fourteen years later, he received only $71,000, losing over half of his investment. The purchaser, James O'Donnell of Washington, sold off much of the furnishings and then sold the house to the Church of Christ. Later the church sold it for $40,000 to Diab & Curran, Boston developers, who planned to convert the house into apartments. Chetwode's final owner was socialite Phoebe Andrews, who had a vision of converting the house into a gallery and arts center. Unfortunately, these plans never came to fruition because of a fire that swept through the structure in January of 1972.

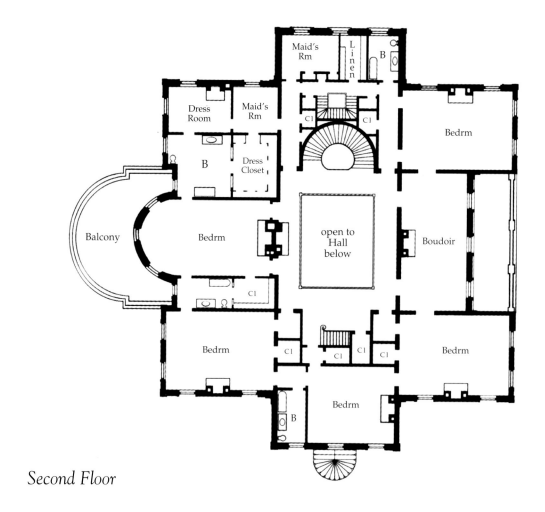

Second Floor

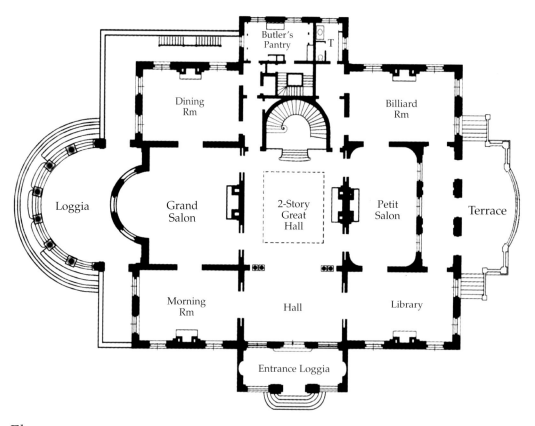

First Floor

WHITEHOLME

MRS. HENRY BARTON JACOBS

John Russell Pope, 1901-1903

In 1872, Mary Sloan Frick, a member of a well-connected Baltimore, Maryland, family and the daughter of attorney William F. Frick, married Robert Garrett. Mr. Garrett's father was John W. Garrett, president of the Baltimore & Ohio Railroad, and his grandfather Robert, an Irish immigrant, was a successful merchant and shipper. A decade after their marriage the Garretts hired Stanford White of McKim, Mead & White to design a house at 9-11 Mt. Vernon Place in Baltimore. Soon after moving into the Italian Renaissance–style house, and following the death of his father in 1884, Garrett succeeded to the presidency of the Baltimore & Ohio Railroad. Thereafter, his health began a precipitous decline, forcing him to retire from business affairs within three years. Dr. Henry Barton Jacobs, a specialist in tubercular medicine brought in from Boston, was his personal physician.

In 1896, Garrett died, leaving his widow a fortune that was estimated to be $20 million. After three years of mourning, the childless widow reentered the social world by acquiring the Stick Style Hitchcock-Travers house that sat on a three-acre estate on the corner of Narragansett and Ochre Point Avenues in Newport. Mrs. Garrett approached John Russell Pope, who was just beginning his career, to greatly enlarge the structure. She would share the house with Dr. Jacobs, whom she married on April 2, 1902. Dr. Jacobs's mother was a descendent of Peregrine White, the first child born in the Plymouth Colony, while on his father's side he was a descendent of Priscilla and John Alden.

During this period older houses like the Hitchcock-Travers residence were either razed and replaced with a new structure or were so completely incorporated into a new design that there was little external evidence of their existence. At Whiteholme a

View From Entrance Piers (Courtesy of the Preservation Society of Newport County)

North View (Courtesy of the Preservation Society of Newport County)

novel approach was taken: the new larger addition was built in front of the older house, with the latter now being relegated to the subservient role of an adjunct service wing. Siting the old structure behind the western wing of the new construction allows the original house, with the help of carefully positioned shrubs and trees, to become virtually invisible.

Pope's finished structure was in the classical Italian manner, although overlaid with a distinctly French sensibility in its proportions, detailing, and window treatments. An angled entrance pavilion is centrally placed within the inside intersection of the two symmetrical wings comprising the architect's L-shaped design. This pavilion is on an axis with the similarly angled gate piers located at the intersection of the two avenues fronting the property. From these piers, a drive bordered by Chinese gingko trees leads to an oval-shaped gravel entrance court.

The house is of brick and concrete construction, whose surface is veneered in stucco with composition decorative detailing. On either side of the wrought-iron entrance doors, which are surmounted by a glass and iron marquee, are placed two-story Ionic columns that are paired with squared pilasters of the same order. They support a deep entablature with a cornice held aloft by scrolled brackets. Above this is placed a roof balustrade augmented with classical urns. At the ends of both wings are single-story loggias capped by a classical parapet with corner urns. The south, or garden, façade, is executed with the same fenestration and detailing, with a central projecting pavilion balanced by linear wings facing a balustraded terrace. Because the staff accommodations were placed in the Hitchcock-Travers wing, there was no need to have an attic story, which allows the tiled roof to remain shallow, thereby increasing the horizontality of the composition.

The comparatively small estate required that the Hitchcock-Travers house be moved to the western edge of the property to allow Pope's new construction to take center position. This also had the effect of creating wide lawns to the north and east of the house, while a formal dual-axial garden was created to the south. The latter is T-shaped, with

Entrance Façade (Author's Collection)

Garden Façade (Courtesy of the Preservation Society of Newport County)

one arm running parallel to the façade. This aspect of the garden is centered by an antique Italian wellhead from which emanates balancing grass segments whose curved ends are embellished with classical statuary. Surrounding the property is an inner hedge of pink and white mountain laurel, augmented by taller plantings of hawthorn bushes and rhododendron. In the southwest corner of the site the original stable was somehow squeezed into this complex and compact landscaping plan.

Pope collaborated on the interiors of Whiteholme with Jules Allard. Their efforts created a stylish and sophisticated display of Beaux-Arts detailing, primarily in the eighteenth-century French Revival taste. A set of wrought-iron doors open directly into a marble-paved and oval-shaped entrance hall with architecturally treated walls in faux Caen stone. To the right is a staircase, framed by columns, with marble treads and an elaborate wrought-iron railing.

Through balancing columns on the left is a hall with doors leading to the principal entertaining rooms. Straight ahead is the reception room with silk damask wall coverings and Louis XVI wainscoting. West of this is a dining room veneered in Régence-style paneling with silk brocade insets. At the far end of the space is a simple marble bolection fireplace with a carved wooden frame and an overmantel embellished with a gilded cartouche with garlands. The opposite end of the house contains a salon executed in the Louis XV Rococo style, with walls inset by mirrored panels and a ceiling embellished with decorative paintings. Within the north wing of the house is the library, although in the original drawings it was designated as a billiard room.

At the top of the staircase is an oval hall having the same dimensions as the entrance hall below. The north wing has two guest bedrooms that share a bath, while the south wing has three bedrooms,

Drawing Room (Author's Collection)

Library (Author's Collection)

three baths, and a boudoir for Mrs. Jacobs. Most of these rooms are executed with wall moldings and marble fireplaces in the Louis XVI style.

The service wing is connected to the Pope addition by a narrow bilevel corridor that was made long enough to allow for adequate light courts on either side. The first floor of the wing contained the kitchen, serving pantry, housekeeper's office, laundry facilities, and servants' hall. The upper two levels housed over a dozen staff rooms.

Mary Jacobs died in Newport in the fall of 1936. Her husband inherited Whiteholme, but rarely occupied it after her death. Three years later Barton died, and in 1940 the Newport estate was sold to James O'Donnell for $33,000. In September of 1944, O'Donnell sold Whiteholme to Annette T. Philips for $36,000. She held on to the property until July of 1960, when it was sold to Armand L. Bilodeau, whose plan to convert it to rental apartments was never implemented. In 1963, Salve Regina College purchased the property and razed the structure to make room for a student dormitory.

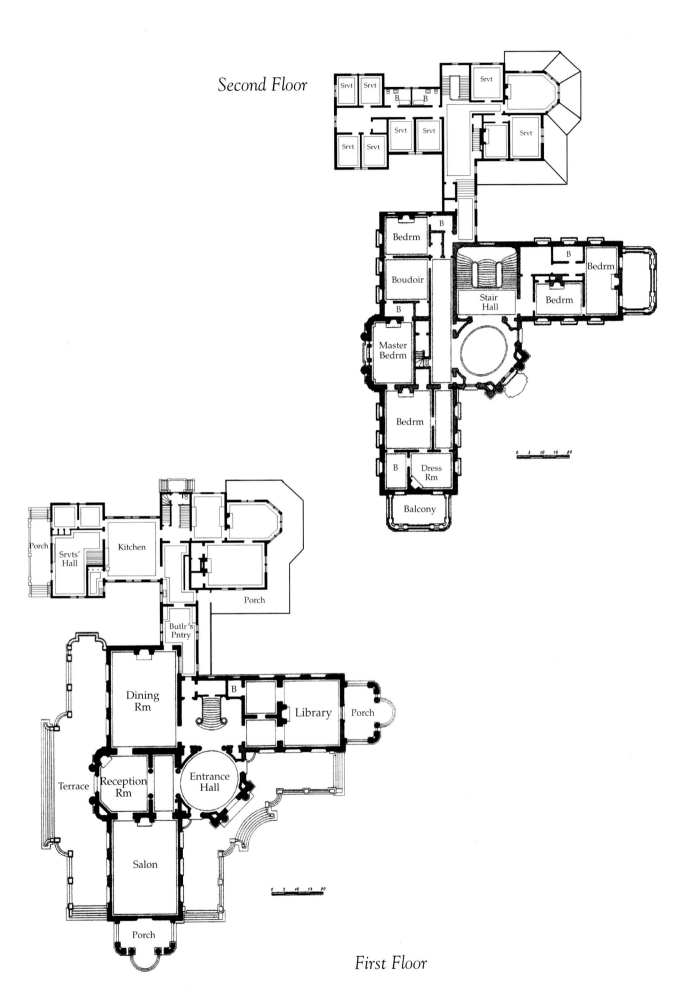

Second Floor

Srvt Srvt
B B
Srvt

Srvt Srvt Srvt Srvt

Srvt

Bedrm
B
Boudoir
B
Stair
Hall
Bedrm
Bedrm
Master
Bedrm
Bedrm

Bedrm

B Dress
Rm

Balcony

First Floor

Porch
Srvts'
Hall
Kitchen

Porch

Butlr's
Pntry

Dining
Rm
B
Library
Porch

Terrace
Reception
Rm
Entrance
Hall

Salon

Porch

CLARADON COURT

EDWARD C. KNIGHT, JR.

Horace Trumbauer, 1903-1904

Glimpsed through dark blue and gilded wrought-iron gates that pierce a high limestone boundary wall, the crisply delineated details of Claradon Court create a sumptuous—yet reserved—statement on Bellevue Avenue. Its architect, Horace Trumbauer, used a proposed house for John Hedworth in Chester-le-Street, County Durham, England, as inspiration. The architect was familiar with the design through a copy in his architectural library of Colin Campbell's Vitruvius Britannicus, which was first published in 1715. The Palladian-style villa was commissioned in 1903 by Edward Collings Knight, Jr., a sugar-refiner and railroad executive from Philadelphia, and his wife, the former Clara Dwight, granddaughter of the prominent Philadelphia merchant Isaac Waterman.

The central mass of Claradon Court is almost an exact replica of Campbell's design, while the wings show some deviation—particularly in Trumbauer's decision not to incorporate the English architect's decorative cupolas. A simple pediment supported by attached Doric columns surround a set of mahogany entrance doors that are surmounted by an arched, metal-framed transom. Quoins define the elevation's corners, while an urn-embellished balustrade—that sits upon a dentiled cornice—caps the composition. The first-floor windows are surmounted by abbreviated entablatures, while those above are graced with alternating triangular and segmental pediments. The single-story wings at either side have similar detailing, but rather than being capped by a roof balustrade, they have blind parapets instead.

The garden façade is similarly finished, but in 1910 single-story wings were added at either end, which are connected along the principal garden elevation by a Doric-

Entrance Gates (Gary Lawrance Collection)

Entrance Façade (Gary Lawrance Collection)

columned loggia. This loggia replaced a canvas-covered awning that had been installed soon after the home's completion in 1904 and which was a popular spot for al fresco entertaining for the Knights. Just prior to these additions, Knight had acquired an additional six acres of land directly behind the house, which gave Claradon Court direct ocean access for the first time. On a portion of the new acreage Trumbauer also designed a substantial brick and stone carriage house in an early Georgian vernacular. Situated behind the carriage house are cutting gardens that are protected from ocean winds by high brick walls.

While the exterior of the house is predominately Campbell's invention, the interior plan shows little resemblance to the Hedworth plan. Trumbauer created fewer rooms, but on a larger scale, better suited to the entertaining needs of Newport. Even though the Parisian decorator Jules Allard worked on Claradon Court's interiors, most of the rooms are executed in the English Georgian manner. The visitor enters the house through a

Garden Façade (Gary Lawrance Collection)

Terrace (Gary Lawrance Collection)

Garden Façade with Additions (Courtesy of the Preservation Society of Newport County)

small marble vestibule that accesses a marble-paved entrance hall. At the far end of the hall is a curved staircase that has white Carrara marble treads and an ornate wrought-iron railing. At either side of this hall one finds the two principal entertainment rooms of the house. The drawing room and the dining room each measure 23 by 40 feet and are the largest rooms in the house. They are decorated with simple wall moldings, dentiled cornices, and white marble mantelpieces. The wing wrapping around the northern end of the entrance court holds a card room, as well as two chambers reserved for bachelor guests. A well-hidden staircase from the basement services this wing so that dirty linens would never be seen traversing the main rooms of the house. (In the 1970s this wing was reconfigured by combining the card room and one of the bedrooms to create a large master bedroom.) After several seasons in the

house the Knights needed more entertaining space, so they added the two previously mentioned wings onto the back of the house. The northern wing holds a Georgian-style paneled library, while the opposite wing is filled with a French-style trellised breakfast room designed by André Carlhian.

Upstairs there are four bedrooms—each with bath—and a sitting room. When originally built, there was another villa sitting directly behind Claradon Court obscuring the water view. Because of this the Knights had their master suite facing Bellevue Avenue. This suite, executed in the French taste, has elaborate French wall moldings and Louis XVI–style marble mantelpieces. The remaining bedrooms on this level are executed with simple applied wall moldings and English wooden mantelpieces.

Clara died in 1928, and the following year

Entrance Hall (Gary Lawrance Collection)

Dining Room (Gary Lawrance Collection)

Library (Courtesy of the Preservation Society of Newport County)

Knight moved to a less elaborate Trumbauer-designed house called Stonybrook in neighboring Middletown. Claradon Court was purchased by Colonel and Mrs. William Hayward of New York. The colonel was a lawyer and a World War I hero, while his wife Mae (Maysie) was the daughter of Martin Cadwell of Connecticut. She divorced her first husband, Selden B. Manwaring of Hartford, in 1914 in order to marry the older (and much richer) Morton F. Plant of New York and New London, Connecticut. Plant even adopted Maysie's son Paul from her earlier marriage. Paul Manwaring Plant, for whom the word "playboy" was coined, gained

notoriety in the 1930s when he married actress Constance Bennett in the garden of his mother's Newport home. Mrs. Hayward was a collector of fine and decorative art, and her changes were limited to improving the collection in the house and changing its name from Claradon Court to Clarendon Court. This modification was probably done to eliminate any lingering associations with the earlier mistress of the house rather than to honor the famous minister of Charles I.

After the colonel's death in 1944, Maysie married once again, this time to John E. Rovensky, the president of the American Car & Foundry Com-

Creating Allée – Carriage House in Background (Newport Historical Society)

pany. After his wife's death in 1956, Rovensky continued to summer at Clarendon Court for an additional fourteen years—until his own death in February 1970. The house was then sold by Rovensky's daughter to utilities heiress Martha (Sunny) Crawford von Bulow and her husband Claus, a former associate of J. Paul Getty's. A couple of exceptional taste, they filled the house with quality antiques and fine art pieces—predominately of English origin from the eighteenth and early nineteenth centuries. The grounds were improved when the landscape firm of Innocenti & Webel removed

a hillock that had always deprived the first-floor rooms of an ocean view. By doing so, they also created an elegant allée to the sea. (Claus Von Bulow was later tried and convicted of trying to kill his wife by insulin injection that left her in an irreversible coma. He was later acquitted during a second trial.)

In 1988 fine art and antique dealer Glenn C. Randall and his wife Patricia purchased the house and are currently in the process of converting a former service wing into a gallery for their collection.

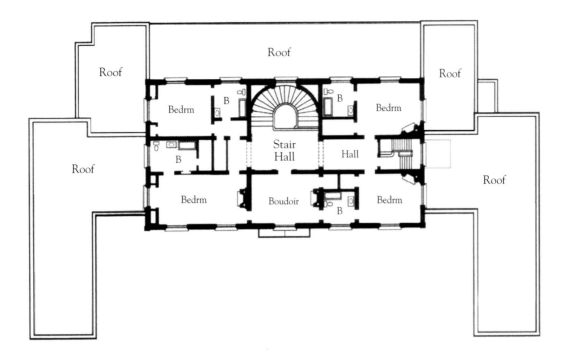

Second Floor

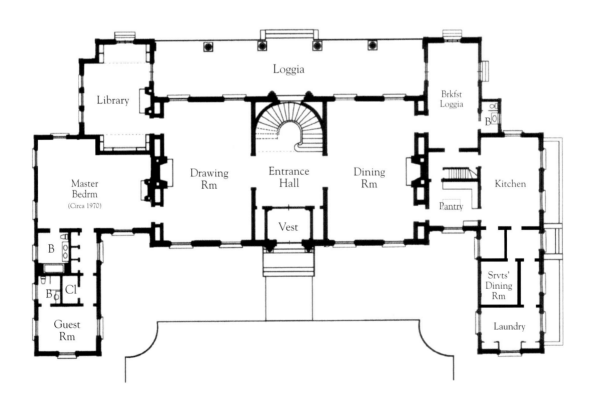

First Floor

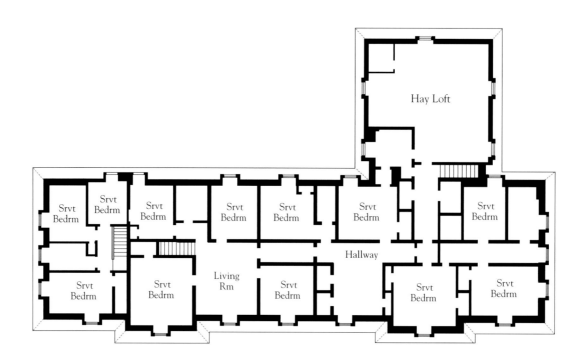

Carriage House, Second Floor

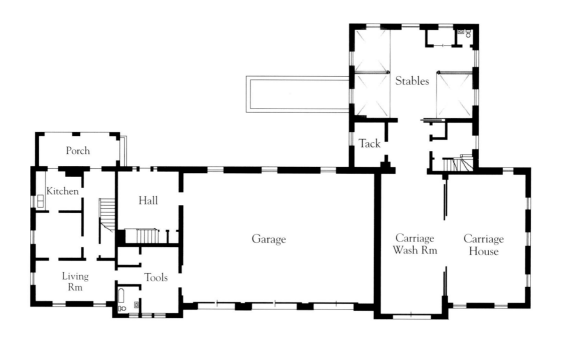

Carriage House, First Floor

ARMSEA HALL

GENERAL FRANCIS VINTON GREENE

Hoppin & Koen, 1901

In 1870, General Francis Vinton Greene graduated at the head of his class from West Point. After spending four years with the International Boundary Commission staking out the nation's northern border with Canada, he took a position under the secretary of war in the Grant administration. He was then sent to Russia as a military attaché to accompany the Russian army in their war with Turkey. In 1889 he joined the New York National Guard as a major and was later promoted to general by President McKinley during the Spanish-American War. Pursuing business interests after the war, Greene was elected president of the Barber Asphalt Paving Company in 1901, where he was instrumental in the creation of the Asphalt Trust.

While at Barber he and his wife Belle purchased a seventeen-acre waterfront parcel in Newport, on the East Passage of Narragansett Bay facing Jamestown and the Dumplings. Unlike the residential crowding experienced on Bellevue Avenue, this substantial parcel of land on Ridge Road allowed for greater seclusion. To insure privacy Green erected a ten-foot-high brick wall along his Ridge Road frontage; the wall's decorative focus was a set of wrought-iron gates supported by ball-capped brick and limestone piers. Behind this wall Greene constructed a thirty-room house designed by Francis Laurens Vinton Hoppin, of the firm of Hoppin & Koen. The architect received the commission because he was a family relation of Greene's. Hoppin's design reflected the neoclassical revival design of American houses being constructed at the end of the eighteenth century, which incorporated Adamesque decorative detailing similar to that found on English and Irish houses of that period. At Armsea Hall the scale was increased to encompass the needs of an early-twentieth-century American plutocrat

Entrance Façade (Gary Lawrance Collection)

Water Façade (Gary Lawrance Collection)

Portico Detail (Gary Lawrance Collection)

and his family. Dependencies included a gate lodge, stables, and an automobile shed that included its own electric generator.

Constructed of wood with a veneer of stucco, Armsea Hall has a three-story central section bracketed by two-story wings. The multifaceted design is capped by a seamed copper roof. The façade facing the water has a stately portico supported by four massive, fluted Corinthian columns crowned by a pediment whose tympanum is embellished with a central shield-shaped window surrounded by carved relief swags. This pediment is attached to the third-floor elevation, which is visually separated from the lower floors by an encircling cornice line that surrounds the tops of the adjacent side wings as well. Simple pilasters divide the linear wall mass, which is embellished with decorative swags and inserted with round openings with uniquely designed rectangular window framing. Topping the house is a series of decorative urns that punctuate the roofline. Within the portico below, a door surmounted by a broken pediment is flanked by framed decorative niches. A

Entrance Hall (Gary Lawrance Collection)

Living Room (Gary Lawrance Collection)

Dining Room (Gary Lawrance Collection)

Reception Room (Gary Lawrance Collection)

wrought-iron balcony designed in the same manner as the structure's crowning widow's walk sits above the door. Framing the portico are broad Palladian windows, which allow quantities of light to penetrate the first-floor rooms within. The wings at either side are wrapped by single-story loggias that are capped by a balustrade. These loggias are hung with canvas awnings during the season, allowing them to become a shaded oasis from the summer sun.

The entrance front is less successful because of the need for a service wing that extends awkwardly forward from the left wing, causing this elevation to lose its symmetrical form. Extending even farther is a large decorative trellis screen in the French eighteenth-century taste that separates the graveled entrance forecourt from an adjacent service yard. The main entrance to the house is defined by a T-shaped porte-cochère, surmounted by a balustrade that projects from the central mass with the forward, wider end being the drive-through position.

One enters the house through a vestibule located beneath the landing of the principal staircase. The adjacent, paneled stair hall leads to a wide transverse hall that connects the four entertaining rooms of the house. The paneled reception room walls are done in shades of pink and white, while the mantelpiece and doorways are surmounted by richly molded broken pediments. The living room occupies the entire south wing and has walls painted white that incorporate bookcases fronted by decorative leaded-glass doors. Above the cases runs a deep red frieze. The three tapestries that hang from its walls are the chief decorative feature of the room. The dining room is found at the opposite end of the house and is embellished with a white-painted wainscot surmounted by walls covered with striped green silk. Completing the family apartments on this level is a cozy study for General Greene. In the service wing can be found the butler's pantry, kitchen, and servants' dining room. Be-

Boudoir (Gary Lawrance Collection)

Bedroom (Gary Lawrance Collection)

low in the basement is placed a billiard room, a wine room, and laundry and storage facilities. Upstairs on the second level are seven bedrooms, Mrs. Greene's boudoir, and four bathrooms. The service wing contains two staff rooms and bath, while the third floor has an additional eight servant rooms, plus a playroom for the Greene children.

Within two years of its completion Armsea Hall was sold. In 1904 it was purchased by Charles Frederick Hoffman, whose fortune was derived from inherited Manhattan real estate. He was president of the Union Club, treasurer of the Cathedral of St. John the Divine, and a trustee of Columbia University. The new owner improved the estate by adding expansive vegetable and formal gardens. Hoffman died in 1919 while in Newport. His funeral was held at Armsea Hall. His widow, Zelia K. Preston Hoffman, soon moved to England, although she continued to return to Newport each summer. At her death in 1929 the house was bequeathed to her daughter Marion.

Marion and her husband, stockbroker Aymar Johnson, occupied the house only periodically.

Between visits, the Johnsons leased the house to high-profile social types such as the Marquesa de Cuevas, a Rockefeller heiress. Following the Johnsons, there were a string of owners. Under the tenure of Barclay Douglas, the estate was renamed Annandale Farm. In 1945, Annandale Farm sold for $14,500, while seven years later it went for $42,000. In 1962 there was a plan to purchase the estate through private subscription and donate it to the nation as a summer "White House" for John F. Kennedy and his wife Jacqueline, whose mother, Mrs. Hugh D. Auchincloss, summered next door at Hammersmith Farm. The Kennedys had actually leased the house for the 1964 season, but the contract was canceled after the president's assassination. The following year a development syndicate purchased the property for $150,000 but defaulted on its mortgage. Subsequently, it was auctioned in 1968 for $195,000. Later it was purchased by Newport Landscape, Inc., which tore the house down and subdivided the property in 1969.

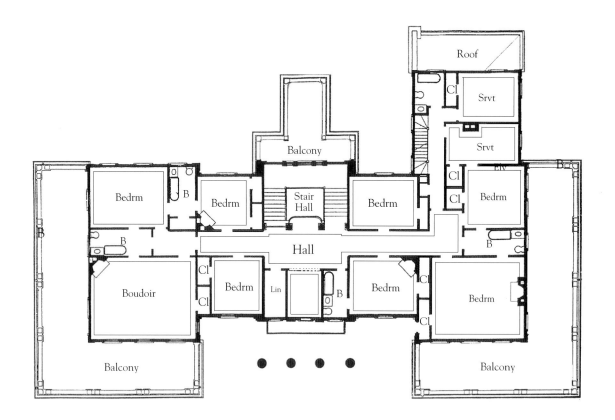

Second Floor

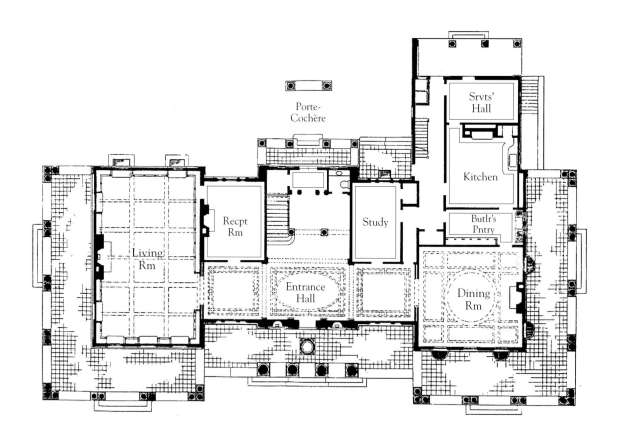

First Floor

HARBOUR COURT

MRS. JOHN NICHOLAS BROWN

Ralph Adams Cram, 1903–1905

John Nicholas Brown was born in 1861, a seventh-generation descendent of Chad Brown, an early settler in Providence Plantations. His father, John Carter Brown, was a successful merchant and manufacturer who died in 1874, leaving the bulk of his estate to his two sons Harold and John Nicholas. After two years at Brown University—named for the family because of their financial support—John Nicholas continued his education by extensive travel and the study of European history, architecture, and languages. After returning home in 1888, he and his brother opened the real estate and mortgage company of J.N. & H. Brown. In 1897 he married Natalie Bayard Dresser, a granddaughter of another Newporter, Daniel Leroy.

Two years later the couple spent their first season together in Newport, where they leased the George Fearing estate on Narragansett Avenue. On February 21, 1900, a son, John Nicholas Brown II, was born. Unfortunately, within two months of his birth, his father contracted typhoid fever and died on the first of May. The family tragedy was compounded when John Nicholas's brother Harold died ten days later in New York, after hurrying back from Europe upon hearing of his brother's death. Since Harold left no issue, the great fortune of John Carter Brown was once again united under the sole principal heir, the two-month-old infant John Nicholas Brown II.

In August of 1903, Natalie Brown purchased an eight-and-a-quarter-acre site in Newport from the estate of Hugh T. Dickey. Located at the intersection of the outer harbor and Halidon Avenue, the property had a 550-foot shore frontage. Ralph Adams Cram, of the Boston firm of Cram, Goodhue & Ferguson, worked very closely with Natalie on the design of the house, which was executed in the French taste of the late-seventeenth-century provincial château. Cram is best known for his collegiate and ecclesiastical Gothic designs; he and Natalie had earlier worked on the design for the Gothic-style Emmanuel Church in Newport, which had been erected as a memorial to her late husband. The choice of style for Harbour Court is based upon Natalie's strong ties to France, having lived there for several years during her youth.

Harbour Court sits majestically on a man-made earthen terrace, with panoramic views overlooking Newport Harbor. It is constructed of brick overlaid with stucco, while decorative elements such as window and door surrounds, as well as corner quoining, are executed in limestone. The entrance to the house is flanked by paired Doric pilasters and a decorative classical frieze that is capped by a wrought-iron balcony. The balcony encloses a tripartite window arrangement, which is surmounted by a single pedimented dormer framed by volutes. Bracketing this are small semicircular glazed openings that help break up the roof mass. The steeply pitched roof of the structure is of slate applied in the traditional European manner, with thicker courses placed at the eave, while diminishing in scale as they rise to the roof ridge. Filling the central position of the harbor side of the house is a covered loggia whose roof is supported by paired columns. The H-shaped plan is augmented by a wing projecting from the southeast corner of the house. This wing has been pierced by a porte-cochère that contains two entrances to the house. A staircase tower has been placed at the juncture of the entrance façade and this wing as a unifying element connecting the two linear plans.

Scattered around the property are numerous

Entrance Court (Author's Collection)

Entrance Court Detail (Author's Collection)

outbuildings. The largest of these is a half-timbered carriage house that contains a five-room groom's apartment and a six-room superintendent's apartment. Directly adjacent to the carriage house is a separate garage for an additional three automobiles. A greenhouse, a poultry house, and an ice house are located nearby, while a small fig house was constructed to protect Natalie's fig trees from harsh New England winters. Built in 1912 along the waterfront, and adjacent to a tiny private beach, is a two-room half-timbered children's playhouse that has its own wood-burning fireplace.

Entering the house through a tiled vestibule, one immediately passes through a set of decorative glazed wrought-iron doors that lead into a 36-foot-long entrance hall paneled entirely in oak. A fireplace is placed directly opposite the entrance as a decorative focus. Paired Doric pilasters support a full entablature, while windows located on either side of the front door have deep paneled reveals. At

Harbor Facing Terrace (Author's Collection)

one end of this hall is the principal staircase, while at the other is an entrance to an office. Of particular interest are the uniquely styled metal light fixtures in the hall that appear to be Gothic in inspiration and may be the only hint in the house of Cram's true architectural preference.

On either side of the hall's fireplace are sets of doors leading to the salon, executed in the Louis XVI style with appropriate paneling and a marble mantelpiece. From this room three sets of French doors open to the loggia, while decorative plaster wreaths with festoons of flowers are found above doorways leading to adjacent rooms. The doorway at the west end of the room leads to the dining room, which is executed in an American Federal Revival style. The fireplace here has Ionic columns that support a decorated frieze and mantelshelf. The room's overdoor rondels contain oil paintings

Gardens (Newport Historical Society, Henry O. Havemeyer Collection)

Hall (Author's Collection)

Drawing Room (Author's Collection)

Dining Room (Author's Collection)

Library (Author's Collection)

of Chinese blue and white porcelain that were executed by Natalie. The library, located at the opposite end of the main block of the structure, has richly molded oak paneling with built-in bookcases. An imported mantelpiece in the Elizabethan manner is the dominant architectural focus of the room.

Suites for both of the principal occupants of the house fill the major part of the second floor. Natalie's apartment consists of a bedroom, morning room, bath, and a chamber for her personal maid. Her son's suite has a night nursery, bath, and a day nursery, as well as an adjacent room for a live-in nurse. Three additional bedrooms and two baths are located on this level, while in the service wing eleven staff chambers are arranged. A spiral staircase leads up to three additional bedrooms in the attic, as well as to a large playroom. This playroom

has a paneled vestibule with a fireplace that was occasionally utilized as a theater for children's amateur productions.

In 1912 alterations were made to the house to make it more compatible with the evolving lifestyles of Natalie and her growing son. These alterations enlarged the library and reconfigured both of the master suites. This work entailed moving a chimney stack and adding a small extension to the eastern end of the house.

Natalie died at Harbor Court on March 23, 1950. Her son then occupied the house until his death in 1979. After his widow, Anne Seddon Kinsolving Brown, died six years later, their children put the house on the market for $4,500,000. After an auction of the home's furnishings in October of 1987, Harbor Court became the Newport headquarters for the New York Yacht Club.

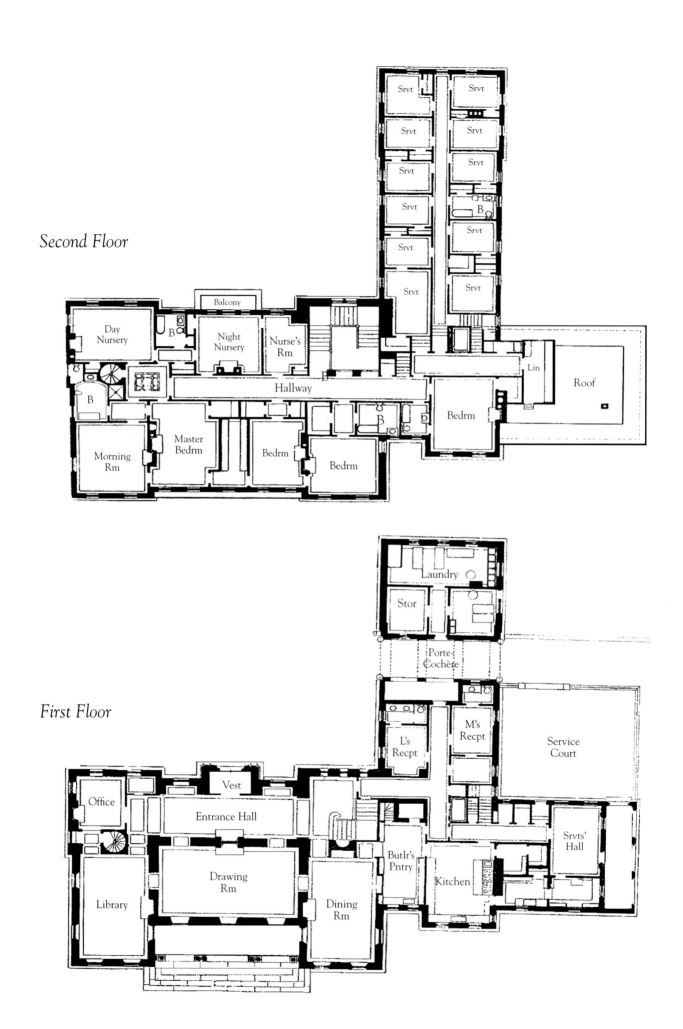

Second Floor

Day Nursery

B

Balcony

Night Nursery

Nurse's Rm

Srvt

Srvt

Srvt

Srvt

Srvt

Srvt

Srvt

Srvt

Srvt

Srvt

B

Srvt

Srvt

B

Morning Rm

Master Bedrm

Bedrm

Bedrm

B

Bedrm

Lin

Roof

Hallway

First Floor

Laundry

Stor

Porte-Cochère

L's Recpt

M's Recpt

Service Court

Office

Vest

Entrance Hall

Srvts' Hall

Library

Drawing Rm

Dining Rm

Butlr's Pntry

Kitchen

CASTLEWOOD

MRS. ÉMILE BRUGUIÈRE AND LOUIS S. BRUGUIÈRE
Edward Payson Whitman, 1904-1906

Of the larger Newport cottages Castlewood is perhaps the least known. A principal reason is its location. An article in the *New York Times* of June 17, 1906, describing the residences erected in the city over the previous year, remarked, "One of them is the handsome French chateau which Mrs. Émile Bruguière has erected on the extreme northern outskirts of the city near Coddington Point, far away from the fashionable section." Although this area, with its bucolic views overlooking the middle passage of Narragansett Bay, was highly desirable in the middle of the nineteenth century, it became overwhelmed with both commercial development and housing for naval personnel by the middle of the twentieth century. Castlewood's demolition by the United States government during World War II to create housing for workers at the Newport torpedo factory was hardly noticed, and by the late 1970s there were few who remembered that the house had ever existed.

Josephine F. Bruguière was the daughter of Peder Sather, who left his native Norway to move to Philadelphia, where he would become a member of the banking firm of Drexel & Company. Sather relocated to San Francisco, where he established the Sather Bank, which eventually became the San Francisco National Bank. Josephine married Émile Bruguière and had four sons. Following the deaths of her father and husband, Josephine left California, dividing her time between a suite of rooms at Sherry's Hotel in New York, her Newport villa, and an apartment in Paris. Mrs. Bruguière shared these three domiciles with her youngest son, Louis S. Bruguière.

Castlewood was designed by New York architect Edward Payson Whitman and was erected between 1904 and 1906. It was sited on the highest elevation of the point,

Entrance Façade (General Research Division, The New York Public Library, Astor, Lenox and Tilden Foundation)

Garden Façade (General Research Division, The New York Public Library, Astor, Lenox and Tilden Foundation)

with expansive views all around. The remnants of an eighteenth-century battery, thought to have been used by the Comte de Rochambeau during the American Revolution, were retained in Castlewood's garden design. If the house had been entirely sheathed in the off-white terra-cotta used in its decorative trim, the rhythmic unfolding of the façade—particularly that found on the waterside—would be decidedly French in inspiration. The use of red brick for the flat wall surfaces, however, provided the elevations with a feeling of the mid-Georgian period found at the end of the eighteenth century in England.

The entrance elevation of Castlewood is a tripartite design; it rests on a raised basement that is topped by a base course of terra-cotta. Corinthian pilasters bracket each section of the façade. The composition is centered on a Doric-columned entrance porch, surmounted by a balustraded balcony with brick piers. This porch is enclosed with glazed wrought iron, making it a protective vestibule for arriving guests on inclement days. Adding additional shelter is a wrought-iron and glass canopy. The first-floor windows all exhibit rounded tops, while a stringcourse separates the top sections of these apertures from the French doors beneath. Above these doors are placed decorative rondels. The second-floor casement windows have bracketed lintels, while their tops support a full entablature. Inserted into the entablature is a frieze of plain brick. At each end of the house are single-story projections: a Doric-columned loggia at the southern end, and an abbreviated service wing at the other. Surmounting the entire composition is a parapet pierced by balusters. Ruining the symmetry of the entrance elevation is an ill-placed service wall extension on the northern end of the façade. The waterfront façade is also a tripartite composition; here a two-story Corinthian colonnade fills the central section. Marble-paved terraces, which are bordered by alternating brick and balustered railings, extend around the west and south elevations. Softening

Hall (General Research Division, The New York Public Library, Astor, Lenox and Tilden Foundation)

the monumental effect of the design are strategically placed potted bay trees and flower-filled urns

Like most Newport houses, Castlewood was designed for grand entertainments. There are five large spaces on the first floor that, when thrown open on gala evenings, can easily accommodate three or four hundred guests. The central block of the structure contains only two rooms: the entrance hall and the living room. The former has a tripartite design separated by paired marble columns. Between the columns on the right side of the room is the principal staircase, which rises to a landing, then turns left to continue its ascent to the second floor. The walls of the hall are sheathed in white marble with a green-marble-inset border, while the ceiling is decorated with an ornately trimmed shallow plaster dome. The living room, located directly behind this hall, is paneled in oak, having a fireplace copied from one at Dorford Hall in Cheshire, England.

The dining room opens from the north end of the living room. Its mahogany paneling supports a deeply covered ceiling centered by a rectangle that is outlined by a decorative plaster border composed of bundled leaves. The most prominent feature of the room is its Sienna marble mantelpiece in an English Renaissance design, which is based on one found at Hatfield House in England.

Filling the southern wing of the house is a salon that faces the water and sits directly behind a library that overlooks the entrance court. The salon is referred to in the contemporary press as the Louis Quinze Drawing-Room, and although it was furnished with eighteenth-century-French-inspired pieces, the decorative detailing of its walls is of the Italian Renaissance. What makes this room innovative is its liberal use of mirrored wall sections that are set within the arched detailing of the wall articulation. A mirrored disc is set into the ceiling above

Salon (General Research Division, The New York Public Library, Astor, Lenox and Tilden Foundation)

Dining Room (General Research Division, The New York Public Library, Astor, Lenox and Tilden Foundation)

Library (General Research Division, The New York Public Library, Astor, Lenox and Tilden Foundation)

the chandelier to enhance its glow at night. The far more somberly finished library is lined with French walnut paneling. Simple Doric pilasters divide the room into sections, while they also support an ornate foliate frieze. The swagged overmantel found above the carved marble chimney is specially designed to frame a portrait of Mrs. Bruguière.

Within two years of taking possession of her opulent new summer residence, Mrs. Bruguière became deep in arrears with her Newport accounts. The trouble culminated in 1908, when a claim was attached to the house. This problem was resolved and attachments removed in June of that year, but in August of 1914 the *New York Times* reported that "to satisfy the claims of Newport trades people the magnificent furnishings of Castle Wood [*sic*], which were bought this week at mortgage sale by the Savings Bank of Newport, will be sold at a Sheriff's sale on Aug. 18 for the benefit of the creditors of Mrs. Emile Bruguière."

On August 10, 1915, Mrs. Bruguière and her son Louis were returning to the United States from France on the White Star steamship *Arabic* when the Germans torpedoed it. Although Louis heroically tried to save his mother by swimming with her upon his chest for some twenty minutes, he was later separated from her while trying to navigate through the debris field. He was saved, but Mrs. Bruguière did not survive. By the terms of her will, she left Castlewood to Louis, but it had been seized the year before.

Arnold Watson Essex of New York and Providence, Rhode Island, then purchased the house from the Savings Bank of Newport. He was reported to be "a man of large means who does not care for society," which made the house—so far away from the frenzied social activity centered around Bellevue Avenue—an ideal residence for the misanthropic new owner. Mrs. John H. Hanan, who occupied the house in the late 1910s, was its final private owner. For many years the structure was used as the Mercy Home orphanage, before being demolished and the land subdivided for development.

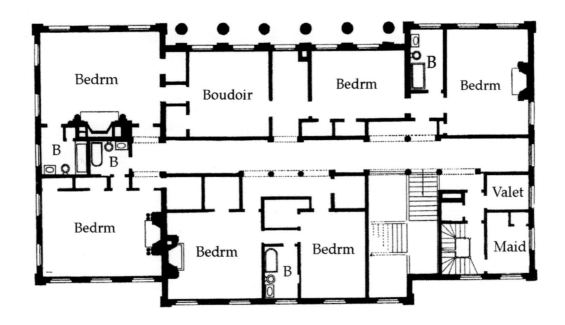

Second Floor

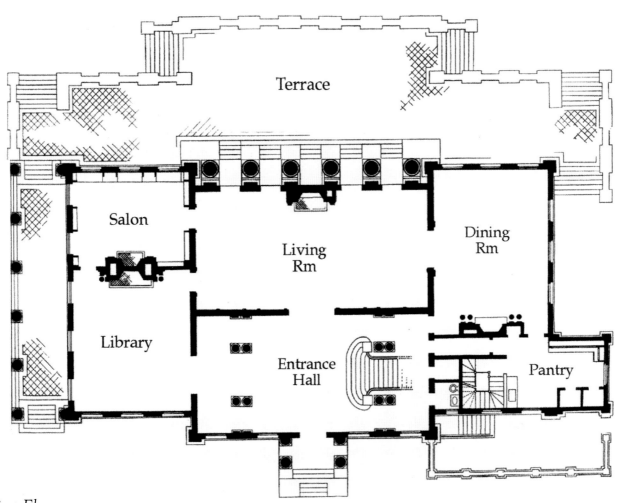

First Floor

SHERWOOD

PEMBROKE JONES

Hoppin & Koen, 1906-1908

I n 1871, New York leather merchant Loring Andrews purchased a five-and-a-half-acre plot on Bellevue Avenue from Edward Willing of Philadelphia. Andrews then commissioned the firm of George Champlin Mason & Son to design a villa in the Stick Style to occupy the site. This villa, which measured 140 by 52 feet and cost $70,000 to construct, was perhaps the most opulent of its era. After Andrews's death in 1875, the house was leased to Theodore A. Havemeyer for several seasons. Havemeyer, from the prominent New York sugar-manufacturing family, eventually purchased the place in September of 1880 and christened it Friedheim—meaning "happy home" in German. Eight years later the Mason firm was recalled to enlarge the house, while also giving it a fashionable Queen Anne Revival appearance.

Soon after Havemeyer's death in 1897 his widow decided to live abroad. For several seasons the home was leased to John Jacob Astor, the son of William B. and Caroline Astor, whose wife was the former Ava Willing of Philadelphia, a member of the same family who had originally sold the property to Loring Andrews over three decades earlier. During the 1901–1902 seasons the house was leased to Pembroke Jones of New York and Wilmington, North Carolina. In April of 1905, Jones purchased the house with the proviso that Theodore's son Henry would retain the name Friedheim, with which he would then rechristen his Newport estate on Harrison Avenue.

Pembroke Jones, whose original fortune derived from the rice-milling industry in Wilmington, North Carolina, and New Orleans, would later invest in railways and shipbuilding. This necessitated the family's move to New York. For several years he and his wife, Sarah Green Jones, resided at 550 Park Avenue but eventually purchased

Entrance Façade (General Research Division, The New York Public Library, Astor, Lenox and Tilden Foundation)

a more substantial residence at 5 East 61st Street. The family retained their southern roots by wintering at Airlie, their North Carolina estate eight miles from Wilmington.

The year following his purchase of the Havemeyer house, Jones hired Francis L. V. Hoppin to reconfigure the house to better suit the family's entertaining needs. In the process Hoppin also transformed it from a somber Victorian villa into a bright classical temple called Sherwood. First he removed the peak roof and gables—as well as most of the third floor. All covered verandas and projections were eliminated, while the architect regularized the elevations and encased them in white stucco with eighteenth- and early-nineteenth-century detailing. The completed work is often cited as resembling the White House in Washington, D.C., because of the

pedimented porte-cochère on the entrance front and a circular portico attached to the garden elevation; but fundamentally the design harkens to the lighter vernaculars associated with the English Regency period in its execution and detailing.

The columns that support the entrance portico have leaf capitals, while the first-floor windows are embraced by elegant Palladian detailing. Placed between the second-story windows are decorated rondels that help to break up the upper wall surface. Above the second-story windows a rosette-embellished frieze supports a fully developed cornice and roof balustrade. A partial third floor is capped by its own cornice and balustraded parapet. At the north end of the house is the service wing added by the Havemeyer family, although newly veneered, while at the south end of the composi-

Garden Façade (General Research Division, The New York Public Library, Astor, Lenox and Tilden Foundation)

Entrance Hall (General Research Division, The New York Public Library, Astor, Lenox and Tilden Foundation)

Reception Room (General Research Division, The New York Public Library, Astor, Lenox and Tilden Foundation)

Dining Room (General Research Division, The New York Public Library, Astor, Lenox and Tilden Foundation)

tion is a single-story veranda whose roof was supported by paired Doric columns. (This veranda was later removed when a ballroom extension was added in 1916.) A newspaper article in October of 1907, at the time of Hoppin's initial renovation, relates that the house is going through a complete metamorphosis: "It looks new in every particular, and when the work is completed it will possibly be found that it would have been as well in the first place to tear down and build up anew." It goes on to say, "The lines of the exterior are so changed that one cannot discover a single suggestion of the old, and what applies to the exterior is practically true of the interior."

Sherwood's major rooms are what would be expected in a Newport villa of this scale. The first-floor entertaining rooms are formal and laid out in such a way that they flow easily into each other, creating functional settings for large-scale enter-

taining. After entering the house through a screen of iron and glass, the visitor enters into a tripartite entrance hall that runs the depth of the house. These sections are divided by the use of Doric columns and pilasters, while the floors are paved with marble-trimmed terrazzo. To gain access to the larger, central division requires ascending a short flight of marble steps. To the right is an archway that leads to the principal staircase with its ornate wrought-iron railing. Beneath this staircase are entrances to a powder room, the service wing, and a billiard room. Across the hall from the staircase is a reception room decorated in the style of Robert Adam. Beyond this is the library, finished with wainscot, ceiling, and mantelpiece in Circassian walnut. In contrast, the upper walls and draperies of the library are hung in green silk damask. On either side of the main hall at the back of the house and overlooking the sloping rear lawn are the drawing

Drawing Room (General Research Division, The New York Public Library, Astor, Lenox and Tilden Foundation)

Library (General Research Division, The New York Public Library, Astor, Lenox and Tilden Foundation)

and dining rooms. At 42 by 28 feet, they are the largest rooms in the house and are both treated in the high-Georgian manner, with fully developed architectural detailing. The dining room has cream-colored walls and a green carpet on the floor with matching silk damask at the windows, while the drawing room located across the hall is painted in two shades of gray, with contrasting trim in white. Here the accent color is a deep cherry-red.

The second floor has six bedrooms and a sitting room, while the third floor guest accommodations have an additional five rooms. There are ten en-suite baths. Mrs. Jones's suite was the most elaborate, executed in the Louis XVI style with crimson hangings and a blanche-brèche marble mantel. Her bathroom has paneled walls above a marble wainscot, and flooring executed in marble tiles. Adjacent to her bath is a dress closet that measures a roomy 14 by 12 feet.

Of the three families associated with the property, the Jones family would be by far the longest in residence. Pembroke Jones died on January 24, 1919, following an operation at the Post-Graduate Hospital in New York. His widow, later married to railroad magnate and renowned art collector Henry Walters of Baltimore, would continue to summer in the house until her death in June of 1943. Sherwood was then inherited by her son Pembroke Jones, Jr., who continued the family's occupancy until his death in 1970. The following year his widow, Paula, would sell the property to the Chartier Real Estate Company for $100,000. While converting the house into apartments, the developer added unsympathetic wings to the garden façade and service wing. Sherwood was later converted into condominiums.

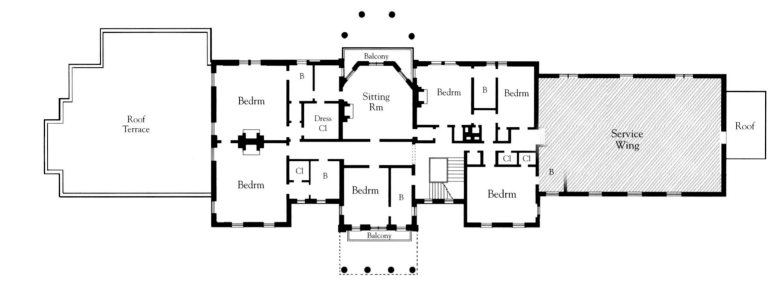

Second Floor

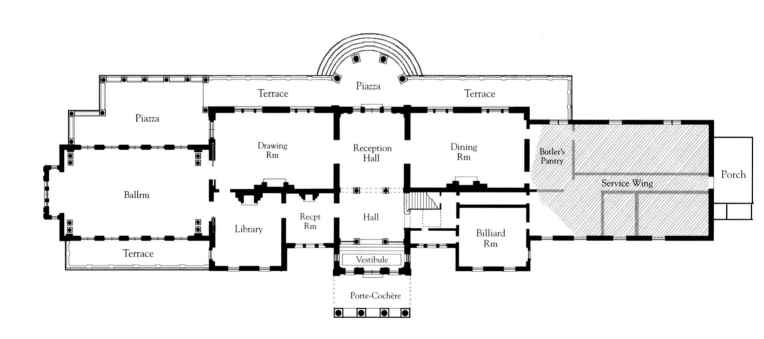

First Floor

BERKELEY VILLA

MARTHA CATHERINE CODMAN

Ogden Codman, Jr., 1910

Martha Catherine Codman was the daughter of John Amory Codman and heiress to a $25 million real estate and mercantile fortune. In her youth she visited Newport with her parents, staying at either the Atlantic House or the Ocean House hotel. Soon after receiving her inheritance in 1897, she purchased a Victorian house on Bellevue Avenue from John G. Weaver. Within a decade she asked her cousin Ogden Codman to design a new house for the property, which was erected just north of where the demolished Weaver house had stood. Placing the new structure in the extreme northwest corner of the property allowed for large formal gardens to be developed to the south and east.

Although Codman is best known for his European Revival residences, at Berkeley Villa he returns to his New England roots for inspiration. The basic shape of this large clapboard house with its dormered and hipped slate roof was borrowed from the eighteenth-century Shirley-Eustis house in Roxbury, Massachusetts, while the Eban Crafts house, Elmwood, also in Roxbury, inspired the double-height entrance projection. Paired Corinthian columns placed upon high rectangular plinths frame the entrance door, and a second-floor wrought-iron balcony fronts what appears to be a set of French doors but are actually two separate windows. Atop the entrance projection is a balustrade that matches that found around a rooftop widow's walk.

A less conventional approach was taken on the south façade. To break up the mass a large central octagonal bay was created that was adapted from yet another Roxbury home—the Perez Morton house, erected in 1796. The bay has three sets of French doors, with a second-floor loggia above; the latter was originally designed to be open

Entrance Façade (Courtesy of the Preservation Society of Newport County)

Garden Façade (Courtesy of the Preservation Society of Newport County)

Yew Garden (Ronald Lee Fleming Collection)

but was eventually glazed-in because of the vagaries of Newport's summer weather.

The oversized doors located at either side of the marble-floored entrance vestibule are embellished with a fanlight and side lights. On either side are niches designed to hold decorative urns or statuary. Next is a small connecting hallway with a door on the left leading to a reception room, while a door on the right accesses the library. Straight ahead lay the decorative pièce de résistance of the house, the staircase rotunda. The rather modest exterior of the house does not prepare one for the sumptuousness of this superbly detailed space. Although principally based on details found at Wardour Castle in Wiltshire, England (designed and executed by the architect James Paine between 1768 and 1776), its dome is closer to that found in Robert Adam's Home House (1777) on Portman Square in London. A handsome, intricately detailed polychrome marble floor supports a spiral staircase that leads to

an encircling balcony at the second-story level. The wall surfaces of the lower floor are rusticated and hold round-topped openings that alternate with similarly shaped niches, while the walls above are divided by evenly spaced Corinthian pilasters that support a full entablature. The dome, with its central oculus, has delicate rondel and garland detailing set within a gridlike format.

The three major entertaining rooms of the house are also executed in the English manner, but from sources taken from structures of a half century earlier. The library, the drawing room, and the dining room are all aligned to take advantage of southern breezes, and overlook a large terrace and formal gardens. The library, located in the southwest corner of the house, has a decorative mantelpiece with a classical landscape painting set within an elaborate frame topped by a broken pediment. Opposite this is a shelved niche with a shell-shaped top that is framed by Corinthian pilasters. The adjacent

Staircase Rotunda (Author's Collection)

Drawing Room (Courtesy of the Preservation Society of Newport County)

paneled drawing room has a mantel reminiscent of William Kent. Above it is another classical landscape. Two more examples of this type of painting are found on either side of the arched set of doors on the north wall that lead to the rotunda. These canvases, which are also arched, are set high in the wall to leave room for rectangular beveled mirrors between them and the chair rail below. On the opposite side of the room is a protruding bay with its three sets of French doors leading to the terrace. Extending to the eastern boundary of the house is the dining room with its simple moldings, a relatively plain mantel and French doors leading to an enclosed terrace. The north end of the room is separated by a screen of Corinthian columns.

To increase privacy none of the principal bedrooms are accessed directly from the rotunda but rather through small connecting hallways emanating from it. The master suite consists of two bed-

rooms, with en-suite baths, separated by an octagonal sitting room, all facing south and overlooking the formal gardens. Two other bedrooms are located on this level, one located at the front of the house, facing the entrance court, while the owner's personal maid may have occupied a smaller one located in the northeast corner of the floor. Between these bedrooms are two small staff rooms. In the attic are two additional guest rooms, a trunk room, and six more staff bedrooms.

The formal gardens that originally graced the estate were executed by Codman but were later redesigned and embellished by the French landscape designer Achille Duchêne. On axis with the drawing room terrace is a tapis vert bordered by floral broderies. Toward the west, a planted formal parterre is dominated by clipped linden trees. To the east of the house is another formally planted space, whose centerpiece features a two-story

Dining Room (Ronald Lee Fleming Collection)

Library (Ronald Lee Fleming Collection)

Bedroom (Courtesy of the Preservation Society of Newport County)

garden pavilion that is based on a prototype erected in 1792 by the Massachusetts architect and wood-carver Samuel McIntire for the garden of Elias Has-ket Derby in Danvers. Extending from the pavilion are graceful wooden fences that arc to embrace an-other parterre, whose central focus is two specimen yew trees.

In July of 1927, Miss Codman entertained two hundred guests at a musicale where the principal entertainer was Maxim Karolik, a Russian tenor who before the Russian Revolution was a featured performer at the Imperial Opera in St. Petersburg. A year later Miss Codman, then almost seventy, and Mr. Karolik, thirty years her junior, were mar-ried in a ceremony on the French Riviera. Al-though initially shocking members of the summer colony, the couple was generally accepted—except by a few Bostonians who continued to dismiss Karo-lik as a "Russian adventurer."

After his wife's death in 1948, Karolik contin-ued summering at Berkeley Villa until his death in 1963. In the mid-1960s the house was acquired by its second owner: singer and actress Jane Pickens

and her husband, stockbroker William C. Langley. She changed the name of the property to Bellevue House, explaining the decision in a *Town & Coun-try* article, "It's the first house on Bellevue Avenue and, since no one else named his house Bellevue, I thought it was logical for me to do so."

Today, Ronald Lee Fleming, the noted preser-vationist and urban planner, owns Bellevue House. He is currently involved with a renovation of the house and grounds, while preserving the beauty and the integrity of the original Codman design. The work includes the addition of a breakfast room whose domed plaster ceiling utilizes an unexecuted Codman design originally intended for Edith Wharton's Newport villa, Land's End. With the help of architect Jon-Paul Couture, Fleming has created two new garden pavilions, both adapted from Samuel McIntire designs in Salem, Massa-chusetts. One replicates a teahouse found at the Beebe-Derby house; the other the cupola of the Branch Church. These structures seamlessly inte-grate with the established architectural framework of the estate.

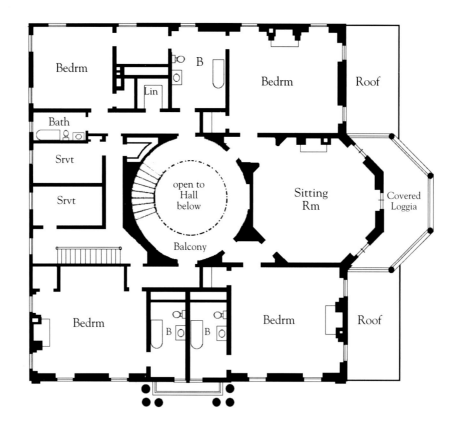

Second Floor

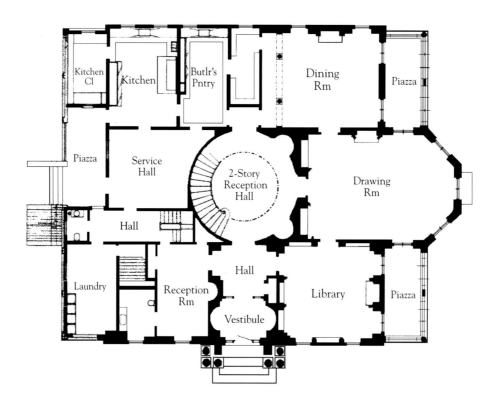

First Floor

BEACON HILL HOUSE

ARTHUR CURTISS JAMES

Howells & Stokes, 1909–1910

Atop the tallest hill on Aquidneck Island—with sweeping ocean views and grounds interspersed with bluestone outcroppings—once stood Beacon Hill House. Its name captures an image from America's War of Independence where a "beacon flashed forth tidings of the approaching enemy." In the nineteenth century it was called Telegraph Hill because its lofty position was used to broadcast to the world the victor in early New York Yacht Club races. It was not the first house to take advantage of this enviable position. During the 1890s Stanford White designed an H-shaped stone house on the site for John H. Glover. This structure was sold in 1900 to J. Edward Addicks, who owned it for eight years before selling it to railroad magnate Arthur Curtiss James.

Originally, James wanted a revamping of the Glover house, but when told about structural defects in the foundation, he decided to build anew. As work was commencing on the house, James had a gate lodge on Brenton Road rushed to completion so he and his wife, the former Harriet Eddy Parsons, would have a roof over there heads for the 1909 season. Elsewhere on the property a large garage complex was built whose basement had to be blasted from solid rock. Along with automobiles, this structure also housed five water tanks that could each hold 50,000 gallons.

The new house measured 165 by 82 feet, and was framed by a 12-foot-wide balustraded terrace. Constructed of rough local bluestone, the home had decorative details of limestone and granite. The entrance façade faced east and was centered by a wrought-iron and glass porte-cochère. Beacon Hill House retained the original H shape of the Glover house, but the architectural firm of Howells & Stokes added

Ariel View of Estate (Courtesy of the Preservation Society of Newport County)

Glover Cottage (Newport Historical Society)

Entrance Façade (Author's Collection)

Rear Façade (Courtesy of the Rhode Island Historical Society)

Blue Garden (Author's Collection – Edward Van Altena photographer)

Swiss Village (Author's Collection)

Gardens (Courtesy of the Preservation Society of Newport County)

projections on every side that nearly doubled its square footage. Sculptural detailing was also added, particularly on dormer windows projecting from the tiled roof.

A narrow galley-shaped entrance vestibule led into a paneled two-story great hall that measured 45 by 23 feet. At one end of the hall was placed an Adam-style mantel, above which a bas-relief overmantel displayed classical imagery. To the right of the fireplace was an organ console whose pipes were visible in the gallery above. At the other end of the hall two broad sets of doors led into a drawing room finished in the Louis XV style, with French walnut boiserie surmounted by an elaborately molded plaster ceiling cove. Stretching along the back of the house in the rear extension were the living and dining rooms, both veneered in matching Jacobean-pe-

riod paneling purchased by Mr. James in England. The wall separating the two spaces could be removed on gala evenings to create a 64-foot-long ballroom. Next to the dining room was an octagonal breakfast room. Bracketing the plan were hexagonal extensions. To the north was Mr. James's mahogany-paneled study, while to the south was the Della Robbia Room. The latter was a conservatory sheathed in earth-toned decorative tiling executed in the style of the famous Florentine family of Renaissance artists.

In 1916, James had a farming complex erected that was rather curiously referred to as the Swiss Village, even though the structures more closely resembled those found in the northern Italian countryside. Designed by Grosvenor Atterbury with rough stone walls and barrel-tiled roofs, the group was designed to be picturesque in the same way that Marie Antoinette's hameau at the Petit Trianon romanticized farm life. The Jameses called it Surprise Valley Farm, as it fit neatly into a newly created dale that had been blasted out of solid rock. Over the years, James continued to buy adjacent estates, bringing his total Newport holdings to 125 acres. It eventually became the largest estate in Newport.

James was not as well known as railroad magnates Jay Gould, James J. Hill, or Cornelius Vanderbilt, but he ended up controlling more trackage that any of them. Born in 1876, he was the grandson of Daniel James, who founded the family fortune in mining operations. His father, D. Willis James, had become a partner in the Phelps Dodge Corporation in 1848, a firm that was instrumental in developing copper and iron mines in North America. Being the sole heir at his father's death in 1907, Arthur Curtiss James inherited a $26 million estate, which chiefly consisted of Phelps-Dodge shares and stock

in the Northern Pacific and Great Northern railroads. By the end of the 1920s he was the largest holder of railroad shares in the country—then valued at over $300 million. James was a devoted yachtsman and a commodore of the New York Yacht Club. Unlike many of his fellow yacht-owning plutocrats, James was a certified captain who could actually navigate his 218-foot fully rigged motor yacht *Aloha*.

Mrs. James was a passionate gardener who developed a hybrid rose that bears her name. At Beacon Hill House she directed the layout of several major gardens; these included a sunken circular garden, a rose garden, and the blue garden, the last generating great acclaim when inaugurated. For the unveiling of the Olmsted-designed garden, Mrs. James entertained her guests with a choreographed piece entitled *Masque of the Blue Garden*. Guests were seated in a blue-canvas-swathed covered stand, while fifty-four professional dancers, musicians, and

Main Hall (Courtesy of the International Tennis Hall of Fame & Museum, Newport, Rhode Island)

Drawing Room (Author's Collection)

Living Room (Redwood Library and Athenaeum, Newport, Rhode Island)

Della Robbia Room (Author's Collection)

singers performed as they cavorted through the garden. Not to be outdone, Mrs. James wore a brilliant sapphire embroidered gown and was addressed as Lady Sapphira throughout the evening.

James retired from active business in 1939 but continued to maintain an office at 40 Wall Street to look after his affairs. This retirement did not last long, because Harriet died of a heart attack in May of 1941, and her husband succumbed to pneumonia three weeks later on June 4. Having no children, the fortune was put to charitable purposes by the establishment of the James Foundation, headquartered at the couple's Park Avenue mansion. In June of 1944, the furnishing of Beacon Hill House

were auctioned and the house, which continued to be owned by the James Foundation, remained empty.

In 1951 the property was deeded to the Roman Catholic Diocese of Providence. Two years later the novitiate of the Order of St. Joseph of Cluny took up residence in one of the smaller structures on the estate, but the main house remained vacant. Because the house sat so far back from any public street, it became a target for looters and vandals who eventually destroyed its beautifully crafted interiors. In May of 1967, a fire completed the devastation, with the charred shell being demolished soon thereafter.

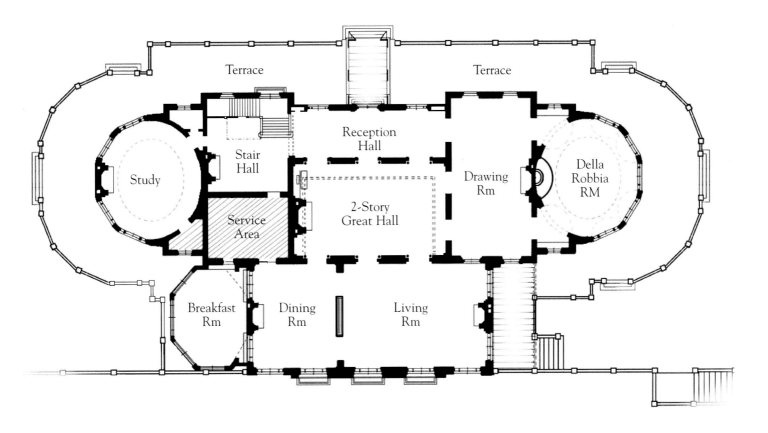

Terrace

Terrace

Study

Stair
Hall

Reception
Hall

Drawing
Rm

Della
Robbia
RM

Service
Area

2-Story
Great Hall

Breakfast
Rm

Dining
Rm

Living
Rm

Note: Plans based on photographs
and written descriptions

First Floor

BONNIECREST

STUART DUNCAN

John Russell Pope, 1912-1914; Addition, 1926

S tuart Duncan, a banker and financier, originally hailed from the Midwest. He and his wife, Jermain Stoddard Duncan, had established themselves in New York by the dawn of the twentieth century. The couple was living in a C. P. H. Gilbert–designed house at 1 East 75th Street, just steps from Fifth Avenue and Central Park. The Duncans were a socially active couple who were already entrenched Newport summer colonists when they began leasing the Henry White estate, Edgerston, on Harrison Avenue. Originally part of the Rutherford Stuyvesant estate, later it had been divided into separate estates, one for White and the other for Arthur Kemp. The Duncans purchased both the White property and the adjacent Kemp estate in 1911, recombining the sites to create the estate they envisioned. The older houses were demolished and replaced with a Tudor-style mansion designed by John Russell Pope called Bonniecrest.

The architect was inspired by the Tudor masterpiece Compton Wynyates, located in Warwickshire, England. This is evident in the warmth of the materials used, the exuberant ornamental chimney stacks, and particularly in the architect's clever adaptation of Compton's famous entrance porch. To achieve an aged appearance Pope carefully selected a warm honey-colored limestone from West Virginia and bricks from several different sources, varying in hue from dark clinker and overburned to light salmon, which were then in turn supplemented by naturally aged used bricks. The textural appearance of the brickwork was additionally heightened by placing much of it in a diaper pattern. Up on the roof, hand-split slate shingles were taken from the outer reaches of the quarry bed, where color is less uniform and the texture varies. All

Entrance Gates (Courtesy of the Preservation Society of Newport County)

Entrance Façade (Courtesy of the Preservation Society of Newport County)

Harbor Façade Detail (Courtesy of the Preservation Society of Newport County)

Long Gallery (Courtesy of the Preservation Society of Newport County)

visible woodwork on the exterior of the house—from molded doorways and half-timbering to the carved decorative bargeboards found surmounting the gables—were treated to enhance this antique appearance. Much of the exterior stonework was sandblasted and beaten with chains to project an aged appearance. Even the flagstones used to pave the harbor-front terrace were culled from a local brook and almost seem to be a natural extension of the adjacent stone outcropping. Crowning the house is a forest of decorative fluted and corkscrewed chimney stacks.

Eschewing the traditional Tudor courtyard plan, the architect selected a linear plan that was better suited for the site and Newport's summer climate. The rambling Tudor style gave Pope the latitude to develop a plan that took full advantage of

summer breezes and sunlight from its rocky site overlooking Newport Harbor. Bonniecrest was erected close to the water's edge, leaving a broad expanse of open lawn between it and the oaken entrance gates on Harrison Avenue. These gates were set within a buttressed framework supporting a lofty stone Tudor arch. The Olmsted Brothers firm accented the grounds with specimen trees and plantings that were specifically placed to heighten the sense of vista and perspective.

On the left side of the entrance porch is found the richly modeled wooden front door to the house. Once inside, the visitor immediately turns right to traverse a narrow hallway that leads to a decorative wrought-iron gate that guards the way to the entrance hall. This artistic piece of ironwork, like others found throughout the house, is the work of

Staircase (Courtesy of the Preservation Society of Newport County)

Samuel Yellin, the renowned master ironworker from Philadelphia. The entrance hall is balanced on one side by a Jacobean-style staircase that has a lion-topped newel and a bank of windows on the other that overlook the water. Extending out of this space is the long gallery, which accesses both the library and the dining room. The gallery is paneled in oak and has a barrel-vaulted ceiling covered in ornamental tracery from which hang period brass chandeliers. Placed on one side of this gallery is an

Living Room (Courtesy of the Preservation Society of Newport County)

Dining Room (Courtesy of the Preservation Society of Newport County)

Library Fireplace Detail (Courtesy of the Preservation Society of Newport County)

antique model of the flagship of Sir Francis Drake. The library walls are covered with linenfold paneling, punctuated by built-in bookcases. A simple mantelshelf supported by carved brackets tops a limestone hearth and surround. At the far end of the gallery is the dining room. A large stone fireplace has a carved frieze that depicts a medieval hunt scene, which is flanked on either side by a carved Tudor rose. This, along with a severely plain overmantel is supported by black and gold marble columns. Above, a plastered tracery ceiling has decorative pendants, while the floor is finished with wide-planked teakwood.

At the opposite end of the house is the living room. At 46 by 28 feet it was originally the largest room in the house. Paneled in oak, as are most of the principal rooms, it boasts a ceiling-high chim-

neypiece adorned with mythical creatures such as griffins and unicorns. The walls of the room are hung with tapestries depicting French country life and hunting. Its high, mullioned bay windows look out to both Fort Adams and the harbor with its myriad boats that fill the view.

Upstairs, the west end of the second floor is filled with Duncans' personal suite, which includes two bedrooms, each with fireplaces, two baths, a dressing room for Mrs. Duncan, and large closets. An additional eight bedrooms, seven with fireplaces, and six en-suite baths complete the family and guest facilities on this level. In the adjacent service wing there are twelve staff rooms and two baths, as well as a large linen closet.

In 1926, Pope was recalled to design a ballroom wing to be added to the west end of the house.

Ballroom Wing (Courtesy of the Preservation Society of Newport County)

Ballroom (Courtesy of the Preservation Society of Newport County)

Because of the enormous scale of the 90-by-60 foot addition, which could have easily overwhelmed the architect's original carefully proportioned work, Pope disguised the exterior of the ballroom to appear as several spaces placed behind gabled extensions and bay windows. The interior of the ballroom is designed to recreate a great Tudor hall, whose beamed English oak ceiling reaches 40 feet. The paneled wainscot is hung with old portraits and antique armor, while the half-timbering found above it is decorated with stags heads and horns.

Stuart Duncan died in 1957. His widow continued to occupy the house, even hosting a ball for a thousand people at the behest of the English-Speaking Union in September of 1962. After her death three years later, the family's collection of English fine and decorative art pieces were dispersed at auction. The following year the estate was sold to the developer Louis F. Chartier. Twenty years later the United States Department of the Interior would remove Bonniecrest and the surrounding estates of Beacon Rock, Beechbound, and Edgehill from the Ocean Drive Historic District because of overdevelopment. Although Bonniecrest still sits majestically on its harbor-front site, regrettably much of the interior work has been altered and subdivided to create condominiums.

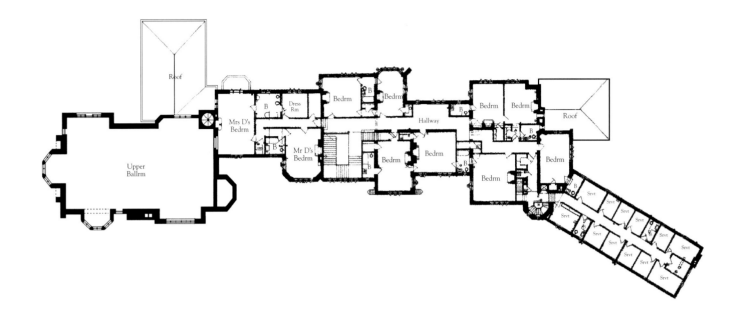

Second Floor

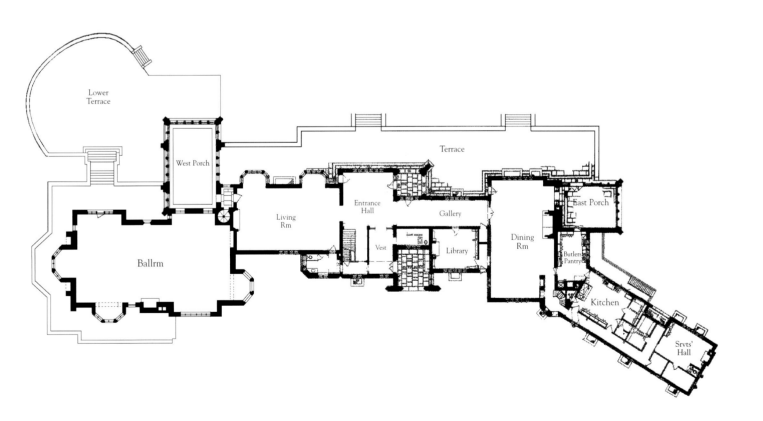

First Floor

MIRAMAR

MRS. GEORGE D. WIDENER

Horace Trumbauer, 1912–1914

In 1911, George D. Widener and his wife Eleanor Elkins Widener purchased the Dr. Christopher M. Bell estate on the cliffs, sited just north of the Ogden Mills cottage on Bellevue Avenue. To augment the site the couple bought the adjoining property of General Francis V. Greene. The combined oceanfront property totaled seven and a half acres, one of the largest parcels to be found on this part of the avenue. Instead of revamping either the Greene or the Bell house, the Wideners elected to replace the two of them with a classical French palais designed by Horace Trumbauer. The interiors were executed by the noted Parisian decorator André Carlhian, while another Frenchman, Jacques Gréber, was put in charge of the gardens. This collaboration produced an inspired conclusion that captured the very essence of French eighteenth-century design and proportion. The couple could well afford this luxurious architectural project, as they were heirs to the Philadelphia traction fortunes of their respective fathers, P. A. B. Widener and William L. Elkins.

The design process began in 1911, and by the spring of 1912 construction was set to begin. In April of that year the couple, along with their younger son Harry Elkins Widener, were returning from a trip to Europe and decided to end their trip with a flourish by booking passage on the maiden voyage of the White Star liner *Titanic*. Eleanor was the only one of the three to survive the tragic sinking. To help distract her during this period of mourning, she immersed herself in two grand architectural projects, the largest being the Trumbauer-designed Harry Elkins Widener Memorial Library that she would give to Harvard University as a memorial to her son. The other would be Miramar.

Entrance Gates (Library of Congress)

Entrance Court View (Courtesy of the International Tennis Hall of Fame & Museum, Newport, Rhode Island)

Miramar is a limestone-sheathed H-shaped structure. A simple rusticated first floor is pierced by symmetrically placed glazed sets of French doors that are topped by rounded lunettes. The central three sets of doors located on the entrance façade are executed in elaborately detailed decorative ironwork. Highly wrought carved trophy panels representing the arts and sciences are placed between the casement windows on the second story. At the top of the composition a classical leaf frieze supports a full cornice and roof balustrade, the latter concealing third-floor dormers set within a seamed copper roof. The architect camouflaged a lower-level service court located at the north end of the house by encasing its walls in vine-covered trelliswork. Consequently, when family members were strolling on the terrace above, they looked down upon what appeared to be a garden court.

The fence enclosing the property is of an intricate design consisting of black wrought-iron sections set upon a limestone base, which is supported by periodic limestone piers. The iron uprights of the fence are designed to resemble Roman fringed spikes. Inserted into runs of these spikes are highly decorative supporting elements centered by masks of Apollo set within sunbursts. Crowning the two entrance gates are Mrs. Widener's initials set within a richly embellished framework.

Because of the limited acreage involved on most Newport estates, a common problem was the placing of service structures so that they wouldn't be seen or, at the very least, not be overtly intrusive to the overall landscape design. At Miramar the architect camouflaged a combined garage and laundry facility so that when viewed from the garden it appears to be a beautifully modeled orangerie.

The formal gardens that were placed between the Bellevue Avenue property line and the front of the house were the most elaborate in Newport. Done in the French classical style, these *parterres* became geometric floral extensions of the house that could be utilized as open-air entertainment

Entrance Façade (Library of Congress)

Ocean Façade Detail (Library of Congress)

spaces for large gatherings. These important gardens were designed by noted French landscape designer Jacques Gréber, while his father Henri-Léon Gréber executed the fountain sculptures.

Miramar's interiors do not deviate from the eighteenth-century theme already established in the structure's exterior elevations and gardens. The

entrance hall has a marble floor with faux Caen stone walls designed in a severe classical manner. Paired Ionic columns that sit on rectangular plinths separate the three grilled apertures facing Bellevue Avenue. The opposite wall holds three balancing sets of French doors that lead to a salon decorated with white and gold Louis XVI–style boiserie. At

Service Court (Library of Congress)

Garage (Library of Congress)

Aerial View (Gary Lawrance Collection)

each end of the salon a white marble fireplace holds the central position. For ease of movement there are five sets of French doors opening onto a broad water-facing terrace that was sometimes covered as a ballroom extension on gala nights. To the south is a smaller salon, or living room, whose walls are covered with a handsome set of antique boiserie of the Régence period. The dining room found at the opposite end of the house is veneered in polychrome marbles in a Louis XVI interpretation of Louis XIV's marbled state apartments at Versailles. Extending from the east ends of both the living room and the dining room are oceanfront projections containing matching conservatories. One has palm trees, a fountain, and comfortable wicker furniture for lounging, while its counterpart, located off the dining room, is used for smaller family meals. Behind the marble staircase with its intricate iron railing is placed a paneled reception room with an adjacent powder room. The principal reception rooms of the house were handsomely accoutred with Eleanor's distinguished collection of fine and decorative art pieces that included Boucher tapestries, Sèvres porcelain, and signed pieces of furniture by eighteenth-century masters. Many of these objects were shipped back and forth seasonally from Newport to her Fifth Avenue townhouse in New York.

On the floor above are ten bedrooms, all with en-suite baths. Overlooking the water on the south-

Entrance Hall (Philadelphia Museum of Art)

Grand Salon (Philadelphia Museum of Art)

Salon Detail (Philadelphia Museum of Art)

Dining Room (Philadelphia Museum of Art)

east corner of the house is a large boudoir for the mistress of the house, as well as an adjoining bedroom. These rooms were finished with restrained Louis XVI paneling in pastel shades, with gilt-bronze light fixtures and hardware adding luster.

Although harkening back to eighteenth-century France, there are aspects of nascent modernity inherent in the design that betray the structure's early-twentieth-century origins. These forward-looking details are experienced in the Spartan detailing of the marble-walled bathrooms and in the use of undivided sheets of plate glass in the first-floor French doors, which effectively integrate indoor areas with the surrounding terraces and gardens. The house also utilized the latest technological advances, including an early air-condition-ing system that worked by drawing cooler evening air into a basement chamber, where it could then be directed by way of an extensive ductwork arrangement to the rooms above.

On August 20 of 1915, the house was officially opened with a ball for five hundred guests. The *New York Times* reported that "Mrs. Widener, wearing a black tulle gown and a string of pearls, received the guests, assisted by her daughter, Mrs. Fitz Eugene Dixon, who wore a costume of silver and gold. The guests danced in the ballroom and on the terrace close to the sea, where they looked upon pretty electrical illuminations in the trees about the cliffs. Three orchestras played." In October of the same year, Eleanor married Dr. Alexander Hamilton Rice, a renowned scientist and world explorer.

Breakfast Loggia (Philadelphia Museum of Art)

In July of 1937, Eleanor died in Paris. Dr. Rice continued to summer at Miramar, having life tenancy of both it and the couple's Fifth Avenue mansion. After his death in 1956, Eleanor's two surviving children, George D. Widener, Jr., and Eleanor Widener Dixon, inherited the Newport estate. With neither wishing to occupy it, they decided to donate it to the Rhode Island Episcopal Diocese. In 1964 it was sold by the diocese to Roy S. Penner for the development of the Miramar School for Girls. The house and grounds, which cost the Widener family $1.5 million a half century earlier, was sold to Penner for a mere $75,000. In 1970 it was purchased by Andrew Panteleakis for $118,000, who maintained it for over thirty years as the headquarters for his American Capital Corporation. In 2005, Panteleakis sold it at auction for $17.5 million, in a way legitimizing Eleanor Rice's original outlay on the property. As of this writing, Miramar is the largest recorded residential sale in Newport County history.

The new owner is David B. Ford, a retired partner of Goldman Sachs. He, with the help of John Tschirch (architectural historian at the Preservation Society of Newport County), are now immersed in a preservation program that will include the restoration of the fencing along Bellevue and Yznaga Avenues, and a rehabilitation of the damaged stonework found on the ocean-facing façades of the structure.

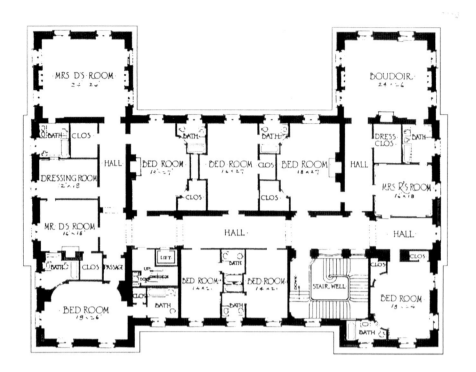

Second Floor

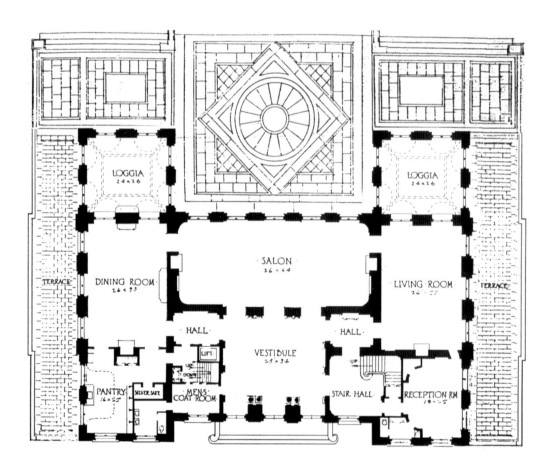

First Floor

CHERRY NECK
BUNGALOW

MRS. F. M. HUNTINGTON WILSON
(MRS. LUCY WORTHAM JAMES)
Delano & Aldrich, 1912-1913

Francis Mairs Huntington Wilson was born in 1876 to Chicagoan Benjamin Mairs Wilson and his wife Francis. In 1897, immediately after graduating from Yale, Huntington was appointed second secretary of the American legation in Tokyo with a promotion to first secretary and chargé d'affaires quickly following. In 1903 he was introduced to an attractive young American tourist named Lucy Wortham Angus James.

Miss James was the great-great-granddaughter of Thomas James, the founder of the Maramec Iron Works in St. James, Missouri—the first major ironworks west of the Mississippi River. Unfortunately, by the time of Lucy's birth in 1880, the ore that had fueled the ironworks had been depleted, resulting in the company's bankruptcy in 1876. Although never destitute, Lucy's childhood was far from luxurious. Fortunately, her grandmother Lucy Ann Dun James had a brother named Robert Graham Dun who founded the Dun & Bradstreet Corporation, one of the country's first credit- and financial-information-reporting institutions. Since Dun had no children, part of his fortune would eventually filter down, through Lucy's father Thomas, to his great-niece.

In May of 1904, Huntington and Lucy were married in Baltimore, Maryland, where the bride had been spending the previous winter. Following a service at Emmanuel Church, there was a breakfast held at the home of the bride's aunt Mrs. George Hamilton Cook. After a brief honeymoon the couple left for Japan. They returned to the United States in 1906, when Huntington accepted the appointment of third secretary of state in the Taft administration. Washington was very hospitable to the young couple, and they were delighted to be back among their countrymen and in their

View From Entrance Pavilion (Collection of the American Academy of Arts and Letters, New York City)

Entrance Pavilion (Collection of the American Academy of Arts and Letters, New York City)

Entrance Façade (Gary Lawrance Collection)

Entrance Detail (Collection of the American Academy of Arts and Letters, New York City)

native culture. The Wilsons became active in Wasington social circles, with Lucy becoming an accomplished hostess. In 1912, when Taft lost his reelection campaign, Huntington resigned his State Department post. Fortunately, by this time Lucy had already received the Dun inheritance, allowing Huntington to retire.

With more leisure time beckoning, the Wilsons purchased a building site fronting Ocean Avenue at Cherry Neck in Newport. According to the 1913 edition of the Newport Social Index, the couple was already ensconced in their new cottage for the season. Cherry Neck Bungalow, as it was christened, was designed by William Delano of the New York firm of Delano & Aldrich. By Newport standards the cottage is rather small, but its innovative design and thoughtful execution lifts it above the ordinary.

Set on a narrow rocky site surrounded by the crashing waves of Cherry Neck, the bungalow is long and low and set within a compact and tightly controlled plan. The entrance to this miniature estate is through a roadside whitewashed-stone pavilion. This structure is capped by a hipped roof punctuated by a single, centrally placed dormer, while below an arched entrance tunnel gives only a glimpse of the house beyond. On either side are placed flat-roofed extensions, a three-car garage to the left and laundry facilities on the right. A flagstone drive is initially flanked by the garage court and a drying yard, which are both succeeded by small rectangular patches of lawn. These in turn lead to a flagstone entrance court that extends to the right, running parallel to the right half of the front façade, terminating with a half-circle arc. Delano designed the low U-shaped structure with a small service wing augmenting its northern end. A long, single-story façade is bracketed by the gabled ends of the two side wings, with a separate gabled entrance porch immediately adjacent to the wing to the left. The latter, with its asymmetrical placement, helps to give the elevation a cozy cottage impression. Of brick construction, the walls are lightly whitewashed to allow for some of the brickwork to show through, thus giving the appearance of natural weathering. A multihued red tile roof, matching that found on the gatehouse, is punctuated by partially inset paired dormer windows with half-timbered and ornamental brick pediments. These elements give color and additional texture to the composition.

The ocean façade has a much more open countenance. A water-facing void is filled with a terrace embellished with awning-adorned windows and doors. The projecting wings at either side help to shelter the space from ocean winds. In season, the terrace would probably be one of the most used areas of the house, either for lounging or for dining

Ocean Façade (Collection of the American Academy of Arts and Letters, New York City)

under umbrellas at breakfast and lunch. The house sits in complete harmony with the surrounding rock ledges, making it in many ways a precursor to the organic architectural theories espoused by the modernist movement in decades to come.

Internally, the principal rooms are focused around the terrace, with a long and relatively narrow living room taking center stage. A dining room fills the north wing, while a master bedroom and bath occupies the other. The latter suite extends through the depth of the structure to the front of the house with a sitting room and two bedrooms, while just off the adjacent entrance hall is a narrow meandering staircase that rises to additional guest rooms in the attic. Along the front of the house facing the courtyard are a drawing room and two guest rooms. The kitchen is found in the northwest corner of the main block, while the neighboring service wing contains a butler's pantry, the servants' dining room, and a covered porch where the Wilson staff could relax and enjoy the sea air when off duty.

Within three years of its completion the Wilsons were divorced. From the day of her final decree the former Mrs. Wilson was forevermore re-ferred to as Mrs. Lucy Wortham James. Keeping title to Cherry Neck Bungalow, she would continue to spend summers enjoying the incomparable views and invigorating air found there. Never forgetting her midwestern roots, she would frequently return to the family home in St. James, where her community work helping the elderly and less fortunate became legendary. Later in life Lucy began repurchasing lost family lands that would eventually become the Maramec Spring Park. Lucy died in January of 1938.

Because of its reasonable size Cherry Neck Bungalow has never languished for occupants. J. Clayton Strawbridge of the Philadelphia department store family purchased the house and changed its name to Normandie, a designation it still retains. In 1961 he and his wife sold the property to Mr. And Mrs. Richard Stackpole of Wayland, Massachusetts, for $57,000, and fifteen years later Ralph and Catherine Gunning paid $190,000 for the choice spot. None of the subsequent owners have altered the house in any substantial way, and each has respected Delano's brilliant architectural concept. Today the house continues to grace the rocky shores of Cherry Neck.

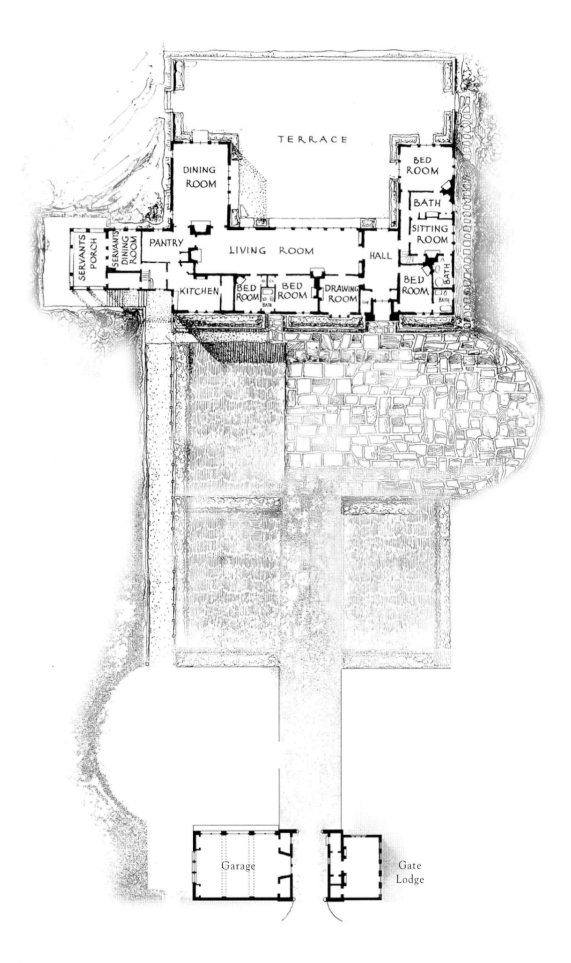

TERRACE

DINING ROOM

BED ROOM

BATH

SITTING ROOM

SERVANTS PORCH

SERVANTS DINING ROOM

PANTRY

LIVING ROOM

HALL

BATH

KITCHEN

BED ROOM

BATH

BED ROOM

DRAWING ROOM

BED ROOM

BED ROOM

BATH

Garage

Gate Lodge

First Floor

SEA VIEW TERRACE

EDSON BRADLEY

Howard Greenley, 1923–1926

This fourteen-acre estate overlooking the ocean at Marine and Wetmore Avenues has gone through several metamorphoses. The fifty-room French château we see today began life as Sea View, a relatively simple clapboarded wooden villa surmounted by a shallow hipped roof with decorative metal cresting. It was erected by architect George Champlin Mason in the early 1870s for James P. Kernochan, the progeny of a prosperous Louisiana sugar planter. Mr. Kernochan's wife Katharine was the daughter of Pierre Lorillard, whose grandfather had founded the tobacco- and snuff-processing firm of P. Lorillard & Company in 1760.

During the following decade the original, simply articulated two-story entrance projection was converted into an opulent Second Empire tower with the addition of another story, which boasted highly decorated window projections highlighted with elaborately treated surrounds. By the mid-1880s the Kernochans had once again enlarged the structure, this time completely encasing the original structure within a Tudor Revival envelope designed by John Dixon Johnston. It remained in this form until 1922, when it was sold by Katharine Pell, the Kernochans' daughter, to Edson Bradley.

Born in New Canaan, Connecticut, Bradley created a fortune as the president of W. A. Gaines & Company, a distillery conglomerate with major interests in the Old Hermitage and Old Crow whiskey brands. By 1905 he had risen to become the official head of "the whiskey trust," controlling 93 percent of the market for sour mash whiskeys in the United States. In 1907, Bradley and his wife—the former Julia Wentworth Williams—purchased a large red brick house just off Dupont Circle in Washington, D.C., that had once been owned by the father-in-law of Alexander Graham Bell,

290

Ocean Façade (Gary Lawrance Collection)

North Façade (Author's Collection)

Gardiner Greene Hubbard. As avid collectors, the Bradleys filled the house with an extensive collection of Chinese porcelains, antique furniture, tapestries, and decorative art pieces that were placed in appropriate architectural settings using sixteenth- and seventeenth-century antique structural elements. The Bradleys also had a summer villa on Alexandria Bay, Thousand Islands, New York, that was also filled with antiques and works of art that the couple had collected. Unfortunately, it was con-

Tower Detail (Gary Lawrance Collection)

sumed by fire in August of 1922, with many works of art being destroyed.

Following the fire, the Bradleys decamped to Newport. By this time Edson was essentially retired. Because his wife's health was beginning to fail, the couple decided to sell the Washington house—with the intention of making Newport their year-round residence. After acquiring Sea View, the couple selected family friend Howard Greenley to revamp and enlarge it at a cost of $100,000. To accomplish

Entrance Hall (Gary Lawrance Collection)

this, the architect was asked to use many interior and exterior elements extracted from the Edsons' Washington house. These included fireplaces, paneling, light fixtures, and even stone elements from the building's exterior. By the time the complicated renovation was completed, Greenley's office had produced over 1,300 drawings.

When finished, the number of rooms now exceeding fifty, it was one of the largest houses in Newport—and certainly the largest built since

Cloister (Gary Lawrance Collection)

before World War I. The 1880s English Tudor–style Kernochan house was completely transformed into an early French Renaissance château. This was accomplished by the elimination of several gabled projections, changing the structure's surface to a chalk-white stucco finish with carved limestone trim and adding two asymmetrically-placed wings to the extant mass. A principal element to the design is a round three-story tower with a conical roof that is placed on the southern façade at the juncture where the old house meets the new west wing.

The tower was strategically placed to camouflage the differing floor levels between the two wings.

Adjacent to the house on the inside of the L created by the addition of the western wing is a broad terrace with an encircling stone balustrade that gives Sea View Terrace its new extended appellation. Another smaller tower sits on the southwest corner of the wing and is filled by a spiral staircase that connects the master bedroom suite with the grounds below. The eastern end of the original structure is extended to include a large solarium

Staircase (Gary Lawrance Collection)

with five sets of glazed French doors facing the sea. Projecting northward is a second new wing, this one devoted entirely to service activities.

Although the gates along Ruggles Avenue are now the main entry to the property, those located on Marine Avenue (at the southwest corner of the property) were originally the principal entrance. These gates open to a long, winding drive that leads past verdant lawns, spectacular water views, and the west wing of the house before finally reaching a porte-cochère in the northwest corner of the struc-

ture. Placing this entrance at the farthest possible distance from the house creates the illusion of an estate of much greater size. On the surrounding property, as well as on noncontiguous parcels of land, were greenhouses, a stone garage for six cars (with a chauffeur's apartment above), a separate seven-room staff cottage, and the original Kernochan brick and stucco stable that Greenley converted into a garage for the storage of an additional ten automobiles.

After passing through a small vestibule, one

Hall (Gary Lawrance Collection)

Living Room (Gary Lawrance Collection)

Dining Room (Gary Lawrance Collection)

Ballroom (Gary Lawrance Collection)

enters a 38-foot-high great hall that has tapestry-covered walls and a floor inset with Hispano-Moresque floor tiles. Straight ahead lies the living room with an English Renaissance–style decorative plaster ceiling and a fifteenth-century French stone fireplace surmounted by a carved Byzantine overmantel from the twelfth century. In the hyphen connecting the west wing to the original structure is a Gothic-style staircase and a round reception room. From the rear of the stair hall one accesses a private family chapel and an adjacent chamber that was used as the family dining room. The paneled main dining room has a Tudor strapwork ceiling, sixteenth-century Flemish tapestries, and furniture of English Chippendale design.

In what was originally the Kernochans' center hall is the stair hall, which still retains a staircase at its north end. Here the décor is derived from the Italian Renaissance, with a particularly fine sculpted wooden and gesso ceiling inset with oil paintings. The largest space in the house is the solarium, which has a terra-cotta-tiled floor and a wall fountain backed by Spanish or Portuguese tiles. The last of the entertainment spaces, the ballroom, is executed in an eighteenth-century manner that exhibits a mixture of Louis XVI and Robert Adam detailing.

Upstairs the family and guest areas are not as elaborately executed but are still embellished with carved woodwork and antique marble fireplaces. The second floor contains a master suite of two bedrooms, a sitting room, two bathrooms, a dressing room, and a room for Mrs. Bradley's personal maid. There are also five additional bedrooms on this level. Located on the third floor are five guest rooms, storage rooms, and a trunk room. The upper levels of the service wing contain twenty-three staff bedrooms that share four bathrooms.

Mrs. Bradley died at Sea View Terrace in August of 1929. Edson then had title to the house transferred to his daughter Julia, who was then married to the Reverend Herbert Shipman, a former bishop of the Episcopal Diocese of New York. In March of the following year, Rev. Shipman died of

a heart attack, leaving Julia and her elderly father in residence. Edson died of pneumonia six years later at the age of eighty-three. Dwindling capital, along with other interests, conspired to keep Julia from regularly occupying the house, but in the summer of 1941 she hosted a fundraising "Ball for Britain" for eight hundred guests. This was the last major social event held at the house. In 1942 the property was deeded to the City of Newport for back taxes totaling $13,697.

During World War II, Sea View Terrace was used as a barracks by the U.S. Army for an antiaircraft battalion. After the war it sat empty, becoming prey to vandals who shattered the stained-glass windows and gouged floors and antique paneling. On May 22, 1949, the City of Newport sold the property to Edward J. Dunn for $8,000. Dunn sold it five months later to Mabel H. Emerson for $24,000, who converted it into Burnham-by-the-Sea, a summer school for girls with a focus on the performing arts. During the remainder of the year it was the Newport School for Girls.

From 1966 to 1971 the house became identified with the television soap opera *Dark Shadows*, which used the exterior of the house for Collinwood, the home of vampire Barnabas Collins. The home's lowest point came a few years later, when it was used as a location for pornographic films. In October of 1975, Sea View Terrace was purchased by Martin T. and Millicent Carey from George W. Emerson, Mabel's son, for over $200,000. The Careys originally intended to turn the house into the Newport Executive Center, a training institute for business executives. These plans fell through, however, with the house remaining largely vacant until 1978, when the couple leased most of the structure to Salve Regina College—retaining limited square footage for personal use. The college, now a university, utilized the upper floor for student housing and placed the music department in the rooms below. Known today as Carey Mansion/Cecelia Hall, it still serves those purposes today.

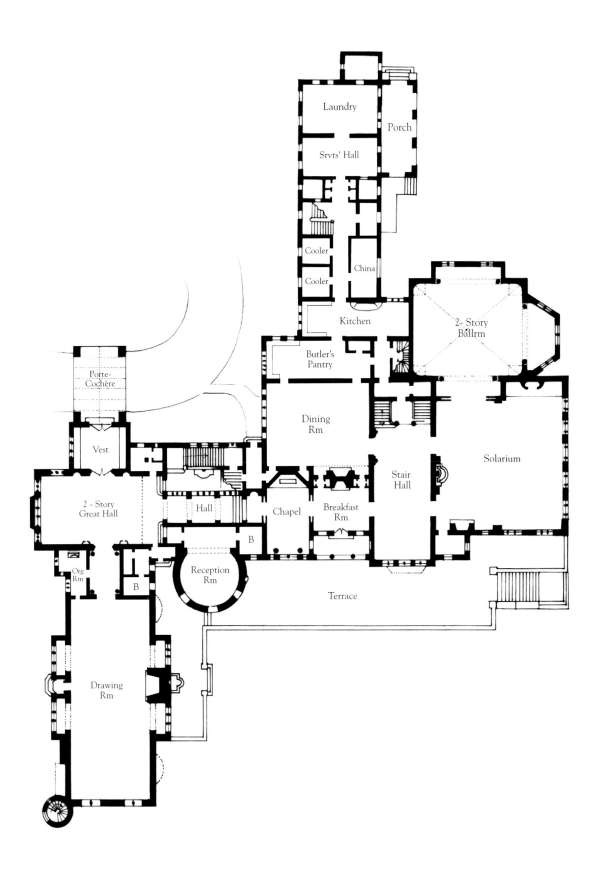

Laundry

Porch

Srvts' Hall

Cooler

China

Cooler

Kitchen

2 - Story
Ballrm

Butler's
Pantry

Porte-
Cochère

Dining
Rm

Vest

Solarium

2 - Story
Great Hall

Stair
Hall

Hall

Chapel

Breakfast
Rm

Org
Rm

B

B

Reception
Rm

Terrace

Drawing
Rm

First Floor

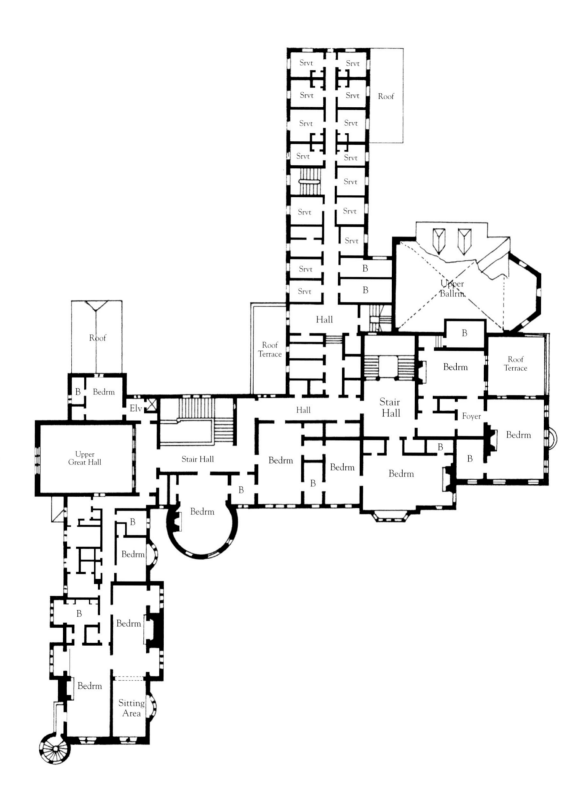

Second Floor

GRAY CRAIG

MICHAEL M. VAN BEUREN

Harrie T. Lindeberg, 1924–1926

The story of Gray Craig begins in 1892 when Oliver Hazard Perry Belmont, Cornelius Vanderbilt II, and other prominent colonists purchased over a hundred acres of waterfront property in Middletown, Rhode Island, on the outskirts of Newport. The property looks out past Paradise Rock to Sachuest Beach. On the site, these gentlemen created an English-style garden and a menagerie filled with exotic animals and birds, all under the auspices of the Gray Crag Park Association, its name derived from the "rocky pudding ridge, or crag, running along the eastern skyline like a ragged backbone." Soon after its creation the association was dissolved, with Belmont gaining complete control and turning it into a farm and horse-breeding facility.

By 1901, Belmont sold the property to J. Mitchell Clark and his wife Sarah Wood Clark. Two years later the Clarks were living in a crenellated stone castle on the site that had been designed for them by architect Abner J. Haydel. According to contemporary entries in the Newport Social Index, the name of the estate was soon changed to the more elegant-sounding Gray Craig. After Clark's death in 1917 his widow sold the property to J. Lawrence Mott III. A fire in June of 1919 left the structure little more than a gutted shell. In the mid-1920s, Mott sold the ruins to Michael Murray van Beuren, a New York broker, and his wife, the former Mary L. Archbold, whose father, John D. Archbold, was one of the founders of the Standard Oil Company along with John D. Rockefeller.

In 1924, van Beuren hired New York architect Harrie T. Lindeberg to develop plans for an estate that would eventually include a house, stables, a greenhouse complex, a kennel, a superintendent's cottage, an engineer's cottage, and assorted garden

301

Ocean Façade (Redwood Library and Athenaeum, Newport, Rhode Island, Gottsho-Schleissner Photographer)

Porte-Cochère (Library of Congress, Gottscho-Schleissner Collection)

Kennels (Library of Congress, Gottscho-Schleissner Collection)

Stables (Redwood Library and Athenaeum, Newport, Rhode Island, Gottscho-Schleissner Photograher)

Reception Room (Redwood Library and Athenaeum, Newport, Rhode Island, Gottscho-Schleissner Photographer)

Staircase (Library of Congress, Gottscho-Schleissner Collection)

Gallery (Library of Congress, Gottscho-Schleissner Collection)

structures. Although the house was completed two years later, work on the dependencies and gardens would continue well into 1928. Like the Clark house, native pudding stone was used for the home's veneer. Lindeberg chose for inspiration eighteenth-century English manor house forms, but updated with detailing reminiscent of the early-twentieth-century works of Sir Edwin Lutyens. The principal, or south, façade, has a central mass covered by a steep red tile roof with four bays on the second floor but, because they are substantially larger, only three below. The main door at the center of the composition has a richly molded surround capped by a broken segmental pediment enclosing a sculpted cartouche—the whole bordered by simple bronze lanterns. On either side of this central composition are rectangular single-bay projections that break through the roof line and are capped by smooth-cut stone coping trimmed with finial capped urns. Tri-

partite windows found on the first-floor fronts of these wings support shallow limestone and wrought-iron balconies that front a set of leaded French doors surrounded by a simple bolection molding with a flattened, scrolled keystone. Springing from either end of this central mass are narrow, single-story gabled wings that terminate in floor-to-ceiling limestone bays.

Mimicking the earlier house, the entrance drive proceeds directly into a porte-cochère located on the northwest corner of the structure. The porte-cochère is placed in an attached pavilion with its own separate hipped roof and side walls terminating in stone peacocks perched on ball finials. The drive then proceeds through to a service courtyard beyond.

While the exterior of the structure clearly represents Lindeberg's pared-down classicism, the home's interiors are more representative of the

Living Room (Redwood Library and Athenaeum, Newport, Rhode Island, Gottscho-Schleissner Photographer)

elaborate entertainment requirements of Newport. An oval vestibule with mahogany doors leads directly into a narrow entrance hall with pedimented doorways and a polychrome marble floor. To the right, windows open onto a walled garden, while opposite are doors leading to the men's and ladies' reception rooms, the latter with walls adorned with Chinese murals reflected in abundant mirrored trim. Proceeding on, there is an oval-shaped hall containing a graceful cantilevered winding staircase with a delicately crafted iron railing. This staircase springs from a polychrome marble floor emblazoned with a unique sunburst motif, while overhead an eighteenth-century crystal chandelier gives illumination to tapestry-covered walls. To the south a doorway leads to an English Rococo-style reception room that accesses the paneled Georgian library located in the southeastern wing of the house. Extending east from the staircase hall is a pine-paneled main hallway executed in a high Georgian manner, with an elaborately carved cornice and doorways capped by richly molded pediments. The adjacent living room is executed in an eighteenth-century Continental fashion with paneled walls and a marble fireplace. The dining room is located at the far end of the main hall, and is decorated in the Federal style with eagle-embellished console tables and a marble fireplace whose entablature is supported by engaged Ionic columns. Decorative shelved niches bracket the fireplace wall. From the center of the ceiling hangs a twenty-four-light crystal chandelier in the English or Irish manner. A set of doors in the far east wall opens into the private suite of Mrs. van Beuren. This suite consists of sitting room, bedroom, and bath, plus numerous closets. Her husband has an identically sized suite located on the floor directly below. The two suites are connected by a private circular staircase.

Dining Room (Library of Congress, Gottscho-Schleissner Collection)

Library (Redwood Library and Athenaeum, Newport, Rhode Island, Gottscho-Schleissner Photographer)

As the house was rising, Ferruccio Vitale was brought in to tame the rocky landscape surrounding the house. This was accomplished by bringing in several tons of topsoil to smooth out the rough terrain. Immediately adjacent to the principal façade of the house is a partially paved terrace that is fronted by a broad set of six steps leading down to a manicured lawn. At the far end of the lawn is a balustrade bracketed by steps that descend to a tree-framed meadow, with a view of Nelson Pond and the ocean beyond. Two towering elm trees were brought in to frame the principal elevation, which also gave the structure a feeling of great age and permanence. On the north side of the house Vitale created a series of gardens that flowed one into another. These include a boxwood parterre, a horse-shoe amphitheater with reflecting pool, and a walled garden with a cross-axial design centered by a croquet lawn bordered by fruit trees.

Mary van Beuren died in February of 1951, with her husband's death following less than four months later. Gray Craig was inherited by their son Archbold, the founder of *Cue* magazine. He occupied the estate with his wife, the former Margaret Ziegler, and their four children. On December 8, 1974, Archbold died, leaving the estate to his wife. In the mid-1980s the furnishings were auctioned and the home put on the market for $3.5 million. Today, even though the land has been subdivided, with the dependencies on the estate occupied by separate families, it still retains the air of a private estate.

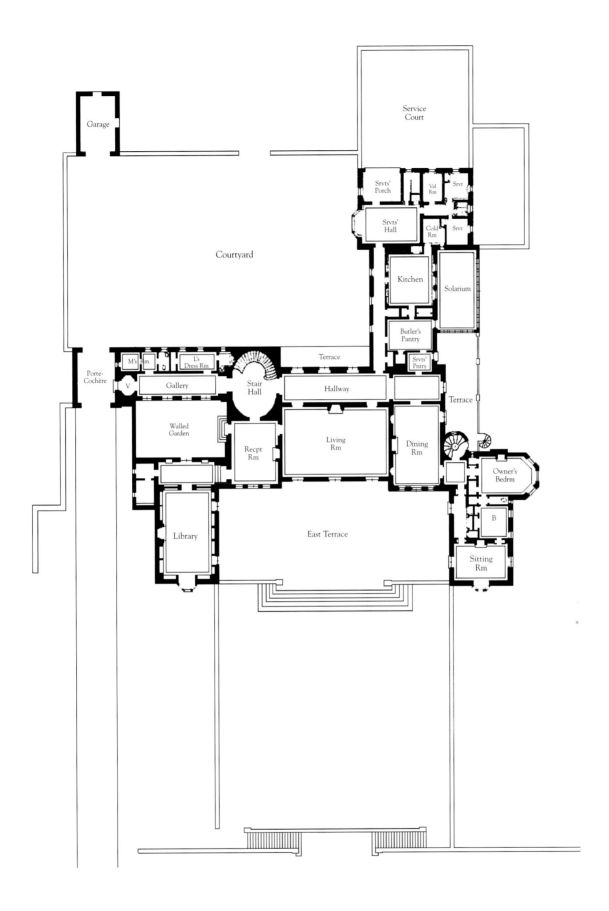

Garage

Service
Court

Srvts'
Porch

Val
Rm

Srvt

Srvts'
Hall

Cold
Rm

Srvt

Courtyard

Kitchen

Solarium

Butler's
Pantry

M's Rm

L's
Dress Rm

Terrace

Srvts'
Pntry

Porte-
Cochère

V

Gallery

Stair
Hall

Hallway

Terrace

Walled
Garden

Recpt
Rm

Living
Rm

Dining
Rm

Owner's
Bedrm

B

Library

East Terrace

Sitting
Rm

First Floor

BOIS DORÉ

WILLIAM FAHNESTOCK

Charles Adams Platt, 1927–1928

In 1922, William Fahnestock purchased the 7.8-acre estate Oak Lawn, located on Narragansett Avenue, that had been developed in the 1850s for Charles H. Russell but had more recently been occupied by the New York banker James Stillman. Four years later the architect Charles Adams Platt was asked to replace the old wooden house on the site with something more appropriate to current tastes. Platt had previously designed Fahnestock's country place Girdle Ridge in Katonah, New York, and remodeled his town house at 22 East 51st Street in the city. Rarely does an architect have the opportunity to work on three residential projects of this scale with a single client, and all with such remarkably good results.

The Fahnestock family descends from Johann Diedrich Fahnestock, who came to this country from Germany in 1726. William Fahnestock was born in Harrisburg, Pennsylvania, in 1857, the son of Harris and Margaret McKinley Fahnestock. The family moved to New York, where Harris became a partner in the banking house of Jay Cooke & Company. At the age of nineteen William obtained a position at the First National Bank of New York, where his father had become a vice president and director. In December of 1880, William acquired a seat on the New York Stock Exchange, and the following year he founded the firm of Fahnestock & Company. In 1898, after firmly establishing his career, William married Julia Goetchius. The couple had a son, William Jr., who followed in his father's professional footsteps.

Bois Doré is difficult to categorize architecturally. It is often referred to as a house in the French taste, and indeed there are many French elements to the design. But the proportion of the house and its hipped roof seem English in inspiration. This feeling is

Entrance Façade (Courtesy of the Preservation Society of Newport County)

Garden Façade (Courtesy of the Preservation Society of Newport County)

Hall and Staircase (Courtesy of the Preservation Society of Newport County)

Loggia (Courtesy of the Preservation Society of Newport County)

enhanced by Platt's use of double-hung instead of traditional French casement windows on the second story, as well as in the attic dormers. Overall, Bois Doré is a well-studied exercise in classical design that successfully melds elements from different design vocabularies. The house cost Fahnestock $434,895, with the stable and service complex adding an additional $10,297 to the tally.

A high stucco wall that runs along Narragansett Avenue is centered by an entrance framed by matching guardhouses with stone sentries of crouching chimeras with faces resembling eighteenth-century French court ladies. A short gravel drive bordered by an allée of pollarded lindens lead to an entrance court and the house. Masonry walls of the structure are punctuated by windows with plain surrounds. Windows on the first floor have arched tops with central keystone detailing that extend upward to a stringcourse that divides the two principal stories. The most ambitious element in the composition is the limestone entrance projection, which has a richly-carved floral swag surmounting the decorative iron and glass doors. Overhead, a perpendicularly positioned oval window is framed by quoin borders and stone urns. Adding drama to the single-story ballroom wing extending from the west end of the house is a series of floral-bedecked stone urns that encircles its roof parapet.

An open, well-thought-out plan allows for the principal entertaining rooms to run across the south façade of the house, ensuring bright airy rooms during the day and cooling breezes at night. An entrance hall extends into a transverse hall that neatly bisects the floor plan. Opposite the entrance and screened by a pair of rectangular fluted columns is the loggia; it has three pairs of French doors, set within a projecting curved bay, that lead to a semicircular brick-and-stone-paved terrace. On either side of the loggia are the living and dining rooms.

Drawing Room (Courtesy of the Preservation Society of Newport County)

Dining Room (Courtesy of the Preservation Society of Newport County)

Ballroom (Courtesy of the Preservation Society of Newport County)

Study (Courtesy of the Preservation Society of Newport County)

These rooms are both paneled in the Louis XVI style and have carved marble mantelpieces as focus points. In the 1960s the dining room décor was augmented by trompe l'oeil murals by Martin Battersby depicting seventeenth- and eighteenth-century French court figures accompanied by depictions of their artistic, intellectual, and architectural patronage. At the western end of the house is the ballroom. Being the largest room in the house, it measures 32 by 64 feet, and gains 3 feet in height by placing the floor six steps below that of the rest of this level. At the far end is a raised orchestra platform, while three sets of arched French doors line each side of the room, allowing for greater ventilation on gala nights. A small study and two lavatories with accompanying dressing rooms complete the reception areas on this level.

The second-floor master suite consists of two bedrooms, two baths, a dressing room, and a boudoir. Three other bedrooms are also placed on this level along with nine staff rooms in the service wing. In the attic are two additional guest rooms, nine staff rooms, and abundant storage facilities.

During the 1929 season the Fahnestocks gave two inaugural housewarmings, the first held on July 17 when they hosted an afternoon musicale and tea for three hundred people. Soprano Erva Giles and tenor Richard Crooks were the featured performers. This was matched the following month by a ball for five hundred guests. A marquee was erected on the south lawn to supplement the ballroom for dancing, while orange and green Japanese lanterns provided light. The shrubbery along the entrance drive was filled with small orange electric lights that were concealed in bunches of ivy.

In July of 1936, Fahnestock died at the age of seventy-eight. His widow rarely returned to Newport after his death, preferring to lease it to others. In March of 1941 the house was sold for $55,000 to Elinor Dorrance Hill, daughter of the founder of the Campbell Soup Company, John T. Dorrance. Her stockbroker husband, Nathaniel P. Hill, was the son of Crawford Hill, who had extensive real estate holdings and mining interests in Colorado. During the 1920s the Hills rented various houses; late in the decade they leased Bois Doré, eventually purchasing it. The couple used the house to throw lavish functions—including debutante parties for their daughters Dorrance in 1946 and Hope in 1952. In 1963 burglars broke into the house through a second-floor window and made off with $300,000 in jewelry. Three years after her husband's death in 1965, Elinor remarried Vice Admiral Stuart Howe Ingersoll, a former commander of the Sixth and Seventh fleets and superintendent of the United States Naval Academy at Annapolis. Elinor continued to occupy Bois Doré seasonally until her death in 1977.

Carolyn Skelly Burford, the Oklahoma oil heiress, purchased Bois Doré for $360,000 in 1978. Bois Doré was again the target of thieves when $2 million in jewels was stolen in 1984; a maid and an accomplice were found responsible. Carolyn's troubles were still not over: two years later she awakened to the sounds of a knife-wielding burglar making off with $3 million in jewels. Skelly died in 1996. In October of 2004, David and Candice Keefe bought Bois Doré for $3.7 million.

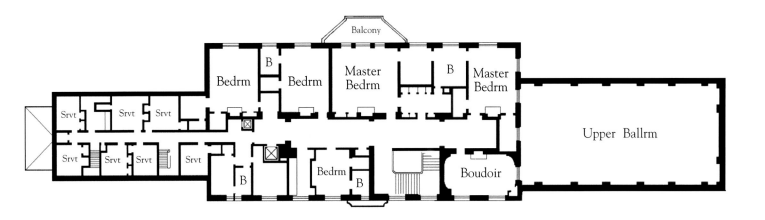

Second Floor

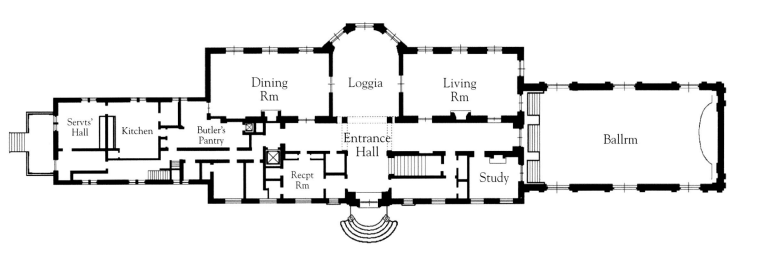

First Floor

THE WAVES

JOHN RUSSELL POPE

John Russell Pope, 1928-1930

A rocky promontory located at the end of Ledge Road was acquired in the mid-1890s by Charles Warren Lippitt, then governor of the state of Rhode Island. Lippitt came from a well-respected Providence family with roots going back to the seventeenth century. His father, Henry Lippitt, had also served as governor, and his brother Henry F. Lippitt was a United States senator. Charles Lippitt's political career greatly benefited from his business success in the manufacturing and banking fields.

By June of 1895 the walls were rising on what the family would soon call The Breakwater, while local wags referred to it as Lippitt's Castle because of its many round towers with crenellated tops. The rocky site engendered construction difficulties that required a large stone platform to be constructed for the house to sit upon. This platform was extended past the outer walls of the house to create terraces and ambulatories on which to take in the ocean views. Thirty years later a devastating fire at The Breakwater turned it into a burned-out shell. It sat for several years as a ruin until about 1926, when it was completely demolished—except for the thick stone walls of the foundation. When architect John Russell Pope purchased the property from an heir of Governor Lippitt in the fall of 1928, he decided to incorporate this remaining bulwark into the plan for his new home: The Waves.

By the mid-1920s, Pope had already distinguished himself in a career primarily devoted to major residential works as well as civic structures such as the Union Station in Richmond, Virginia (1913–1919). He would later become even better known for his federal commissions in Washington, D.C., such as Constitution Hall (1914–1932),

Aerial View (Author's Collection)

Northwest View (Library of Congress, Gottscho-Schleissner Collection)

Terrace Detail (Gary Lawrance Collection)

the National Archives Building (1930–1933), and the Jefferson Memorial (1935–1937) design, not completed until 1943). The selection of Newport for Pope's summer house was dictated by his wife's family and their social connections. His wife, Sadie, was the daughter of Pembroke Jones, whose Belle-vue Avenue cottage Sherwood was designed by Francis Hoppin.

Even though both houses utilized the same plat-form, The Breakwater was tall and assertive—de-signed to dominate the site, while Pope's work at The Waves seems to discreetly sprawl over its rocky site. The architect chose the Tudor-Cotswold style for the house because of its easy adaptability to an uneven terrain. As at Bonniecrest, Pope's other Tu-dor-style house in Newport, the materials used were carefully selected and orchestrated to create an ap-pearance of antiquity. With its asymmetrical mass-ing and warm honey-colored stone walls, the ocean façade of the house clearly proclaims the Cotswold

Garden Court (Library of Congress, Gottscho-Schleissner Collection)

Loggia (Library of Congress, Gottscho-Schleissner Collection)

Studio (Library of Congress, Gottscho-Schleissner Collection)

Entrance Hall (Library of Congress, Gottscho-Schleissner Collection)

Staircase (Library of Congress, Gottscho-Schleissner Collection)

Main Hall (Library of Congress, Gottscho-Schleissner Collection)

cottage to be its inspiration. Here the eaves are lower, with the principal second-story windows partially encased in stone-gabled dormers, which are themselves seamless extensions of the lower wall plane. The central mass holds a leaded-glass bay set between a leaded window on the left and a heavy wooden door that is surrounded by additional tiers of windows. At either side of the central façade Pope placed timbered porches that created transition areas between the cozy, low-studded interior spaces and the surrounding sun-drenched terrace. These covered spaces also help alleviate any awkwardness in junctures with the retreating wings found at either end.

The north side of the house is planned around a garden court protected from the Atlantic winds by the main body of the house and its sheltering wings. The wing to the east contains the dining room and service facilities; and because of the topography, it has an exposed lower level adjacent to Ledge Road. The wing at the opposite end of the house holds the main entrance and allied reception facilities. Within the courtyard the structure has a stone-sheathed first floor surmounted by half-timbering and stucco walls at the second-floor level. A constant eave line gives this façade a more uniform aspect—one not generally associated with the Tudor Revival style. The court-embracing wings of the house are attached to wall extensions that maneuver to connect with Pope's studio on the far side of the courtyard. Executed in the same half-timbered and stucco Tudor motif, it has a traditional cottage-like appearance inside the courtyard but has an outer wall pierced by a modern floor-to-ceiling leaded window. The high slate roof of the structure is capped by a decorative weathervane in the shape of a fifteenth-century ship. Inside, it is sparsely furnished and appears in contemporary photographs to be more a peaceful retreat for the architect than a working studio.

Living Room (Library of Congress, Gottscho-Schleissner Collection)

Dining Room (Library of Congress, Gottscho-Schleissner Collection)

Library (Library of Congress, Gottscho-Schleissner Collection)

The Waves is not entered at its center, but by an entrance porch placed at the end of the west wing. The circular forecourt is framed by one of the original tower foundations of the Lippitt house. A heavily molded door leads into a rectangular stone-paved entrance hall whose walls are textured to resemble stone. Ahead lay a paneled gallery with a run of mullioned windows overlooking the garden court. A doorway located opposite these windows leads into a paneled Georgian library with built-in bookcases and a corner fireplace embellished with a split pediment overmantel. At the end of the gallery is the principal staircase, framed by a shallow paneled arch. At the base of the staircase an adjoining transverse hall runs parallel to a living room that fills the center of the ocean side of the house. The living room has wooden paneling in the simplest early Georgian manner, with strong moldings and no carved ornamentation. The decorative focus of the room is on two large portraits executed by English painter Wilford Deglan that are prominently placed at either side of the fireplace. These paintings represent Mary and Jane Pope, the architect's two children. At the far end of the transverse hall is the dining room with its triple French doors opening onto the garden, while beyond lay the butler's pantry, kitchen, and other service areas.

On August 9, 1937, Pope became ill at The Waves. He was taken back to New York for medical treatment but died on the twenty-seventh of the same month. Two days later a funeral service was held at Trinity Church in Newport for the sixty-three-year-old architect; he was buried at the Berkeley Memorial Chapel Cemetery in neighboring Middletown. Sadie and her surviving daughter continued to inhabit The Waves until the start of World War II, when it was used to house military personnel. After the war the house was acquired by Mrs. John F. C. Bryce. In 1950 it was purchased by Frazier Jelke, who converted it into eight apartments—a development that became the salvation of many Newport houses during this period. Four years later Louis Chartier purchased the waves from the Frazier Jelke Foundation for $95,000, as an investment. It has since been converted into condominiums. Although there have been many alterations to the structure, both inside and out, The Waves remains true to Pope's original vision.

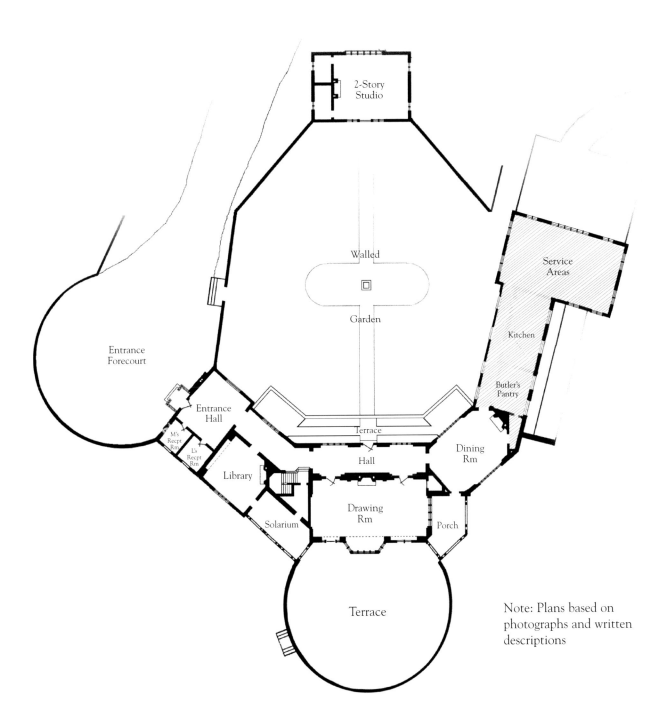

2-Story
Studio

Walled

Service
Areas

Entrance
Forecourt

Kitchen

Garden

Entrance
Hall

Butler's
Pantry

M's
Recpt
Rm

L's
Recpt
Rm

Terrace

Dining
Rm

Library

Hall

Drawing
Rm

Solarium

Porch

Terrace

Note: Plans based on
photographs and written
descriptions

First Floor

CHAMP SOLEIL

LUCY DREXEL DAHLGREN

Polhemus & Coffin, 1929–1930; additions, 1944

Champ Soleil was constructed in 1929 for Lucy Drexel Dahlgren, following the designs of the New York firm of Polhemus & Coffin. Mrs. Dahlgren was the granddaughter of Joseph W. Drexel, cofounder of the banking house Drexel & Company in Philadelphia. Married to stockbroker Eric B. Dahlgren in 1890, the couple divorced twenty-three years later. In 1928, Lucy began developing plans for a new summer house in Newport; three years later, in September of 1931, Champ Soleil was officially opened with a musicale and tea.

After Lucy's death twelve years later, Champ Soleil was purchased by Robert Wilson Goelet, the only son of real estate magnate Ogden Goelet. Goelet had inherited the estate of Ochre Court upon the death of his mother in 1929 but now wanted something smaller and easier to maintain. He asked Polhemus & Coffin to update the house by augmenting the service wing and adding a large dining room addition to the northwest corner of the garden elevation.

Sitting behind a wrought-iron fence and screened by towering trees, the five-and-a-half acre estate is a haven of tranquility. The house is an amalgam of two centuries of Gallic architectural elements. The high-pitched roof is evocative of a provincial seventeenth-century French manor house, while in contrast, the decorative detailing relates to the more sophisticated elements associated with smaller eighteenth-century royal châteaux. The central projecting entrance pavilion of the structure is an interpretation of La Lanterne, the hunting pavilion erected by Louis XIV at Versailles. The stucco veneer of Champ Soleil is embellished by limestone trim. The stucco was originally painted off-white to contrast with the stone elements, but in recent years it has

328

View Through Entrance Piers (Author's Collection)

been painted to match the limestone in an attempt to give the exterior a more unified appearance. Stone is used for window and door surrounds, the stringcourse that divides the first and second floor, and quoining that brackets and defines the linear divisions of the elevation. Carved floral elements such as those found inside the dentiled central pediment and the bas-relief floral swag panels inserted between the first- and second-story windows add gaiety to an otherwise austere design.

The west, or garden, façade has a similarly detailed tripartite arrangement with symmetrically placed door and window openings. The principal difference here is that the central decorative pediment is now segmental in composition. Projecting from the north end of the symmetrical mass is the Goelet dining room and a recessed two-story service wing with a walled courtyard to shield deliveries from view.

The visitor enters the house through a set of

Entrance Façade (Author's Collection)

Garden Façade (Author's Collection)

richly molded oak doors surmounted by a glazed wrought-iron transom. Inside, one is welcomed by an entrance hall that is paved with a light-colored speckled marble inset with small squares of black marble, the latter set on the diagonal. The walls are paneled in a provincial interpretation of the Louis XV vernacular. At the far end of the space is a wall of paned glass, interrupted by a centrally placed set of French doors that lead to a broad garden terrace.

The library's beautifully carved Régence oak boiserie is antique. It is the highest-caliber finish in the house, and was probably installed by Robert Goelet during the 1940s renovation. A side hall contains a marble staircase embellished with a decorative wrought-iron railing accented with gold-leaf detailing. Bracketing the staircase are the men's toilet and a coat closet. This hall terminates at a set of doors that lead into the living room. The 35-by-

South Façade (Authors Collection)

Garage (Author's Collection)

24-foot living room has walls covered in a simply modeled Louis XV boiserie painted in colors ranging from pale blue to cream. One enters the space by descending a short flight of steps that are framed by railings similar to that found on the principal staircase. Lowering the floor 2 feet gives this room higher ceilings and a greater sense of spaciousness. The inside wall of the room is centered by a Louis XV–style chimneypiece in a heavily veined deep reddish marble, with baseboards encircling the space marbleized to match. The room extends through the structure with two windows at each end, while the south wall has three sets of French doors that lead to a paved terrace and a secluded parterre garden.

The original dining room is sheathed in simple paneling and embellished with a Louis XV marble mantelpiece. This room was later utilized as a sitting room by the Goelets. To the left of the room's fireplace is a door leading to a small paneled and marble-floored anteroom whose décor features mirrors and built-in display cabinets. It, in turn, leads to the Goelet addition. As in the living room, one descends into the new dining room, which was also used as a ballroom when needed. It was decorated by the firm Jansen with Louis XVI moldings inset with plaster panels of classical imagery. Gilded console tables on opposite walls are surmounted by mirrors that reflect light from a Louis XVI–style crystal chandelier. At the far end of the room, in place of the traditional fireplace, is an eighteenth-century faience stove capped by a chimney in the shape of a palm tree adorned with frolicking cherubs.

The second floor contains a master suite consisting of two bedrooms, a sitting room, and two baths. The larger of the two sleeping chambers has a marble fireplace and French-inspired moldings on the walls, while the smaller has pine paneling. The

Dining Room (Paul Manno Collection)

Library (Paul Manno Collection)

Sitting Room (Original Dining Room) (Author's Collection)

chatelaine's bath is one of the more elaborate spaces in the house and exhibits a high Edwardian sensibility in an elaborate Louis XVI Revival mode. One of the two arched window openings in the bathroom is entirely filled by a floor-length lighted mirrored panel that can swing open when not in use. There are three additional bedrooms on this level as well as staff chambers.

The meticulously landscaped estate is a mixture of formal and informal areas. Designed by the renowned landscaping firm of Innocenti & Webel for Robert Goelet during the 1940s, there are large stone terraces that overlook formal parterres and sweeping lawns lined with specimen shrubs and trees.

Later, Champ Soleil was purchased by artist, writer, and international sportsman Russell B. Aitken and his wife Annie Laurie, the widow of Pittsburgh utilities magnate George Crawford. It was under the latter occupancy that the garden directly off the rear terrace was redesigned into a formal croquet court. The court is bordered with boxwoods, while carved horse heads modeled on those at the Parthenon once graced the four corners. The crowning embellishment is a circular garden pavilion, which is based on Marie Antoinette's Temple of Love at the Petit Trianon. Completing the estate is a four-car garage and a gate lodge.

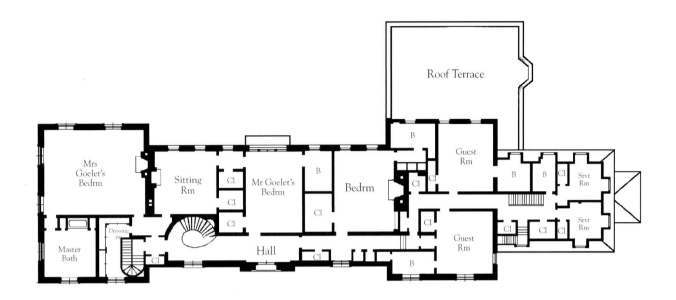

Second Floor

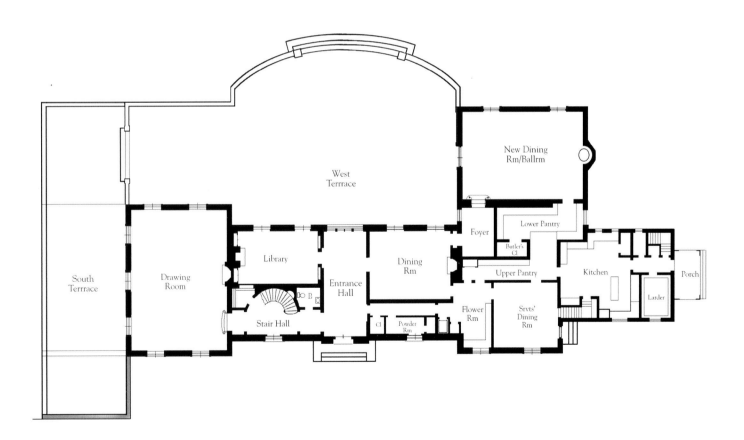

First Floor

FAIRHOLME

COUNT ALPHONSO VILLA

Dwight James Baum, 1929-1930

Beneath the beautifully articulated Tudor detailing of this picturesque abode lays a Stick Style dwelling erected in 1875 for Fairman Rogers of Philadelphia. Rogers, who came from a well-connected Quaker family, was a professor of engineering at the University of Pennsylvania when he asked Frank Furness of the firm of Furness & Hewitt to design a home for his Ochre Point site. This was the first house built on what was until then the sixty-acre Ochre Point Farm. Although plans had been made as early as 1862 to subdivide and develop the oceanfront setting into roughly twenty-five lots, Rogers would actually be the first to begin the process when he purchased the property in September of 1874. On the twelfth of that same month, the Newport Mercury reported that Professor Rogers "will begin at once the erection of a fine house."

By May 20 of the following year the *Newport Mercury* was reporting that this "cottage by the sea" was almost completed. With the mass being 60 by 115 feet and two and one-half stories in height, it was one of the largest villas erected in Newport up to that time. Furness also designed a carriage house for Rogers that still exists on what is now a separate parcel of land.

In the early 1890s, Fairholm (then without the letter *e*) was leased by another couple hailing from Philadelphia, the John R. Drexels. Mr. Drexel was the son of Philadelphia banker Anthony J. Drexel and grandson of Francis M. Drexel, cofounder of Drexel & Company. He and his wife Alice eventually purchased the property. After acquiring Fairholm the Drexels broadened their social horizons by moving their principal residence to New York, leaving the more conservative social environment of

Entrance Façade (Redwood Library and Athenaeum, Newport, Rhode Island, Gottscho-Schleissner Photographer)

their native city. Major changes were soon to envelop Fairholm in an effort to bring the now twenty-year-old house up to current standards. The Drexels began eliminating many of the Victorian excesses of the original design by covering most of the wooden Stick Style characteristics in either brick or shingle. At the west end of the ocean façade a large three-story tower was added, which balanced an extension made to the west end of the front of the house. As significant as these alterations were, the greatest change came at the roof, or third-floor, level, where all the jerkinhead gables and dormers were replaced with pointed gables having elaborate bargeboard detailing. The twisted chimneystacks were simplified and the roof covered in slate. These pseudo-Tudor changes would foretell

Entrance Porch (Redwood Library and Athenaeum, Newport, Rhode Island, Gottscho-Schleissner Photographer)

Ocean Façade (Library of Congress, Gottscho-Schleissner Collection)

later alterations, but at this time the house was effectively transformed into a Victorian Queen Anne–style cottage. In 1909, Horace Trumbauer added a ballroom and enlarged the servants' wing. Trumbauer was also responsible for updating the principal entertaining spaces, changing the East-lake-inspired interiors of the Rogers era into European-style period rooms.

By the end of the 1920s the Drexels had moved to Paris and rarely visited Newport. In 1929 the family sold Fairholme (by now with an *e*) to Count Alphonso Villa and his wife, the former Helen Lip-

Ocean Façade Detail (Redwood Library and Athenaeum, Newport, Rhode Island, Gottscho-Schleissner Photographer)

Tower Detail (Redwood Library and Athenaeum, Newport, Rhode Island, Gottscho-Schleissner Photographer)

pincott of Philadelphia. The count hired the New York architect Dwight James Baum to completely revamp the house into an approximation of one in Tudor England. The architect was able to transform an essentially weak and disjointed composition into a cohesive and orderly presentation within a single design idiom. This was accomplished by encasing the existing shell in stucco and half-timbering, with the latter filled with elaborate brick nogging. The waterside tower was altered by removing the

Living Room (Redwood Library and Athenaeum, Newport, Rhode Island, Gottscho-Schleissner Photograher)

Dining Room (Redwood Library and Athenaeum, Newport, Rhode Island, Gottscho-Schleissner Photographer)

Salon (Redwood Library and Athenaeum, Newport, Rhode Island, Gottscho-Schleissner Photographer)

Ballroom (Library of Congress, Gottscho-Schleissner Collection)

shingled roof and extending the brickwork up to a stone-capped, crenellated top. The second- and third-floor levels of the tower were given stone-mullioned windows with diamond-paned leaded-glass windows, a theme carried out throughout the design. A new ocean-facing covered porch has a stone-capped parapet centered by the Villa family coat of arms. The buttressed corners of the porch frame five round-topped openings, while two matching bays fill each end.

Throughout the design Baum used distressed wooden fittings and frames to give the structure a sense of great age. This is particularly evident in the tripartite entrance porch, with its beautiful Gothic balustrade guarding a richly molded wooden door. To add additional texture to the entrance façade the architect created a two-story projecting bay window whose wall surfaces are veneered in decorative lead panels. Topping the entire composition are seven towering Tudor chimneys, no two exactly the same.

The house is entered through the original Rogers entrance hallway that still extends through to the rear of the house. Here the paneling has been updated and the balcony opening to the second-floor hallway above has been closed. To the west are found the library and a paneled family living room, while behind them are a Louis XVI–style salon and the ballroom, whose walls are embellished with decorative trelliswork. To the east of the main hall are a reception room and a Georgian-style dining room. Farther along is a service wing that includes the pantry, kitchen, servants' hall, cold room, and laundry. The second floor holds six bedrooms, two dressing rooms, five bathrooms, and six staff rooms, while the third floor has an additional eight bedrooms, five baths, and six more servant rooms.

In 1942, Fairholme was purchased by financier Robert R. Young, best known for wresting control of the New York Central Railroad away from the Vanderbilt family. Young's wife, Anita O'Keeffe Young, was the sister of artist Georgia O'Keeffe. The couple often entertained social luminaries such as the Duke and Duchess of Windsor at Fairholme and at Montsorrel, their Palm Beach estate. The Youngs' most important alteration to the property was the replacement of the lily-pond garden located on the west end of the estate with a walled swimming pool and changing pavilion. A retractable glass window was inserted into the pool's perimeter wall that faces the sea.

Mr. Young committed suicide in 1958. His widow continued to summer in Newport until her own death in 1985. Its next owner, John Masheks, began an extensive renovation of the house and grounds. In 1992 publishing heiress Janet Annenberg Hooker acquired the property, and continued to oversee and augment improvements initiated by her predecessor. At her death five years later, the property was inherited by her son Gilbert S. Kahn. In the year 2000, Mr. Kahn and his partner John J. Noffo Kahn held a party at Fairholme to celebrate the home's 125th anniversary. At this function the Kahns thoughtfully invited the descendants of all previous owners of the estate.

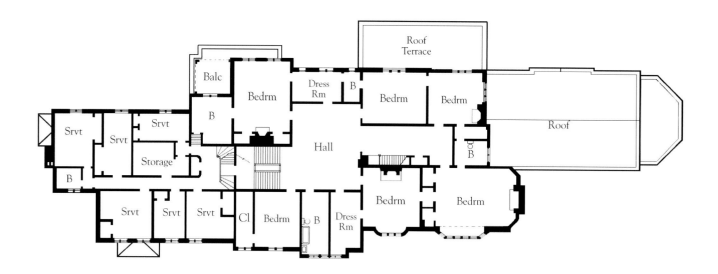

Second Floor

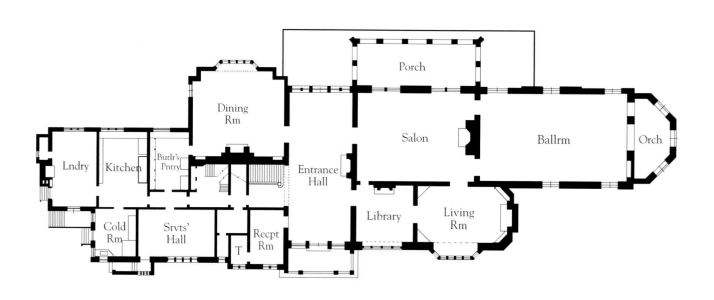

First Floor

TERRE MARE

VERNER Z. REED, JR.

James C. Mackenzie, Jr., 1934-1935

Terre Mare is the last of the great houses erected in Newport. Even though the structure has many architectural similarities with earlier residences such as Idle Hour and Vernon Court, it holds a unique spot in the history of Newport because of its setting. Terre Mare's story begins late in the winter of 1933 and the early part of 1934 when Ethel Davies Thacher and Charles Warren Lippitt sold four different parcels of land on Cherry Neck to Verner Zevola Reed, Jr. These transactions cumulatively created an oceanfront estate of almost nine acres. Reed, his wife Gladys, and their two sons (Verner Z. III and G. Peter Quentell) had been leasing Sea Edge on Price's Neck since 1931.

Reed was the son of Verner Z. Reed, Sr., a Denver capitalist who established a fortune in mining, banking, oil, and ranching—most of it in Colorado and Wyoming. At Reed's death in 1919 a majority of the estate was inherited by his wife, but a portion also went to his son, who spent much of it on a luxurious lifestyle centered in New York, Pine Hurst, North Carolina, and Newport.

With this fortune to back him, in 1934 Reed began his building campaign. He hired architect James C. Mackenzie, Jr., to develop plans for the spectacular Cherry Neck site. Daringly, the house was sited on a rock ledge directly at water's edge. During severe weather conditions the Reeds—as well as future occupants—would regret this choice.

The central mass of Terre Mare is capped by a slate hipped roof in the seventeenth-century manner, embellished with pairs of soaring, attenuated chimney stacks at each side. The rubble-stone walls of the house have limestone quoins, window surrounds,

Aerial View (Author's Collection)

Entrance Façade (Courtesy of the Preservation Society of Newport County)

Ocean Façade Detail (Courtesy of the Preservation Society of Newport County)

and stringcourses—one of the latter separates the two principal levels of the structure and the other is placed at the sill level of the second-story windows. Curved wings at either side reach out to embrace an elliptically shaped courtyard centered by a limestone entrance surround whose subtle Louis XVI detailing has been distilled into an Art Deco motif.

The ocean-facing elevation exhibits a different perspective because it sits elevated upon a broad, half-circle terrace. The tripartite design of this elevation has a two-and-a-half-story central mass bracketed by one-and-a-half-story projecting wings. Set within one wing is a single-story loggia, whose roof is supported by paired Ionic columns.

Garage (Courtesy of the Preservation Society of Newport County)

The front door opens into a small open vestibule with a short flight of curving steps on either side that lead up to a balcony, with the main transverse hall beyond. On each side of this vestibule is a small reception room, while across the hall are symmetrically placed sets of doors, separated by a decorative wall mural. At one end of the hall is an octagonal space that contains a marble staircase with a Direc-

toire-style wrought-iron railing; at the opposite end is an enclosed smaller spiral staircase that leads up to a master bedroom suite. Three major entertaining spaces fill the ocean-facing central block and balancing wings. In the middle the living room has simply molded walls, a white marble Louis XVI–style mantel, and overdoor lunettes containing classical paintings in grisaille, while three sets of French

East Loggia (Courtesy of the Preservation Society of Newport County)

Staircase (Courtesy of the Preservation Society of Newport County)

doors on the south side of the room open onto a loggia. East of this space is a paneled library and to the west is the dining room, which has Louis XVI detailing, rectangular overdoor paintings, and a large western-facing bay window. The eastern wing of the house has an Art Deco morning room, with an adjacent chart room. A curved, open loggia with statuary niches at either end comes next, while farther along is an art studio. Service areas are placed within the curve of the western wing. The second floor has five bedrooms, each with bath, plus a master suite. Found on the floor above are four additional guest rooms. In the service wing is a housekeeper's suite and seven staff bedrooms.

The Reeds formally opened the house with a dinner party in August of 1935. The family generally stayed until October, when it was time to return to New York. These plans were interrupted in September of 1938 when a massive hurricane struck Newport, inflicting heavy damage to the property. Water crashed through the French doors, causing flooding throughout the basement and first floor of the house and forcing the Reeds to seek shelter at the nearby Frazier Jelke estate. Afterward, repair work was expedited because the Reeds wanted Terre Mare ready for the 1939 season.

In the early 1940s there was yet another hurricane: although not quite as destructive as the 1938 storm, it was responsible for enough damage to convince the Reeds to give up and sell Terre Mare. In 1945, Mrs. John R. McLean of Dallas, Texas, pur-

chased it for $110,000. Elizabeth McLean moved into Terre Mare, jokingly referring to it as Hurricane Hut. During 1954 the house was leased to William L. Van Alen when Hurricane Carol hit, requiring the family and servants to evacuate the property. While trying to reach safety at his brother's estate Avalon (located across Ocean Drive on higher ground), a wave swamped both the fleeing Van Alen automobiles. Three servants were killed.

In 1955, Texas oilman Thomas W. Blake purchased the house, renaming it Seafair in an attempt to disassociate the house from its troubled past. In the late 1950s and early '60s, Blake tried in vain to sell Seafair. In 1965, he was finally able to sell part of the property, which included the house, to Erwin Davlin, the owner of the Standard Fittings Company. Davlin later acquired the remaining original acreage, bringing the estate back to its 1934 size.

In 1983 a proposal for transforming Seafair into a luxury hotel was withdrawn because of objections by neighbors. In 1986, Davlin successfully proposed converting the house to condominium use. In 1992 the largest part Seafair—some 14,000 square feet—was sold to Richard Dvorak of Wakefield, Rhode Island, for just over a million dollars. After completing a thorough renovation, Dvorak was convicted for tax evasion and sent to prison. The twenty-room unit was then acquired by Richard Bready for $2.5 million. In the now seventy-year tug-of-war between man and nature on Cherry Neck, Seafair seems, for the moment, to be winning.

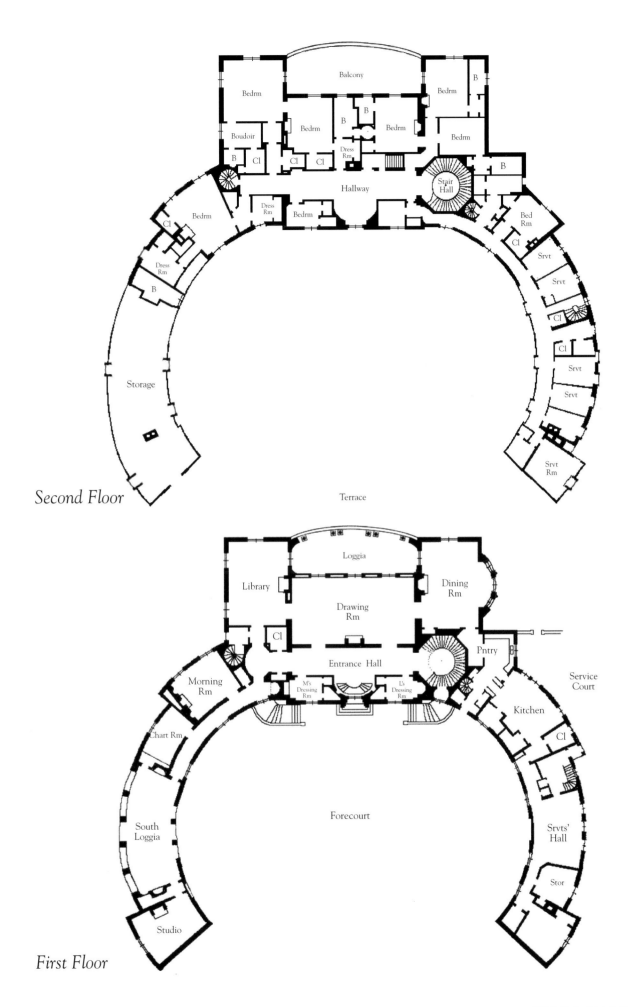

Second Floor

Balcony

Bedrm

Bedrm

B

Bedrm

Bedrm

Boudoir

B

Cl

Cl

Cl

Dress Rm

Hallway

Stair Hall

Bedrm

Dress Rm

Bedrm

Bed Rm

Cl

Srvt

Srvt

Cl

Dress Rm

B

Cl

Srvt

Srvt

Cl

Storage

Srvt Rm

Terrace

First Floor

Loggia

Library

Drawing Rm

Dining Rm

Cl

Entrance Hall

Pntry

Morning Rm

M's Dressing Rm

L's Dressing Rm

Service Court

Kitchen

Chart Rm

Cl

South Loggia

Forecourt

Srvts' Hall

Studio

Stor

SELECTED CATALOG

1880–81. Château-Nooga. Christopher Columbus Baldwin. George Brown Post, Architect. Extant. (Author's Collection)

1882–83. Vinland. Catherine Lorillard Wolfe. Peabody & Stearns, Architects. Enlarged by Peabody & Stearns in 1907-10 for Hamilton McKown Twombly. Extant. (Author's Collection)

1882–83. Greystone. Fitch J. Bosworth. George Champlin Mason & Son, Architects. Razed. (Redwood Library and Athenaeum, Newport, Rhode Island)

1882–84. William G. Weld Villa. Dudley Newton, Architect. Extant, altered. (Redwood Library and Athenaeum, Newport, Rhode Island)

1884–86. H. A. C. Taylor Villa. McKim, Mead & White, Architects. Razed. (Redwood Library and Athenaeum, Newport, Rhode Island)

1884–86. Commodore William Edgar Villa. McKim, Mead & White, Architects. Extant. (Author's Collection)

1885–86. Mid-Cliff. Miss Carolyn Ogden Jones. Peabody & Stearns, Architects. Extant. (Author's Collection)

1885–87. The Cloisters. James P. Kernochan. John Dixon Johnston, Architect. Razed. (Author's Collection)

1885–88. Inchiquin. John O'Brien. John Dixon Johnston, Architect. Extant, altered. (Author's Collection)

1887–88. Oak View. William Osgood. Harding & Dinkelly, Architects. Extant, altered. (Newport Historical Society)

1887–88. Lindenhurst. John M. Hodgson. John M. Hodgson, Architect. Extant. (Author's Collection)

1887–88. Edgehill. George Gordon King. McKim, Mead & White, Architects. Extant. (Newport Historical Society)

1887–89. Ivy Tower. Harriet N. Pond. John Dixon Johnston, Architect. Extant. (Author's Collection)

1888–89. Ocean Lawn. Mrs. William Gammell. Peabody & Stearns, Architects. Extant. (Courtesy of the Preservation Society of Newport County)

1889–90. Althorpe. John Spencer Thomas. Peabody & Stearns, Architects. Extant. (Courtesy of the Preservation Society of Newport County)

1890–91. Roslyn. William Grosvenor. William Ralph Emerson, Architect. Extant. (Author's Collection)

1890–91. Rockhurst. Mrs. H. Mortimer Brooks. Peabody & Stearns, Architects. Razed. (Author's Collection)

1889–92. Indian Spring. Joseph R. Busk. Richard Morris Hunt, Architect. Extant. (Author's Collection)

c. 1894. Whitehall. David King, Jr., McKim, Mead & White, Architects. Burned. (Author's Collection)

1893–95. Beechbound. William Burden. Peabody & Stearns, Architects. Extant, altered. (Courtesy of the Preservation Society of Newport County)

c. 1895. Belmead. George S. Scott. Bruce Price, Architect. Extant. (Author's Collection)

1895–96. Landfall. Alfred M. Coats. Ogden Codman, Jr., Architect. Extant. (Author's Collection)

1895-96. Seabeach. Mrs. Charles Coolidge Pomeroy. Ogden Codman, Jr., Architect. Extant. (Author's Collection)

1897-98. Beach-Mound. Benjamin Thaw. Henry Ives Cobb, Architect. Extant. (Author's Collection)

1897-98. Ridgemere. Miss Fanny Foster. Peabody & Stearns, Architects. Extant. (James Amodeo Photographer)

1898-99. The Breakwater. Charles Warren Lippitt. Robert H. Robertson, Architect. Razed. (Author's Collection)

1900. Wayside. Elisha Dyer, Jr. John Dixon Johnston, Architect. Extant. (Newport Historical Society)

1899-1902. Ellen Mason Villa. Irving Gill, Architect. Extant, altered. (Author's Collection)

1902. Gray Crag. J. Mitchell Clark. Abner J. Haydel, Architect. Burned. (Author's Collection)

1902–03. Faxon Lodge. Frank K. Sturgis. Ogden Codman, Jr., Architect. Extant. (Courtesy of the Preservation Society of Newport County)

c. 1907. Avalon. Edward S. Rawson. Architect unknown. Burned, razed. (Author's Collection)

c. 1915. Rock Cliff. Frederick Lathrop Ames (originally Thomas Cushing house, George Champlin Mason, Architect). Remodeled c. 1910, Architect George Champlin Mason, Jr. Extant. (Courtesy of the International Tennis Hall of Fame & Museum, Newport, Rhode Island)

1916. Ayrault House. Virginia Scott Hoyt. Cross & Cross, Architects. Extant. (James Amodeo Photographer)

1920–22. The Glen. Moses Taylor V. John Russell Pope, Architect. Extant, additions. (Author's Collection)

1922–24. Eagle's Nest. F. Frazier Jelke. Aldrich & Sleeper, Architects. Extant. (Author's Collection)

1925. Stonybrook. Edward C. Knight, Jr. Horace Trumbauer, Architect. Extant. (Author's Collection)

1929. Idle Hour. Mrs. Frederick Allen. Frederic Rhinelander King, Architect. Extant. (Author's Collection)

1930. Little Clifton Berley. Mrs. Douglas Cameron. Charles Barton King, Architect. Extant. (Author's Collection)

1932. Ker Avor. Snowden Fahnestock. Russell & Clinton, Architects. Extant. (Author's Collection)

ARCHITECTS' BIOGRAPHIES

DWIGHT JAMES BAUM

Born in Little Falls, New York, Dwight James Baum (1886–1939) studied at Syracuse University, where he graduated in 1909. In 1915, Baum opened up an office in the bucolic Riverdale section of the Bronx in New York. He became known for his brick Georgian and Dutch Colonial Revival houses, many erected in the Fieldston section of Riverdale. Also a writer, he published articles on American Colonial architecture and remained a longtime architectural consultant for *Good Housekeeping* magazine. In 1930, Baum won the Bronze Medal Award of the Better Homes of America Association for the best-designed small house plan built between 1926 and 1930. Two years later he won a Gold Medal for his work from the Architectural League of New York. Although principally known for his restrained works in traditional Colonial and Georgian styles, one of the architect's best-known design's is Ca d'Zan, the highly elaborate Venetian Gothic residence of John and Mabel Ringling in Sarasota, Florida. The alterations to Fairholme for Count and Countess Alphonso Villa in 1929–1930 constitute Baum's only known work in Newport

CARRÈRE & HASTINGS

John Mervin Carrère (1858–1911) and Thomas Hastings (1860–1929) first became acquainted as students at the École des Beaux-Arts in Paris. After graduation they returned to the United States and apprenticed at the firm of McKim, Mead & White. In the mid-1880s the architects left and opened their own firm, with Henry Morrison Flagler becoming one of their first clients. Flagler was just then developing southern Florida into America's winter playground, and the fledgling firm was asked to design the Ponce de León (1885–1887) and the Alcazar (1886–1888) hotels in St. Augustine. (The firm subsequently designed Flagler's Palm Beach mansion, Whitehall, in 1902.) Although these early hotels were designed in a vaguely Moorish-Spanish taste, the firm became better known for its full-blown Beaux-Arts neoclassic styles, predominately in the French taste. The Modern French-style Henry T. Sloane house (1896) on East 72nd Street in New York, accented with florid limestone detailing, established a design philosophy that was often repeated during the following decades. Other important New York works include the Staten Island Ferry Terminal (1905), the New Theater (1909), the Manhattan Bridge (1909), and the New York Public Library (1911). In Washington, D.C., the firm designed the Office Building for the U. S. House of Representatives (1904), and the Arlington Memorial Amphitheater. In 1898, Mrs. Richard Gambrill asked Thomas Hastings to design Vernon Court on Bellevue Avenue in Newport. Rather surprisingly, the only other Newport commission for this prolific and well-respected New York firm was the design of a fountain for Colonel George R. Fearing in 1902.

OGDEN CODMAN, JR.

Ogden Codman (1863–1951) was born into a wealthy Boston Brahmin family whose financial reverses in the mid-1870s led to an eleven-year European expatriation. Thus, at a young age, Codman was exposed to European architecture and culture. He returned to the United States in 1882 and enrolled in an architectural training program at MIT. Chafing at the highly structured manner of education, he soon left MIT to take up an apprenticeship at the Boston architectural firm of Andrews, Jacques & Rantoul. By 1891, Codman had opened his own office on Chestnut Street. An early triumph was a commission from Edith Wharton to redecorate her Newport home Land's End, located at the end of Ledge Road in Newport. He and the author soon collaborated on a book entitled *The Decoration of Houses*, which articulately espouses their emerging design ethic, based on classical proportion and simplicity. Although Codman has principally been identified with his interior work, which was highly architectural in nature, he was also an accomplished architect with nearly thirty complete structures to his credit. In 1894, Codman received a high-profile commission from Cornelius Vanderbilt II to decorate the second- and third-floor rooms

at The Breakers in Newport. Because much of his work was by now being generated by New York–based clients, Codman decided to move to that city and open an office at 5 East 16th Street. This office flourished until the advent of World War I. Because Codman's high-style interior finishes were manufactured in either France or England, his work came to a complete standstill. After the war, instead of reopening his office, Codman chose to retire and move to France. There he soon began designing La Leopolda, his home on the Riviera, which happily occupied many years of his retirement. His complete Newport houses include Seabeach (1896) for Mrs. Charles C. Pomeroy, Landfall (1896) for Alfred M. Coats, Villa Rosa (1900) for E. Rollins Morse, Faxon Lodge (1903) for Frank K. Sturgis, and Berkeley Villa (1910) for his cousin Martha Codman. His major interior works are seen in the Harold Brown Villa (1893), Edgemere (1897) for Nathaniel Thayer, High Tide (1900) for William Starr Miller, Quatrel (1900) for Edgerton Winthrop, Hopedene (1903) for Mrs. E. Hope Gammell Slater, and Chateau-sur-Mer (1903) for George Peabody Wetmore.

CRAM, GOODHUE & FERGUSON

Ralph Adams Cram (1863–1942) was born in Hampton Falls, New Hampshire, into a clerical Unitarian family. At the age of eighteen, he moved to Boston to begin a five-year apprentice at the firm of Rotch & Tilden. He later continued his studies in Rome, where he became enamored of the Gothic Revival style. In 1890, Cram opened an office with Charles Francis Wentworth. The firm quickly became a specialist in ecclesiastical and collegiate architecture. Within a few years Bertram Grosvenor Goodhue (1869–1924) and F. W. Ferguson became partners in the firm. The firm of Cram, Goodhue & Ferguson had much success with high-profile structures such as the new St. Thomas Church (1906–1914) located on Fifth Avenue at 53rd Street in New York. Soon after the plans for St. Thomas's were completed, Goodhue left the firm, while the firm of Cram & Ferguson continued with such notable commissions as the Cathedral of St. John the Devine in the Morningside Heights section of Manhattan. Of the firm's many Collegiate Gothic structures, the four they designed for the campus of Princeton University are perhaps the finest. As Princeton's consulting architect between 1907 and 1929, Cram is directly responsible for the overall look of the campus as we know it today. As a noted scholar, Cram wrote extensively on the subject of Gothic Revival architecture in many publications, including *Church Building* (1901), *The Gothic Quest* (1907), *The Ministry of Art* (1914) and *The Substance of Gothic* (1916). Cram obtained the firm's three Newport commissions because of his personal association with the venerable Brown family of Providence. The first was for Emmanuel Church on Spring Street, built as a memorial for John Nicholas Brown (1904). The second was Harbour Court, the Newport house of Brown's widow (1905). The last was a chapel at St. George's School, a project backed by John Nicholas Brown II (1922–1928).

DELANO & ALDRICH

William Adams Delano (1874–1960) and Chester Aldrich (1871–1940) met while working as designers at Carrère & Hastings. They had each studied at Columbia and at the École des Beaux-Arts. The firm of Delano & Aldrich was formed in 1903, and one of its first commissions was Kykuit, the Rockefeller house in Pocantico Hills, New York. They received this plum commission because Mrs. Rockefeller was a relative of Chester Aldrich's. The office developed a reputation for its chaste and elegant country houses, most designed in an Americanized interpretation of the English Georgian tradition. Examples include Highlawn House (1910) in Lenox, Massachusetts, for W. B. Osgood Field; Woodside (1916) in Syosset, Long Island, for James A. Burden; and Oak Knoll (1918) in Mill Neck, New York, for Bertram G. Work. The firm's New York City works are equally illustrious and include the Colony Club (1916), the Harold I. Pratt house (1920) at 58 East 68th Street, the Francis

Palmer/George F. Baker house (1917, 1928) at 75 East 93rd Street and the Willard Straight house (1915) at 1130 Fifth Avenue. The firm's only Newport project was Cherry Neck Bungalow for Mrs. F. M. Huntington Wilson in 1913.

HOWARD GREENLEY

Educated at Trinity College in Hartford, Connecticut, Howard Greenley (1874–1963) went on to study at the École des Beaux-Arts in Paris. He entered private practice in 1902. Early in his career he executed country houses on Long Island, New York, for Charles A. Coffin (c. 1910) and Anson W. Burchard (1906). In New York City he designed the classical fourteen-story Beaux-Arts–style Prince George Hotel on East 28th Street in 1904, and its 1912 addition. A decade later, he designed the Corning Free Academy in Corning, New York, in the Romanesque Revival style. His only Newport project was the renovation and enlargement of Sea View Terrace for Edson Bradley, completed in 1926.

HOPPIN & KOEN

Francis L. V. Hoppin (1867–1941) was born in Providence, Rhode Island. He originally intended to pursue a career in the military but switched his vocation to architecture. He received his education at Brown University and MIT, furthering his architectural education by a long sojourn to Paris. Upon his return to the United States, Hoppin apprenticed in the offices of McKim, Mead & White, where he would meet his future professional collaborator Terrence A. Koen (1858–1923). Hoppin & Koen was founded in 1894, with a third partner, Robert Palmer Huntington, joining the firm two years later. The firm's major residential work includes The Mount (1902) in Lenox, Massachusetts, for Edith and Teddy Wharton, and Ashintully (1912) in neighboring Tyringham for Robb de Peyster Tytus. In Newport, Hoppin's two major projects were Armsea Hall (1901) for General Francis Vinton Greene, and Sherwood (1908) for Pembroke Jones.

HOWELLS & STOKES

Many great-house architectural practitioners came from well-to-do families from whose established professional and social networks they could cull clients. An example of this dynamic is the fashionable practice established by partners John Mead Howells (1868–1959) and Isaac Newton Phelps Stokes (1867–1844). Stokes was the son of a New York banker and philanthropist, whereas Howells came from a prominent New England family; his father was novelist William Dean Howells. Stokes first became acquainted with Howells when they were both at Harvard in 1880s. After graduation Stokes entered the School of Architecture at Columbia University and afterward joined Howells in Paris, where they both studied at the École des Beaux-Arts in 1896 and 1897. Upon their return they formed a partnership based in New York. Over the years, the firm created important examples of early-twentieth-century architecture such as St. Paul's Episcopal Chapel at Columbia (1913) and the Chicago Tribune Tower (1923), the latter in association with Raymond Hood. Howells was an authority on American Colonial architecture and wrote extensively on the subject. These works include *Charles Bulfinch* (1908) and *Lost Examples of Colonial Architecture* (1931). Stokes was passionately interested in the history of New York City and was editor of the six-volume *Iconography of Manhattan Island* (1915–1928). The firm's single Newport project was the 1909 commission of Beacon Hill House for Arthur Curtiss James.

RICHARD MORRIS HUNT

Richard Morris Hunt (1827–1895) is the father of American architecture. He is responsible for establishing the profession with set fees and services that, for the first time, put architects on a par with other professionals such as doctors and lawyers. Born in Brattleboro, Vermont, at a young age his mother took him to live in Europe. He became the first American to graduate with an architectural degree from the École des Beaux-Arts in Paris. Upon his return to the United States in 1855, he opened an office in New York. His first major project was the Studio Building on West 10th Street (1856), where he later opened his own atelier based on Beaux-Arts principles, providing instruction to a new generation of American architects. His pupils included such luminaries as Henry Van Brunt, Frank Furness, and George Brown Post. In Newport, Hunt had strong familial connections, and by the early 1860s he was establishing his reputation with his important Stick Style houses, which included the Thomas Hitchcock house (1861), the J. N. A. Griswold house (1864), and Hypotenuse (1871) his own house on Catherine Street. By the 1880s, Hunt had returned to his high Beaux-Arts classical training when economic circumstances gave him a group of clients who represented the country's new moneyed elite. Now, with seemingly unlimited budgets, Hunt became known for his François I châteaux and neoclassical mansions. Chief among these are his Newport commissions, most completed in the 1890s. In 1888, the design process began on Ochre Court for Ogden Goelet and Marble House for William K. Vanderbilt. In 1889, Hunt created Indian Spring for Joseph R. Busk in an organic mode that sits beautifully on its rocky, windswept Ocean Avenue location. In 1894, he completed Belcourt for Oliver Belmont in a style reminiscent of Louis XIII's hunting lodge found at the core of the palace of Versailles. His final Newport contribution, and perhaps his greatest, is The Breakers for Cornelius Vanderbilt II, completed within weeks of the architect's death in 1895.

CHARLES EAMER KEMPE

Charles Eamer Kempe (1837–1907) was born at Ovingdean Hall, near Brighton, England. He originally intended to become a clergyman, but as an undergraduate at Pembroke College, Oxford, he realized that a speech impediment would forever impede his ability to evangelize the Christian message. Instead, he began an apprenticeship with the architectural firm of George Frederick Bodley, an exponent of the Gothic Revival style. He was given the opportunity to decorate the interiors of All Saints-

Jesus Lane in Cambridge and St. John the Baptist in Liverpool in the "correct" Gothic manner. He went on to become a specialist in the design and installation of stained-glass windows, with his first documented window design being the Bishop Hooper Memorial window in Gloucester Cathedral of 1865. Much of his work is inspired by fifteenth-century English stained glass that he considered the most harmonious with the new Gothic structures that they were designed to embellish. By 1888 his studio and offices moved to 28 Nottingham Place in Central London, where he employed a staff of over fifty. Kempe became a friend of James J. Van Alen, who asked him to develop plans for his Newport house (1884–1887), which was to be based on the Elizabethan manor house Wakehurst Place in Sussex. He also helped Van Alen collect antique fittings and stained glass with which to create an appropriate period environment.

HARRIE T. LINDEBERG

Known for his country-house practice, Harrie Thomas Lindeberg (1880–1959) is best remembered for his eclectic English styles that are imbued with a modern sensibility, although never at the expense of warmth or vitality. Born in Bergen Point, New Jersey, to parents of Swedish descent, Lindeberg studied at the National Academy of Design in New York. He apprenticed at the firm of McKim, Mead & White, where he reputedly served as a design assistant on the 1905–1906 addition to the James L. Breeze estate in Southampton. The following year he and another McKim, Mead & White alumnus, Lewis Colt Albro (1876–1924), formed the firm of Albro & Lindeberg, which lasted until 1914, when the latter decided to go out on his own. Lindeberg became a fashionable country-house practitioner, with a client list that included such notables as P. D. Armour, Irving Brokaw, Nelson Doubleday, Horace Havemeyer, James Stillman, and R. T. Vanderbilt. Lindeberg's single Newport commission was Gray Craig for Michael van Beuren (1923) which actually sits in neighboring Middletown.

JAMES C. MACKENZIE, JR.

James Mackenzie was a New York City–based architect who specialized in middle- and upper-bracket residential projects. Typical of his work was a 1930 commission to design a house for John Sloane of the W. & J. Sloane company at 48–50 East 92nd Street, on a plot of land that measured 40 by 100 feet. Mackenzie's other New York work includes the Union Apartments on East 105th Street (1926), the Sheepshead Bay Housing Development in Brooklyn, and the Administration Building on Governors Island. Farther afield, Mackenzie was responsible for the design of the United States Training School in Memphis, Tennessee. In 1949, the National Park Service contracted the architect for a $500,000 improvement program for the Statue of Liberty on Bedloe's Island (now known as Liberty Island). His responsibilities included a new landing pier and six smaller structures for island residents and staff. In association with architect Philip Ives he designed a 1950 luxury housing development on North Manursing Island near Rye, New York. His only known work in Newport is Terre Mare, the Cherry Neck residence of Verner Z. Reed, Jr., completed in 1935.

MCKIM, MEAD & WHITE

Charles Follen McKim (1847–1909), William Rutherford Mead (1846–1928), and Stanford White (1853–1906) headed what may have been the most influential architectural firm in the history of New York. McKim studied at the École des Beaux-Arts from 1866 to 1870. He then returned to New York, where he began working in the office of Henry Hobson Richardson. In 1873 he left Richardson to go into partnership with William Mead. His new partner was from Brattleboro, Vermont, and educated at Amherst before traveling to Florence to study Renaissance architecture. In 1879, the multitalented Stanford White, who had also apprenticed in Richardson's office, joined the firm. Included in its vast volume of work are structures as far-flung as the New York Life Building in Kansas City (1890) and the American Academy in Rome (1914). Closer to home are the Metropolitan

Club (1894), the Tiffany & Company Building at 37th Street and Fifth Avenue (1906), and the Gorham Company Building (1905). One of the firm's larger commissions was the original Madison Square Garden, which sat on the block bounded by 26th and 27th streets, and Madison and Park avenues (1891). In 1906 an ex-lover's husband murdered Stanford White while he was attending a show at the Madison Square roof garden. In Newport the firm is best known for its strikingly original Shingle Style work of the 1880s, but by the end of the decade they had moved on to become a principal proponent of the Colonial Revival movement. Their Newport work includes The Casino (1879–1891), Kingscote addition for David King, Jr. (1882), the Samuel Tilton house on Sunnyside Place (1882), the William Watts Sherman house renovation (1882), the Isaac Bell house (Edna Villa) (1883), Villano for Mrs. Frances L. Skinner (1882), the Samuel Coleman house (1883), the Charles M. Bull house (1883), Ochre Point for Robert Goelet (1884), the Commodore William Edgar house (Sunnyside) (1886), Berkeley House for LeRoy King (1886), the H. A. C. Taylor house (1886), Berry Hill for John H. Glover (1887), Edgehill for George Gordon King (1888), Beacon Rock for Edwin D. Morgan III (1891), Rosecliff for Hermann and Theresa Fair Oelrichs (1902), and Oakwood for George Gordon King (1902).

DUDLEY NEWTON

One of Newport's most prolific nineteenth-century architects, Dudley Newton (1845–1907) apprenticed for six years under the city's other preeminent nineteenth-century architect, George Champlin Mason, Sr. (1820–1894). His first commissions were the St. Spyridon Greek Orthodox Church (1865), and the local police station (1867), but he soon branched out into residential works such as his 1870 renovation of Belair for George Henry Norman, a house originally designed by Seth C. Bradford (1801–1878) in 1850. His most important contribution to the architectural profession was his design for the Newton Roof, patented in 1872. This roof design is based on the Mansard style, but with an important indentation where the roof joins the house that prevents water from ever seeping into the wall plane below it. During the 1870s, Newton became known for his Stick Style houses, such as the George Clarence Cram house on Purgatory Road in neighboring Middletown and the Henry H. Swinburne house at 97 Rhode Island Avenue, both completed in 1876. In the following decade, Newton developed Shingle Style plans for Hawkshurst for Caroline Seymour (1884) and Bethshan for Major Theodore Kane Gibbs on Gibbs Avenue (1884), as well as large stone houses such as the villa he designed in 1864 for William G. Weld on Bellevue Avenue. In 1888, James J. Van Alen asked Newton to implement the imported plans for Wakehurst that had been originally developed in England by Charles Eamer Kempe. His other two contributions to the Revival movement in Newport are the baronial Harold Brown Villa of 1894, and Crossways for Stuyvesant Fish, completed four years later.

PEABODY & STEARNS

Peabody & Stearns rose to national prominence with commissions extending along the East Coast from Maine to Georgia, and out west to Colorado. Boston's most prolific firm was created when architect Robert Swain Peabody (1845–1917) and engineer John Goddard Stearns (1843–1917) formed a partnership in 1870. Peabody graduated from Harvard in 1866, and then went on to study at the École des Beaux-Arts, while Stearns apprenticed at the firm of Ware & Van Brunt. One of Peabody & Stearns's earlier works was the 1877 commission for Pierre Lorillard's Newport home, The Breakers, later replaced by R. M. Hunt's work. By 1886, it had become the leading architectural firm in New England. Because of its prominence, the firm was selected to participate in the World's Columbian Exposition in Chicago in 1893. Other major works include the St. Louis Museum of Fine Art (1879–1891) and the Union League Club in New York (1881); while in Boston, they designed the Exchange Building (1887–1891) and the Custom House Tower (1909–1910). The firm was active in Newport from 1871 until around 1910. They designed works such as the Frederick S. C. D'Hauteville cottage (c. 1871), Weetamore (Edgemere) (1872) for Nathaniel Thayer, Vinland (1882–1885) for Catherine Lorillard Wolfe, Honeysuckle Lodge (1886) for Joseph Fisk, Mid-Cliff (1886) for Caroline Ogden Jones, Rough Point (1887–1891) for Frederick Vanderbilt, Ocean Lawn (1888–1889) for Mrs. William Gammell, Althorpe (1889–1890) for John Thompson Spencer, Rockhurst (1890–1891; additions 1893 and 1896) for Mrs. H. Mortimer Brooks, and Bleak House II (1892–1893) for Ross R. Winans. Later works in the European Revival styles include Beechbound (1893–1895) for William Burden, Shamrock Cliff (1894–1896) for Gaun M. Hutton, Ridgemere (1897–1898) for Miss Fanny Foster, and Hopedene (1899–1902) for Elizabeth Hope Gammell Slater.

CHARLES ADAMS PLATT

A New York City native, Charles Adams Platt (1861–1933) began his career as an artist studying at the National Academy of Design. In 1882, he went to Europe to study for five years, after which he returned home to join the workshop of sculptor Augustus Saint-Gaudens. A decade later he exhibited his paintings in Europe, while studying classical Italian gardens. In 1894 he and his brother published an influential work entitled *Italian Gardens*. From this, he began designing gardens for wealthy Bostonians at the estates of Weld and Faulkner Farm. He also began designing houses for friends in the artistic community of Cornish, New Hampshire, which launched his career as an architect. Platt designed many city and country houses, as well as apartment buildings. Larger projects include the Freer Gallery of Art in Washington, D.C., and Phillips Andover Academy in Massachusetts. Platt's sole Newport commission was Bois Doré, the William Fahnestock house on Narragansett Avenue, completed in 1928.

POLHEMUS & COFFIN

The fashionable architectural firm of Henry M. Polhemus (1891–1970) and Lewis A. Coffin (1892–1963) focused on country houses in styles ranging from rustic American Colonial Revival farmhouses to adaptations of provincial French châteaux. In 1921, Scribners published the architects' work *Small French Buildings: The Architecture of Town and Country, Comprising Cottages, Farmhouses, Minor Chateaux or Manors with Their Farm Groups, Small Town Dwellings, and a Few Churches*. Two years earlier, Coffin and Arthur C. Holden had released *Brick Architecture of the Colonial Period in Maryland and Virginia*. Much of their work is located in suburban areas surrounding New York. These works include the Albert Barnes Boardman house in Southampton, New York (1923), Falaise, for Harry F. Guggenheim in Sands Point, New York (with associate architect Frederick J. Sterner) (1923), The Cedars for Charles A. Blackwell in Brookville, New York (c. 1926), Woodford for Nevil Ford in Lloyd Harbor, New York (c. 1930), Mille Fleurs for Mrs. Daniel Guggenheim in Sands Point, New York (c. 1931), and Château O'Brien for Katherine Mackay in Southampton, New York (c. 1925). The firm's nonresidential work includes the Baker Field Boathouse for Columbia University (1930), Barnard College Memorial Gates (c. 1926), and the Johnson Athletic Center at Choate (1931). Their only Newport work is the 1929 design of Champ Soleil for Lucy Drexel Dahlgren. The firm returned to alter the house when it was occupied by Robert Wilson Goelet.

JOHN RUSSELL POPE

One of America's most distinguished architects, John Russell Pope (1874–1937) is best remembered for his classical civic works in Washington, D.C. These projects include the National Archives Building (1929–1935), the National Gallery of Art (1935–1941), and the Jefferson Memorial (1935–1943). His work was international in scope, exemplified by his work at the British Museum (1930–1939) and the Tate Gallery (1929–1937), both in London. The architect was born in New York, where his father John Pope (1820–1881) was an accomplished portrait painter and his mother Mary Avery (née Loomis) was a piano teacher and landscape painter. In the fall of 1888, Pope entered the City College of New York. Three years later he enrolled in Columbia University's Department of Architecture in the School of Mines. In 1895, the year following his graduation from Columbia, Pope won the first McKim Scholarship to the American Academy in Rome. In 1897 he began three years of study at the École des Beaux-Arts in the atelier of Henri Deglane. In 1900 he returned to New York and found employment in the office of Bruce Price before opening his own office in 1905 (even though he seems to have had clients before finally opening his independent practice). The architect's initial work centers on country-house designs, which quickly became the driving force in the early years of Pope's practice. Included in the impressive roster are the W. R. Stow house (1903) in Roslyn, New York, the residence of Mrs. William K. Vanderbilt, Jr. (c. 1911) in Jericho, New York, the Ogden L. Mills house (c. 1915) in Woodbury, New York, and the Andrew V. Stout house (1917) located in Red Bank, New Jersey. In Newport, Pope was responsible for the design of Whiteholme (1901–1903) for Mrs. Henry Barton Jacobs, Bonniecrest (1912–1914; addition, 1926) for Stuart Duncan, alterations to Chateau-sur-Mer (c. 1915) for the Wetmore family, and The Glen (1921–1923) for Moses Taylor V, and his own house, The Waves (1928–1930).

HORACE TRUMBAUER

Horace Trumbauer's (1868–1938) family hailed from Bucks County, Pennsylvania, but the architect was born in the Frankford section of Philadelphia. When he was nine yeas old, his family moved to suburban Jenkintown, Pennsylvania. There he attended public schools until he was fourteen years old, when he took a job as a messenger boy at the prestigious Philadelphia architectural firm of George & William Hewitt. With talent and drive

Trumbauer worked his way up through the ranks, from drafting to design work. At the age of twenty-one, the architect opened his own firm. Only three years later he received his first major residential commission when William Welsh Harrison asked him to design Grey Towers in Glenside, Pennsylvania. His office was eventually responsible for over 1,100 commissions; these included major civic works in his hometown such as the Free Library and the Philadelphia Museum of Art, as well as important commercial structures like the Widener Building in Philadelphia and the New York Evening Post building in downtown New York. Trumbauer became best known for his residential work for prominent American families such as the Vanderbilts, Wideners, Dukes, Drexels, and Goulds. In Newport, his works include The Elms (1899–1901) for E. J. Berwind, Chetwode (1900–1902) for W. S. Wells, Claradon Court (1903–1904) and Stonybrook in Middletown (1927–1928), both for E. C. Knight, Jr., and Miramar (1912–1914) for Eleanor Elkins Widener. Trumbauer's remodeling jobs include Quarterfoil (1901) for W. E. Carter, Sea Weed (1902–1903) for Thomas Dolan, Belcourt (1910) for Perry Belmont, Rough Point (1922–1923) for J. B. Duke, and Beaulieu (1930) for Cornelius Vanderbilt III.

WARREN & WETMORE

Whitney Warren (1864–1943) was born and raised in New York City. At the age of twenty, after briefly studying at Columbia, he went to Paris to study at the École des Beaux-Arts. He entered the École in 1887 and studied at the atelier of Honoré Daumet and Charles-Louis Girault. After leaving the École, he remained in France, furthering his architectural education for ten more years. Warren eventually returned to New York, and in 1896 joined Charles D. Wetmore (1867–1941) in founding the firm of Warren & Wetmore. Wetmore was born in Elmira, New York, and graduated from Harvard in 1889. The firm's New York works include the New York Yacht Club (1900), Grand Central Terminal (1913), the Biltmore Hotel (1914), and the Aeolian Building

(1924). Warren founded the Beaux-Arts Institute of Design in New York, and always considered the Louvain Library restoration in Belgium to be his favorite project. High Tide (1900), the William Starr Miller house, would be the firm's only major residential Newport work, although Warren designed the Newport Country Club (1894) two years before his partnership with Wetmore.

EDWARD PAYSON WHITMAN

After graduating from MIT in 1892, Edward Payson Whitman (1869–1940) continued his architectural studies in Europe for two years. Later he returned to New York as a designer in the firm of McKim, Mead & White. After this apprenticeship Whitman decided to open his own office in New York. During the late teens or early twenties, he moved to northern California, where he continued his architectural practice for the next quarter of a century, principally in Alameda County. For his last commission, Whitman designed the new City Hall for Hayward City, California. The architect's only Newport project was for Castlewood, the Coddington Point estate of Mrs. Émile Bruguière and her son Louis.

BIBLIOGRAPHY

BOOKS

Abbott, James Archer. *Jansen*. New York: Acanthus Press, 2006.

Aldrich, Nelson W., Jr. *Old Money*. New York: Alfred A. Knopf, 1988.

Allen, Armin Brand. *The Cornelius Vanderbilts of the Breakers*. Newport, R.I.: Preservation Society of Newport County, 1995.

Aslet, Clive. *The American Country House*. New Haven, Conn.: Yale University Press, 1990.

Auchincloss, Louis. *The Vanderbilt Era*. New York: Charles Scribner's Sons, 1989.

Baker, Paul R. *Richard Morris Hunt*. Cambridge, Mass.: MIT Press, 1980.

———. *Stanny: The Gilded Life of Stanford White*. New York: Free Press, 1989.

Balsan, Consuelo Vanderbilt. *The Glitter and Gold*. New York: Harper & Brothers, 1952.

Bedford, Steven McLeod. *John Russell Pope: Architect of Empire*. New York: Rizzoli International Publications, 1998.

Brandt, Clare. *An American Aristocracy, The Livingstons*. Garden City, NY: Doubleday & Company, Inc., 1986.

Brough, James. *Consuelo*. New York: Coward, McCann & Geoghegan, 1979.

Bryan, John M. *G. W. Vanderbilt's Biltmore Estate*. New York: Rizzoli International Publications, 1994.

Burden, Shirley. *The Vanderbilts in My Life*. New Haven, Conn.: Ticknor & Fields, 1981.

Churchill, Allen. *The Splendor Seekers*. New York: Grosset & Dunlap, 1974.

Codman, Florence. *The Clever Young Boston Architect*. Augusta, Maine: KJ Litho, 1970.

Cortissoz, Royal. *Domestic Architecture of H. T. Lindenberg*. New York: William Helburn, 1940, reprint New York: Acanthus Press, 1996.

Cowles, Virginia. *The Astors*. New York: Alfred A. Knopf, 1979.

Craig, Theresa. *Edith Wharton*. New York: Monacelli Press, 1996.

Craven, Wayne. *Stanford White*. New York: Columbia University Press, 2005.

Desmond, Harry W., and Herbert Croly. *Stately Homes in America*. New York: D. Appleton and Co., 1903.

Dorsey, John. *Mount Vernon Place*. Baltimore: Maclay & Associates, 1983.

Downing, Antoinette F., and Vincent J. Scully, Jr. *The Architectural Heritage of Newport Rhode Island,1640–1915*. New York: Clarkson N. Potter, 1952, 2d. ed. rev., 1967.

Elizabeth, Lady Decies. *Turn of the World*. Philadelphia: J. B. Lippincott Co., 1937.

Elliott, Maud Howe. *This Was My Newport*. Cambridge, Mass.: Mythology Co., 1944. Reprint, New York: Arno Press, 1975.

Ferree, Barr. *American Estates and Gardens*. New York: Munn & Co., 1906.

Folsom, Merrill. *Great American Mansions*. New York: Hastings House, 1963.

————. *More Great American Mansions*. New York: Hastings House, 1967.

Foreman, John, and Robbe Pierce Stimson. *The Vanderbilts and the Gilded Age*. New York: St. Martin's Press, 1991.

Friedman, B. H. *Gertrude Vanderbilt Whitney*. Garden City, N.Y.: Doubleday & Co., 1978.

Garman, James E. *A History of the Gentlemen's Farms of Portsmouth, RI*. Portsmouth, R.I.: Hamilton Printing, 2003.

Garrison, James B. *Mastering Tradition: The Residential Architecture of John Russell Pope*. New York: Acanthus Press, 2004.

Goldsmith, Barbara. *Little Gloria…Happy at Last*. New York: Alfred A. Knopf, 1980.

Gréber, Jacques. *L'Architecture aux États-Unis*. Paris: Payot, 1920.

Griswold, Mac, and Eleanor Weller. *The Golden Age of American Gardens*. New York: Harry N. Abrams, 1991.

Grosvenor, Richard. *Newport*. Beverly, Mass.: Commonwealth Editions, 2002.

Hoyt, Edwin P. *The Vanderbilts and Their Fortunes*. Garden City, N.Y.: Doubleday & Co., 1962.

King, Robert B. *The Vanderbilt Homes*. New York: Rizzoli International Publications, 1989.

Lehr, Elizabeth Drexel. *"King Lehr" and the Gilded Age*. Philadelphia: J. B. Lippincott Co., 1935. Reprint, New York: Arno Press, 1975.

Lessard, Suzannah. *The Architect of Desire*. New York: Dial Press, 1996.

Lowell, Guy, ed. *American Gardens*. Boston: Bates & Guild, 1902.

Mann, William d'Alton. *Fads and Fancies of Representative Americans at the Beginning of the Twentieth Century*. New York: Town Topics Publishing Co., 1905. Reprint, New York, Arno Press, 1975.

Mason, George Champlin. *Newport and Its Cottages*. Boston: J. R. Osgood & Co., 1875.

Metcalf, Pauline C., ed. *Odgen Codman and the Decoration of Houses*. Boston: Boston Athenæum, 1988.

Morgan, Keith N. *Charles A. Platt*. New York: Architectural History Foundation, 1985.

Ormond, Richard, and Elaine Kilmurray. *John Singer Sargent*. New Haven, Conn.: Yale University Press, 2002.

Pardee, Bettie Bearden. *Private Newport*. New York: Bullfinch Press, 2004.

Patrick, James B., ed. *Newport Landscapes*. Newport, R. I.: Preservation Society of Newport County, 2000.

Patterson, Augusta Owen. *American Homes of To-Day*. New York: Macmillan Co., 1924.

Patterson, Jerry E. *The Vanderbilts*. New York: Harry N. Abrams, 1989.

Pennoyer, Peter, and Walker, Anne. *The Architecture of Delano & Aldrich*. New York: W. W. Norton & Co., 2003.

————. *The Architecture of Warren & Wetmore*. New York: W. W. Norton & Co., 2006.

Phelps, Harriet Jackson. *Newport in Flower*. Newport, R. I.: Preservation Society of Newport County, 1979.

Platt, Frederick. *America's Gilded Age*. Cranbury, N.J.: A. S. Barnes and Co., 1976.

Pons, Bruno. *French Period Rooms, 1650 -1800*. Dijon, France: Éditions Faton, 1995.

Rector, Margaret Hayden. *Alva, That Vanderbilt-Belmont Woman*. Wickford, R. I.: Dutch Island Press, 1992.

Rieder, William. *A Charmed Couple, The Art and Life of Walter and Matilda Gay*. New York: Harry N. Abrams, 2000.

Robinson, Bill. *Legendary Yachts*. New York: David McKay Co., 1971, rev. 1978.

Roth, Leland. *A Monograph of the Works of McKim, Mead & White, 1879-1915*. New York: Architectural Book Publishing, 1915. Reprint, New York: Arno Press, 1977.

Rybczynski, Witold. *A Clearing in the Distance*. New York: Scribner, 1999.

Schezen, Roberto. *Newport Houses*. New York: Rizzoli International Publications, 1989.

Schnadelbach, R. Terry. *Ferruccio Vitale*. New York: Princeton Architectural Press, 2001.

Sheldon, Sidney. *Artistic Country-Seats: Types of Recent American Villa and Cottage Architecture with Instances of Country Club-Houses*. New York: D. Appleton & Co., 1887.

Sherman, Joe. *The House at Shelburne Farms*. Middlebury, Vt.: Paul S. Eriksson, 1986.

Sinclair, David. *Dynasty: The Astors and Their Times*. New York: Beaufort Books, 1984.

Sirkis, Nancy. *Newport: Pleasure and Palaces*. New York: Viking Press, 1963.

Sloane, Florence Adele. *Maverick in Mauve*. Garden City, NY: Doubleday & Co., 1983.

Stasz, Clarice. *The Vanderbilt Women*. New York: St. Martin's Press, 1991.

Stein, Susan R., ed. *The Architecture of Richard Morris Hunt*. Chicago: University of Chicago Press, 1986.

Stuart, Amanda Mackenzie. *Consuelo and Alva Vanderbilt*. New York: HarperCollins Publishers, 2005.

Tadgell, Christopher. *Ange-Jacques Gabriel*. London: A. Zwemmer, 1978.

Tebbel, John. *The Inheritors*. New York: G. P. Putnam's Sons, 1962.

Towner, Wesley. *The Elegant Auctioneers*. New York: Hill & Wang, 1970.

Van Rensselaer, Mrs. John King. *Newport, Our Social Capital*. Philadelphia: J. B. Lippincott Co., 1905. Reprint, New York: Arno Press, 1975.

Vanderbilt, Arthur T., II. *Fortune's Children, The Fall of the House of Vanderbilt*. New York: William Morrow and Co., 1989.

Vanderbilt, Cornelius, Jr. *Farewell to Fifth Avenue*. New York: Simon & Schuster, 1935.

————. *Queen of the Golden Age*. New York: McGraw-Hill Book Co., 1956.

Vernay, Arthur Stannard. *Decorations and English Interiors*. New York: William Helburn, 1927.

Warren, Charles D. *The Architecture of Charles A. Platt*. New York: Acanthus Press, 1998.

Wharton, Edith, and Ogden Codman, Jr. *The Decoration of Houses*. New York: Charles Scribner's Sons, 1897. Reprint, New York: Arno Press, 1975.

White, Samuel G. *The Houses of McKim, Mead & White*. New York: Rizzoli International Publications, 1998.

Widener, P. A. B. *Without Drums*. New York: G. P. Putnam's Sons, 1940.

Williams, Henry Lionel and Ottalie K. Williams. *America's Small Houses*. New York: A. S. Barnes and Co., 1964.

———. *Great Houses of America*. New York: G. P. Putnam's Sons, 1966.

———. *A Treasury of Great American Houses*. New York: G. P. Putnam's Sons, 1970.

Wilson, Richard Guy. *McKim, Mead & White, Architects*. New York: Rizzoli International Publications, 1983.

Wright, William. *The Von Bülow Affair*. New York: Delacorte Press, 1983.

Wurman, Richard Saul. *The Newport Guide*. Newport, R. I.: Initial Press Syndicate, 1995.

Yarnall, James L. *Newport Through Its Architecture*. Newport, R. I.: Salve University Press, 2005.

Zimmermann, H. Russell. *Magnificent Milwaukee, Architectural Treasures 1850–1920*. Milwaukee: Milwaukee Public Museum, 1987

PERIODICALS

American Architect and Building News
American Homes & Gardens
Architect
Architectural Forum
Architectural Record
Architectural Review
Architecture
The Brickbuilder
Country Life in America
House and Garden
Illustrated American
Journal of the Society of Architectural Historians

The Magazine Antiques
New York Architect
New York Times
Town & Country

AUCTION CATALOGUES

Christie's New York
Doyle New York
Parke-Bernet Galleries, New York
Sotheby's New York

OTHER

Newport Gazette
Newport Mercury Almanac
Newport Social Index
Wilson, Barbara. *Landscape Preservation: The Glen Farm Portsmouth, Rhode Island. Refuse Policy Alternative*. Amherst, Mass.: Graduate School of the University of Massachusetts, Department of Landscape Architecture and Regional Planning, May 1991.

ARCHIVAL MATERIALS

Gary Lawrance Collection
Historic New England, SPNEA Library and Archives, Codman Papers, Boston, Massachusetts
Lenox Library Associations, Reference Department, Lenox, Massachusetts
Library of Congress, Prints and Photographs Division, Washington, D.C.
Metropolitan Museum of Art, Codman Papers, New York, New York
New York Public Library, New York, New York
Newport Historical Society, Library and Print Department, Newport, Rhode Island
Peabody & Stearns Papers, Fine Arts Department, Boston Public Library, Boston, Massachusetts
Preservation Society of Newport County, Newport, Rhode Island
Redwood Library and Anthenæum, Newport, Rhode Island
Richard Marchand Collection
Salve Regina University Archive, Newport, Rhode Island

INDEX